# WINNING
# the RACE
# for VALUE

# WINNING the RACE for VALUE

## Strategies to Create Competitive Advantage in the Emerging "Age of Abundance"

### Barry Sheehy, Hyler Bracey, Rick Frazier

**amacom**

American Management Association

New York • Atlanta • Boston • Chicago • Kansas City • San Francisco • Washington, D.C.
Brussels • Mexico City • Tokyo • Toronto

*HD*
*30.28*
*S427*
*1996*

**Library of Congress Cataloging-in-Publication Data**

Sheehy, Barry.
    Winning the race for value : strategies to create competitive
  advantage in the emerging "age of abundance" / Barry Sheehy, Hyler
  Bracey, Rick Frazier.
      p.   cm.
    Includes bibliographical references and index.
    ISBN 0-8144-0354-9
    1. Strategic planning.   2. Management.   3. Competition.
  I. Bracey, Hyler.   II. Frazier, Rick.   III. Title.
  HD30.28.S427      1996
  658.4′012—dc20                                          96–22693
                                                              CIP

Printing number

10 9 8 7 6 5 4 3 2 1

To Bernard Vick and my other teachers over the years, who taught me to think, and Father Alan Cox, a priest, who taught me to act, and to my loving family, Christine, Kelly and James, who have borne the consequences without complaint.

*—Barry Sheehy*

To my friends and business associates, Jack Rosenblum, Aubrey Sanford, and Roy Trueblood, who prepared me for this stage in my career; to the clients and employees of The Atlanta Consulting Group, who have been my teachers; and to my beautiful wife, Cass Flagg, for her loving support.

*—Hyler Bracey*

To my parents, Helen and Richard, who told me to "go ahead—try it" and then supported me whenever I failed; and to Carol, my wife, for doing the same.

*—Rick Frazier*

# Contents

# Acknowledgments

James O'Toole, Executive Director of The Leadership Institute, has a rule which states, "Whenever about to congratulate oneself on having an original idea, before going public, remind yourself that the odds are, Aristotle had it first!" O'Toole's Rule reminds us of how much we have benefited from the work of others in formulating our ideas for this book. The works of several authors and scholars served as both a source of information and inspiration in our research and deserve special recognition. They include: Nuala Beck, Peter Drucker, Diane Francis, Jonathan Rauch, Paul Romer, Barbara Tuchman and Margaret Wheatley. Some recent writings by Peter Drucker fueled our confidence that this book was indeed worth writing. The fresh insights of economist Paul Romer led us to believe our hypotheses would, at a minimum, turn out to be more right than wrong. Barbara Tuchman, in her own brilliant way, gave us a perspective of the past which proved invaluable for writing about the future. Nuala Beck's insightful analysis of the new economy, *Shifting Gears*, was immensely helpful in formulating the early chapters of this book. Diane Francis' work, *A Matter of Survival*, helped clarify and shape our ideas on globalization and the role of government in the new economy. Jonathan Rauch's compelling book, *Demosclerosis: The Silent Killer of Government*, was instrumental in shaping our thinking on the danger posed by special interest politics. We would like to acknowledge the work of David J. Morrison and Adrian Slywotzky of Corporate Decisions, Inc., whose concept of value migration represents an elegant and compelling way of describing the phenomenon of value in motion. We would also like to thank Joel Rosenfeld and the Strategic Planning Institute for giving us access to the PIMS Database. We are indebted to Margaret Wheatley, whose profound work, *Leadership and the New Science*, greatly influenced our thinking on the learning organization. Finally, Don

Tapscott's *Digital Economy* was invaluable in shaping our thinking regarding trends such as disintermediation and innovation.

The errors and omissions contained in this book belong solely to the authors, but as to its strength, there are many people to thank. Among these are colleagues, clients, and friends. But a special debt of gratitude to our editor, Dale Fetherling, whose insightful recommendations, advice and, on occasion, forbearance, made this work possible. We also must thank Jerry Eastridge for stalwart support in word processing, and Candy Baxter, Lou Savary, Kathlyn Horibe and Robbie Hunt for their outstanding copy editing and editorial advice. To Paige Moody and Jack Rosenblum, who provided valuable assistance in preparation and project management. This book has been a playground of learning for us, but none of this learning would have been possible without the support and sponsorship of clients and colleagues. They have been our true teachers. Those who have been especially helpful are: Ken Chenault, Randy Christopherson, Jim Clemmer, Carlyle Crothers, Cal Darden, Bob Drummond, Frank Erbrick, Alexandra Golinkin, Harvey Golub, John Hagerman, Joe Kielty, Jim Kelly, Jane Lee, Jon Linen, Gerry McDonough, Art McNeil, Joe Moderow, Oz Nelson, Morris Perlis, James Robinson III, Tom Ryder, Terry Smith, Andy Somers, Bonnie Stedt, Cal Tyler, Tom Weidemeyer, Clinton (Bud) Yard, and Tommaso Zanzotto.

Other important sources are to be found in our Bibliography and Notes at the end of this book.

# Part I

# A New Order Born of Chaos

# 1
# Through the Looking Glass

*How queer everything is today! And yesterday, things were just as usual. I wonder if I've been changed in the night . . . but, if I'm not the same, who in the world am I? Ah, that's the great puzzle?*

—Alice, from Lewis Carroll's
Alice in Wonderland

Wayne Gretzky will be remembered as one of the greatest hockey players to ever lace up skates. He was once the subject of a study to discover the physical traits and athletic skills which accounted for his extraordinary success. The study concluded Gretzky's success was not due to his size or physical prowess; he is neither as big nor strong as other stars in the National Hockey League. When asked what he thought made him different from other players, Gretzky replied, "Most players tend to play where the puck is, whereas I play where the puck is going to be."

If you've seen him play, you know this is true. His uncanny instinct for anticipating the movement of the puck is without equal, and has led him to being universally hailed as "The Great One."

That ability to look ahead, to discern a future trajectory, to think several steps in advance of our peers is an increasingly valuable skill in another arena, too. The underpinnings of the world in general, and business in particular, are changing so quickly that anticipating today's problems is no longer enough. We have to focus on tomorrow's.

Tomorrow's issues are tough, because as never before, the economic ground is shifting beneath our feet. Events once considered isolated foreign phenomena—an interest rate rise in Europe, or the fall of a government in Asia—now reverberate in the local economy as well, sending shudders through even the smallest businesses. Meanwhile, power here and abroad is shifting from producer to consumer . . . and from traditional institutions to individuals.

As a result, old business certainties are crumbling. Strategies which always succeeded, structures which always worked, products which always sold, and markets which always performed are no longer as effective. It isn't that they've gone from "always working" to "always failing." Change is never that simple. Yet, increasingly, with ever-greater regularity, the old formulas and the old organizations are losing their power. All around us, we see evidence of the old post-war world coming unhinged.

Japan, Inc., thought to be invincible, hits a wall, and the European "miracle" of the 1970s slows to almost a stop in the '80s. At the same time, Mexico, which balanced its budget and reduced its debt, experiences a near-meltdown, economically.

IBM, Wang, Pan Am, Westinghouse, Sears and GM, all paragons of American corporate power a couple of decades ago, stumble, or even disappear. Suddenly, little Southwest Airlines and its clones, not giant American Airlines, become the new models of aviation profitability! AMR, American's parent company, earns more money from its SABRE reservation system than from the whole airline! *How can that be?* How can moving little bits and bytes around, which is what a reservation system does, turn more profit than flying people around the world?

The U.S. economy, thought by many to be in terminal decline a decade or two ago, comes roaring back. In the process many Fortune 500 companies drop from the list like flies. Meanwhile, exciting new companies are launched daily and unemployment falls to 30-year lows—*yet* millions lose their jobs in layoffs.

Yes, something out of the ordinary is happening here. But what? And *why?*

Our world, like Alice's, has turned upside down. Think, for example, of the astounding speed with which communism was virtually swept away. In a matter of *months*, what then-President Bush labeled "a new world order"—and Zbigniew Brzezinski more accurately called "a new world disorder"—was upon us. Now, breakdowns and dislocations are becoming more common as old rules, assumptions and institutions are swept aside. Shocks and surprises, some pleasant, others less so, will continue to be the order of the day. Yet, out of this apparent chaos, the world likely will emerge safer and richer.

## Seeing a Pattern

Most people fail to see this pattern beneath the flurry of activity and headlines . . . or fail to see any pattern at all. The closer they look, the more confused they become.

The key is not to look closely, but from afar. If you step back far enough, you begin to see the contours of the historic changes we are witnessing. In broad outline, they are characterized by the emergence of a knowledge-based, global economy, where everything affects everything else. No person or corporation, indeed, no nation or society, is an island. None are free from global economic influences and the shifting patterns of what constitutes value. What is going on globally and what is happening in your town and your business are inextricably linked and will define tomorrow's winners and losers.

Low interest rates in the United States, for example, can cause stock prices to rise in Malaysia. Advances in wireless communications in Latin America may force a Maine mail order firm to revamp its marketing. When American homeowners decide to refinance their mortgages, they stir up a storm in the Treasury bond market. Futures contracts traded in Chicago can undermine the Japanese Finance Ministry. In short, the economic world has become integrated and, increasingly, we are all in the same boat whether we like it or not.

Meanwhile, we are undergoing a Knowledge Revolution that stands many of our old precepts about the economy on their heads. Information, not raw materials, capital or labor, is the new key to economic power. The consumer, not the producer, is becoming dominant in deciding what is produced, where, and at what price. As the flow of information grows, so does the flood of discounters, warehousers, consolidators, catalog merchants, and consumer buying guides. Already looming on the horizon: global electronic shopping.

Look around and you will see product after product being commoditized. You find yesterday's expensive mechanical calculator displaced by digital hand-held machines, so cheap you don't even bother to have them repaired. If one stops working, you simply buy another. The same is true of most electronics today, including VCRs, radios and even televisions. The same process is at work in financial services, transportation, telecommunications and most key sectors of the economy.

## Trends to Watch For

New rules, new incentives and new trends are emerging to impact the economy. Among these are phenomena with strange-sounding names like disintermediation, transmigration, integration, prosumption and commoditization. We will discuss each of these in the course of this work. The first, disintermediation, is the most intriguing and potentially the most lethal. *Disintermediation* occurs when a competitor uses a new distribution channel to get between you and your customer. These new competitors *transmigrate* from other sectors of the economy into your backyard and disintermediate traditional customer-supplier relationships. As an example, look at how a host of financial service companies today are establishing banking-like relationships with traditional bank customers. This is classic disintermediation in action. Transmigration and accompanying disintermediation are occurring throughout our economy today. If you look carefully, you will see it happening in transportation, financial services, travel, retailing and a host of other industries.

*Digital integration* is another trend impacting business today. Digital integration entails organizations using information technology to closely interlink their business processes with those of other partners, creating a transparent, seamless value proposition. The highest order of integration allows suppliers to partner with customers to create new products. In essence, customers and suppliers become part of the same enterprise. As for *innovation*, it is a theme which will appear again and again throughout this book, along with its reverse image, *commoditization.*

These trends are reshaping our economy. Business and government must learn to master them or be mastered by them.

Today's economy is changing so quickly that it leaves little room for slow learners. On these issues, there are none but the quick or the dead.

## Two Seismic Forces

This book is about two seismic forces intersecting. One force is moving us from an economy based on the nation-state to one based on global markets; the other is moving us from a manufacturing and service-based analog economy to one based primarily on commercialized knowledge and digital information.

The convergence of these two trends marks the arrival of a new era of abundance, along with a "new" consumer unlike any the marketplace has known before. Armed with access to information and global competitive options, this buyer is now at the controls. Daily, in thousands of ways, customers are using this power to drive up quality and drive down price.

The merging of these two seismic forces has tremendous and largely favorable implications for society as a whole, especially over the long term. We are on the cusp of a new era of abundance that signals the arrival of more opportunity, wealth and freedom. However, this era will also bring more competition, more change and more challenge.

In the short term, this puts tremendous pressure on leaders and managers, in business and government alike, to perceive and keep pace with this change. As we will see in the course of this book, those who operate with theories, systems and structures designed for an age of scarcity are especially handicapped.

## Reshaping Our Economy

Our aim in writing this book is to help decision makers better manage globalization and the massive shifts in economic value which lie ahead. We will explain how shifts toward information and knowledge as the key sources of value are reshaping our economy and restructuring business and government. By "value," of course, we mean economic value, what consumers believe is the overall worth of a given product or service.

Value is shifting today because consumers are redefining what constitutes wealth. Such changes often begin subtly, scarcely noticed by the big players in an industry. Then the changes snowball. For example, think of how quickly digital sound systems overwhelmed analog systems; or how cable TV cut into the networks' audience and were themselves undercut by small dish satellites. In a world where the consumer is increasingly in control, value is a *sine qua non* for economic success. Organizations unable to provide value are headed for trouble and it's becoming more difficult to do so because the market's definition of value is shifting in new directions and taking on new forms.

As the economy shifts toward a new order driven by knowledge and information, the best way to add value will be by making a product or service more knowledge-intensive. That means bringing more technology and/or knowledge to bear on the output.

Value has become a by-product of knowledge. Adding value and adding knowledge or information are becoming synonymous. Today, technology is fast becoming the most important manifestation of commercialized knowledge. In any case, the line separating technology and knowledge is blurring. Today, most automobiles carry more-value added electronics than they do steel. For example, the Ford Taurus of the early 1990s contained 600 dollars worth of steel and 800 dollars worth of electronic components. In a sense, it was more a piece of information than a piece of metal.

## U.S. Competitive Recovery

We are experiencing nonlinear, almost quantum changes that make it difficult to predict tomorrow's business environment. However, we *can* make assumptions about its nature and shape based on trends which are *already* shaping our economy. Today, more Americans make computers than cars. Health care and medical-related industries are bigger than oil refining, automobiles, textiles, steel and mining *combined*. Software, practically nonexistent 20 years ago, now is a $42 billion-a-year business. Employment in knowledge-intensive sectors is growing quickly, in some cases at double-digit rates.

These facts just hint at the shift to information- or knowledge-added value in recent years. There are many more signs that will continue to appear as consumers increasingly view information and knowledge as the key sources of value or as their definition of what constitutes value, or worth, changes.

Shifting value was at the core of the U.S. competitive recovery over the past decade. At the height of the U.S. economic malaise in the late 1970s and early '80s, the U.S. economy seemed on death's doorstep. Everywhere there were industries in trouble: steel, autos, machine tools, textiles, consumer electronics. Even semi-conductors, an industry we invented, seemed destined for the scrap heap. The future belonged to Japan, not the United States.

But the U.S. economy didn't die; it rebounded with amazing strength, creating 25 million jobs. Exports boomed and our share of worldwide manufacturing rose an astonishing five percentage points, from 15% to more than 20%, and is *still* growing. The U.S. regained its position as the world's leading producer of semi-conductors and the world's largest exporter of goods and services. By the mid-1990s, the U.S. economy was judged to be the most cost-competitive in the world.

## Shedding Our Old Industrial Base

How did the U.S. pull it off? In short, by responding quickly to a massive shift in value. In the past 25 years, the U.S. deployed three times as much computing power per capita as any other industrial region. In doing so, it created tens of millions of jobs in high-knowledge industries. The U.S. became the world leader in the proportion of its working age population with jobs, while creating employment for some 12 million immigrants.

Everywhere during this period, information and knowledge took on new importance. During the 1980s, the whole world was starting to shed its old industrial base and transition to a 21st century economy, but the U.S. did it faster than anyone. In leading this transition, U.S. industries added technology and improved quality. They invested more than a trillion dollars in new plants and equipment. They pared costs, scrapped obsolete systems, and shifted to a new kind of economy rooted in changed customer requirements and driven by knowledge and information. As we will show, this new economy is still largely misunderstood by U.S. business, government and the press.

Even as America's new economy was being born, parts of its old economy—steel, autos, textiles, and so on—staged an amazing comeback. It is their story which attracts the most attention. However, the real news of the '80s was not the recovery of the old industries but the rise of others in which information, not capital or labor, was the critical resource. Even the resurgence of the smoke-stack industries was largely the result of adding value by applying knowledge and information technology.

It is no accident that as the auto industry began cautiously hiring again in the '90s, the hiring profile was dramatically different from that of the 1980s. Suddenly, a high school and college education became essential criteria for working on the assembly line. Detroit was looking for knowledge workers.

Similarly, what consumers considered *value* in 1980 was largely obsolete by the early 1990s. They expected different things from products and services, and they expected them delivered faster and at lower prices. Music audiocassettes, ubiquitous in 1980, were largely obsolete by 1990. The demand for dedicated word-processing machines in 1980 was incredibly high, but 10 years later, a floppy disk containing a word-processing "program" had virtually eliminated the entire industry. "Bank teller" became a job category under siege as did the all-purpose travel agent and any middleman who could not add unique knowledge to the value chain.

The shift from an analog to a digital, knowledge-driven economy is transforming our definition of value. Like a mighty vortex, today's value is being pulled inwards and commoditized. This commoditization process signals the beginning of an age of abundance; for once at the center of the vortex, value does not disappear; it becomes abundant. A product can be characterized as commoditized when its availability is so great that it must compete primarily on price and/or loses all capacity to command a price premium. But even as old value is being commoditized, it is being replaced by new, largely knowledge-driven value. When dual airbags became standard features on automobiles (i.e., commoditized), car companies didn't stop searching for ways to add value. On the contrary, they put whole armies of designers and engineers to work on developing new features and capabilities which would be perceived by customers as value added. We are transitioning to a new economic paradigm, in which **availability, affordability** and *information* are changing the very nature of economic value. In industry after industry, customers' expectations regarding a product, service, or even the entire industry are changing, setting off a scramble to restore profits and reexamine strategies. Companies everywhere are running a race with shifting value. Those who cannot keep up will find their products and services commoditized in a flash.

To cope, corporate America is restructuring and reengineering itself into a frenzy. Millions of jobs in old-line businesses are being eliminated. Middle managers are becoming an endangered species, and corporate loyalty, like chivalry, seems a quaint relic.

Government, slower and less adaptive, will be hard pressed to keep up. But as we will show in Chapters 10 and 11, falling behind will not be an option. Unless governments can catch up and keep up, they are likely to be "fired" by their constituents. The huge, ponderous apparatus of central government has everywhere become economically inefficient and a hindrance to growth . . . it is simply too slow at "learning." There is a high likelihood that government, as we know it today, will be disassembled in the coming decade and reconstructed within smarter, more manageable parameters.

But in every change, something's lost and something's gained. The coming Age of Abundance will not bring universally good news. There will emerge both new winners and new losers. This new era, and the economy which supports it, will come with different rules. The rewards will be immense for those quick enough to recognize these rules. They will see a new world order taking shape, as different from what it replaces as the Industrial Revolution was from the Agricultural Revolution.

## Counter to Conventional Wisdom

*Why and how is all this happening? Where will it end? How can you thrive amidst the changes?* We will try to shed some light on these questions. Be prepared, though, since much of what we say runs counter to conventional wisdom. For example, the U.S. economy is not getting weaker but stronger. The world will see democracy grow while governments shrink. For corporations, adding value and exceeding customer expectations will take precedence over slashing costs. Knowledge will replace raw materials as the source and object of production. The cost of producing wealth will drop, even as the speed of production increases. We will find ourselves in an Age of Abundance, not sentenced to live in a world of scarcity.

*How do you cope with change of this magnitude?* For starters, do not stand in the way! Position yourself and your organization to move with value, not against it. Lay a foundation based on information and the commercialization of knowledge. Heed the imperatives of abundance, which are outlined in Chapter 12.

Thus, the future is not a complete mystery. New value is taking shape around us every day. Few generations have been so surrounded by opportunity. However, like Wayne Gretzky, we need to look at where the puck is going, not where it is. Clues for doing just that are on display *if* we know what to look for.

# 2

# The New Economy: A Value-Driven Kaleidoscope

*What concerns me is not the way things are, but rather the way people think they are.*

—*Epictetus, Greek philosopher*

There is precedent for today's economic upheaval. The world has been through two previous transformations of equal proportions—the Agricultural Revolution and the Industrial Revolution. However, this revolution is driven not by food production or machinery, but by information. Call it the Information Revolution, or if you wish, the Knowledge Revolution. Whatever you call it, the impact it's having on our economy is profound. The very foundations of wealth and value are being transformed.

In the Agricultural Revolution, land and raw materials were the keys to wealth. In the Industrial Revolution, capital replaced land and raw materials as the source of economic power. Today, knowledge is increasingly the source of wealth and power.

As a result, even the definition of wealth has changed. Three hundred years ago, wealth was associated with owning land and domestic animals. Today, Bill Gates, the founder of Microsoft, owns little in terms of land or factories and, so far as we know, the only animal he owns is a dog. Yet he is one of America's richest, most influential people.

Revolutions are disruptive. Each of the previous economic revolutions exerted tremendous pressure for change. That change ultimately overwhelmed the status quo, creating new institutions and new elites. Outdated technologies, ideologies and political structures were cast aside or swept away. This is precisely what is happening today.

The Knowledge Revolution, what futurist Alvin Toffler calls the Third Wave, marks the end of the dominance of manufacturing. Now, value is created by the ability to put information to work, to commercialize knowledge.

Sensing this transition, parts of the developed world are already looking back on yesterday's industrial epoch with historical curiosity. In Germany, what was until 1987 the country's largest steel plant has been turned into a museum and declared a world heritage site. Consider the speed of this transition. In less than ten years, this plant went from being a mainstay of the German economy to being a museum. This is precisely what's happening in sector after sector of our old analog economy.

Old sectors of the economy are being rendered obsolete because the Knowledge Revolution has rearranged the factors of production in a profound way.

---

**Information Revolution Value Inputs**

I
M
P
O
R
T
A
N
C
E

↑

1.  Knowledge

2.  Capital

3.  Labor

4.  Raw Materials

---

Knowledge is now the most important factor in raising productivity and adding value; raw materials the least important. This explains why natural resources generally are 20% less expensive today than in 1980, 50% cheaper than in 1950, and 80% cheaper than in 1920.

Capital, though important, is generally abundant, at least for jurisdictions that make money welcome. Labor also is readily available, but, as we will see, the type of labor required by the new information economy differs markedly from that of the old analog service and industrial economy.

## Heart of the New Economy

The microchip drives the Knowledge Revolution as powerfully as the internal combustion engine drove the Industrial Age. "The heart of this new economy is the tiny microprocessor, the transistor-packed silicon chip that combines with clever software and laser optics to make possible what we glibly call the Information Age," wrote John Huey. "The microprocessor has been around for more than 20 years, but its power has been increasing exponentially, and it now has become an essential, affordable, ubiquitous fixture in our lives."

Imagine you receive one of those greeting cards that plays "Happy Birthday" when you open it. After it brings a smile to your face, you casually toss it into the wastebasket. Huey reminds us that "you've just discarded more computer processing power than existed in the entire world before 1950."

In fact, computing power doubles every 18 months and is now 8,000 times less expensive than it was 30 years ago. This staggering increase in productivity is having a profound impact on our economy.

## Historic Threshold

So much has been written about the Information Age that it seems almost like old news. In reality, the line separating the analog and digital economies has only recently been crossed. It was only in the early 1990s that American business began spending more money on information technology than on all other forms of capital investment combined—all the machinery needed for services, manufacturing, mining, agriculture, construction and the like. This represents an important and historic economic threshold.

It means we will see the importance of highly skilled knowledge workers rising as that of low-skilled production workers declines. This process is under way and explains part of the growing pressure on the blue-collar middle class.

Today's most valuable employees are well-educated knowledge workers. They no longer "mass produce" things. Instead, they provide service by bringing knowledge and technical expertise to bear on their work. In this new economy, workers are less likely to tie themselves for life to factories or large corporations as they did in the past in exchange for economic security.

Even the term "worker" is becoming obsolete because many knowledge workers are really individual contributors to the wealth-creation process. More and more "workers" are choosing to contribute in ways other than full-time employment as they search for "dejobbed" security.

The contingent workforce, which includes many knowledge workers, now numbers over 40 million in the United States. This group—temporaries, part-timers, the self-employed, and consultants—has grown 57% since the 1980s. People are learning to care for themselves and their families by planning their own careers and building their own retirement funds. By the turn of the century, it is likely that less than half the workforce in the developed world will be holding conventional full-time jobs.

The new knowledge worker is generally more self-reliant and arguably more self-centered than yesterday's employees. They also seem more intent on making a difference in the world and adding value to their work. Even Generation "X" is turning out to be different. Denied a free ride to success and burdened with a huge public sector debt run up by their parents and grandparents, they are distrustful of large institutions and intent on finding their own way. In fact, Generation "X" may turn out to be the most entrepreneurial Americans ever.

As the economy shifts to this new order, there will be an increasing emphasis on adding value by adding information–based technology. As that technology moves "downstream," it will impact not just the way something is made but how it is distributed and used. We will see higher and higher ratios of value-added knowledge being applied to products and services.

Where value moves, margins and profits soon follow. Those industries with the highest ratios of knowledge workers and commercialized knowledge to invested capital will command the highest margins and pay the highest salaries. Those with low or declining knowledge-value ratios will find margins eroding and pay scales declining. Already, we can see software profits which are four times higher than comparable hardware profits.

## Cars, Bombs, Airplanes, and Toilets

Bombs, though not on everyone's shopping list, provide a classic example of how the economy is shifting toward the application of technology to enhance performance. In World War II, "dumb iron bombs" (as they were called in the trade), guided by little more than gravity, were lucky to land within a mile of their target. To compensate, planes had to drop tons and tons of bombs over each target. In fact, it took 9,000 bombs—that's right, *9000!*—to guarantee that one of them hit within a 100 foot by 30 foot target area. In Vietnam, by contrast, it took only 400 bombs to accomplish the same task.

Today, bombs made intelligent by adding laser-guidance, self-adjusting fins, and optical-tracking mechanisms—all communicating via a battery of silicon chips—can be aimed with unbelievable accuracy and reliability. The target that took 9,000 bombs to hit in World War II and 400 iron bombs in Vietnam now can be hit with two. (The second acts as insurance for the first.) Two bombs . . . one target . . . one hit! And with a drastic reduction in civilian casualties, to boot. During the Gulf War, for example, laser-guided bombs accounted for 8% of the ordnance, but were credited with hitting 50% of the strategic targets.

The saga of the bombs tells us a lot about the shape of the future economy. The iron and explosive in the "dumb" iron bomb constituted 90% of the raw materials in the product; the guidance packet in the modern bomb amounts to less than 10%. But the bulk of the value is, of course, in the guidance packet. The information and intelligence added by the laser-guidance package exponentially increases the effectiveness of the total system. One "smart" bomb costs 20 times more than its "dumb" cousin, but is 400 times more accurate and effective. The difference in price and performance is entirely made up of knowledge or intelligence value-added. The smart bomb's inherent value is not in its physical form but in the essential information it carries. In the civilian economy, consumers are increasingly thinking of value in the same way.

For example, look at the automobile. Detroit, slow at first to respond, has taken the industry into the Information Age. Forty or fifty microprocessors sit under the dashboard of most new cars today. (That compares to almost none before 1980.) Micro-processors control all the operations of the engine—fuel mixture, air flow, fuel flow, timing, spark firing order, and transmission. Computer chips control the pulsing of anti-lock brakes, the level-ing function of the air-suspension system, and shut down the fuel pump if the car is hit from behind. Other computer components supply a constant stream of information, ranging from fuel con-sumption and fuel economy, to the number of miles till the next scheduled tune-up. Still more chips run the cruise control, work the lights, govern heat or air-conditioning, display a roadmap screen, play the stereo, and trigger warning bells, buzzers, and artificial voices.

"Think of the automobile as one big system, filled with infor-mation technology," says Joe Gorman, CEO of TRW, the world's fourth-largest maker of auto parts. The average driver is unaware of most microprocessor-controlled functions, although they make the car safer and less polluting as well as more efficient, reliable, longer lasting, and more enjoyable. Detroit, in turn, is making more money by building fewer, but better cars. Everyone benefits as a result of adding tremendous knowledge to what is essentially a late 19th century technology.

We mentioned in Chapter 1 that airline reservation systems, essentially a knowledge-driven process, generate more profit than flying people around the world on a billion dollars' worth of air-craft. Again, that's because the reservation system is more knowl-edge intensive than the traditional airlines they serve. In addition, aircraft maintenance information systems (AMIS) can now keep planes flying more cost effectively than ever before. The use of these systems in the second half of the nineties could determine, in large part, which airlines prevail and which fail. This application of knowledge to the business of managing assets will enable compa-nies to extract more value from existing assets, thus protecting margins.

Airlines were also pioneers in computer-driven revenue man-agement. For more than a decade, airlines have employed large computer systems to manage "yields" on available seat inventory. Using historical models and real time information, these systems enabled airlines to adjust pricing to ensure full loads. Hotels and car rental companies have followed suit with similar yield or revenue management systems. Today, increasing computer power, coupled with declining computer costs, is enabling companies to engage in this sort of knowledge-based pricing. Properly employed, these systems will keep profits from tanking even in environments where prices are under downward pressure.

Speaking of tanks, a Japanese manufacturer has turned the dumb "catch and flush" toilet into an intelligent piece of equipment. Biosensors and microprocessors allow for warming of the seat, cleaning and drying, and provide diagnostic medical information. It can even relay a message to the doctor if something is wrong. If information can be added to increase the value and utility of toilets, it can be added anywhere.

## The New Economy Today

Though we can catch glimpses of the new economy as it evolves around us, it's important to understand that history happens in bits and pieces. The Knowledge Revolution will not occur overnight. If the past is prologue, the old economy and new economy will coexist for a long while in uneasy equilibrium.

With the arrival of the later stages of the Industrial Revolution, cotton and tobacco were already declining industries, but remained important segments of the economy. Even today, as the Information Age dawns, tobacco and cotton remain important crops because people still buy cigarettes and wear underwear. But with each passing day, such crops are less and less central to the future of the economy.

The "underwear" connection provides an interesting look at the application of knowledge to an old analog industry. Playtex, a subsidiary of Sara Lee, sells bras and panties (they call them "intimates") and does so very profitably. However, Playtex *manufactures* very little. It farms out around the world the actual making of its products. This allows Playtex to focus its energies on brand management, distribution and design, and finding out what women really want in "intimates."

Is this an example of the "hollowing out" of the American economy, a retreat from what we have always done best and what has made our economy so strong? Absolutely not. Rather, it is a classic case of following value upstream to the areas of concept and design, where higher margins are found. Playtex employs more people in America today than it ever did as a manufacturer. What has changed is the type of worker it employs and the ratio of knowledge applied to the work.

Calvin Klein has followed a similar strategy, moving out of manufacturing and shifting its best talent into higher knowledge functions such as designing, licensing and brand management. It is no accident that this shift in strategy coincided with a resurgence in Calvin Klein's profits.

Much the same is true of most of today's old analog industries, such as steel, automobiles and mining. These industries remain important and their genesis as part of the old economy does not preclude them from growing and being profitable. However, they can do so only by adding an ever increasing ratio of knowledge to their output.

In fact, we can learn a lot from these old industries as they transition toward higher ratios of information value-added. For example, the cyclical recovery in America's traditional economic base highlights one of the paradoxes inherent in economic growth and transition: *productivity (as presently measured) is often higher in declining and mature industries than in young, immature industries.*

Farming's productivity, for example, has increased incredibly over the past 100 years and continues to improve, even though agriculture is clearly a First Wave relic. Likewise, the productivity of manufacturing has been growing steadily for 150 years, soaring to new heights in the 1980s and early 1990s. Why? Declining industries *must* improve productivity to survive because they cannot count on growth to keep them afloat. Only the lean can survive. (An exception, of course, can be found in state-sponsored monopolies and protected industries where, all other things being equal, service and productivity will decline even as prices increase.)

On the other hand, growth industries focus most of their attention on expanding, thus they tend to be less efficient than mature industries. Eventually, the process rights itself as new industries mature and become more productive. This is precisely what will happen over the next several decades in many new growth sectors of the U.S. economy, such as health care, telecommunications, transportation and tourism.

# Where to Look for the New Economy

How do you identify tomorrow's important industries? The first step, as Canadian economist Nuala Beck wrote in her brilliant analysis, *Shifting Gears*, is: "Find out what's growing and what's not."

Do so, and you will find some surprising trends. For example, at nearly 14% of Gross National Product (GNP), health care and medical related industries represent the largest sectors of the U.S. economy, while information and communications account for 9%. Travel and tourism, now *the world's largest industry* and still one of the fastest growing, is rapidly expanding and has become one of America's chief exports. (Inbound tourism brings in money, just like any outbound export.) Other booming sectors include telecommunications, engineering and scientific equipment, and environmental consulting and equipment.

Another way to identify tomorrow's industries is to find out who is hiring and who is not. Electronics employment, for example, has risen a blistering 18% in each of the past several years. The entertainment business employs more people than the auto industry.

As the new economy expands, the old is slowly receding. Among Fortune 500 companies, the number of jobs declined from 16.2 million to 11.5 million over the past 15 years even though overall U.S. employment rose strongly. (Thirty years ago, manufacturing accounted for 25% of all jobs. Today, it is 16% and falling.)

How can we be expanding and adding jobs while the Fortune 500 firms are laying off millions of people? Because we are in a period of transition, and the old analog economy is disproportionately reflected in the makeup of the Fortune 500. As that "wave" declines, so will the percentage of people it employs relative to the economy as a whole.

Such layoffs, now as well as historically, are not a sign of a dying economy but one being reborn. Throughout the Industrial Revolution, two-thirds of the jobs existing at the beginning of the century were gone by century's end. However, at the end of every century, there were three times as many people at work and both the standard of living and life expectancy were higher.

Unfortunately, governments and many economists continue to religiously track the economic indicators of the old economy, such as housing starts. Forty years ago when housing construction was

7.2% of GNP, it was an important indicator of future economic activity. Today, at 3.5% of GNP, housing is far less important. The same is true of steel, autos and mining.

Tracking these indicators could easily give the impression the economy is decaying. From the perspective of the old economy, the turnaround of the mid-1990s seems little more than a small upward blip in the midst of a long-term cyclical decline. Nothing could be further from the truth.

When computers and semiconductors, communications, entertainment and telecommunications, health and medicine, instrumentation, tourism and high-tech services are tracked, a very different picture emerges. While old analog industries are generally shedding laborers, knowledge-worker employment is expanding briskly. Thanks to new growth industries, overall U.S. employment is very strong as of this writing.

Another statistic which can produce false readings is the trade deficit. The present deficit is exactly what should be expected when the U.S. economy is growing more strongly than most of its trading partners. That's because growing economies tend to suck in imports as well as investments. Far more important to track are America's high-tech trade figures. There the picture brightens considerably as the United States has run, and continues to run, an expanding high-tech trade surplus.

With productivity high in declining analog industries and slowly increasing in new knowledge-intensive industries, the true data on the new economy indicates a boom, not a decline. The United States appears to be transitioning to a knowledge-driven, post-industrial economy faster than any country or region in the world and this bodes well for the future.

## The New Playing Field

To understand what's happening here, it is not enough just to know that the Rust Belt industries will continue to decline in importance, while the knowledge-intensive industries will grow. That is only a by-product of a much larger economic transition involving wholesale shifts in economic power, and those shifts are occurring at multiple levels. Among the most important of these shifts are:

1. From national to global markets
2. From place (geographic location) to people (wherever the customer happens to be)
3. From low knowledge-added to high knowledge-added products and services
4. From the producer to the consumer

## From National to Global Markets

An entrepreneur we know wanted to start a bicycle manufacturing firm. He liked living in the Boston area, so he established his corporate headquarters in Cambridge. However, none of his bicycles are made there, nor are any sold there. His company takes up no more space in North America than a small office with a telephone, computer and fax machine. His investment capital comes from the Near East, the bikes are manufactured in Taiwan, and sold exclusively in Europe.

That small entrepreneur is a paradigm for the future leaders in the New Economy. He looks beyond national borders for solutions to his problems. In a world increasingly connected, we all must develop global solutions.

Think about it. The most pressing problems we face are all transnational in nature: terrorism, nuclear proliferation, environmental degradation, AIDS, the regulation of global financial markets. Even war—one of the original reasons nations were created in the first place—has become a transnational business as shown by the Gulf War coalition and various peacekeeping actions around the globe.

It was less than 500 years ago that French philosopher Jean Bodin conceived the idea of the nation-state, and less than 300 years since it first took physical form in Europe. As the millennium dawns, it appears Bodin's theory is an idea whose time has come— and is *going*. At every turn, global economic forces are wrenching power and prerogatives from national governments, while at the same time local and regional jurisdictions are demanding more autonomy. The nation-state, so familiar to all of us as the locus of power and protection in the 20th century, is caught between powerful centrifugal forces and is being pulled apart.

The decline of national sovereignty may be a scary prospect for some. However, when we examine these centrifugal forces in

detail, we find they are mostly positive, such as the present movement to open markets and bring down trade barriers. In the 1930s,
the world learned the hard way the importance of trade and open
markets. After a murderous run-up in tariffs—a key factor in creating the Depression—trade barriers leveled out and did not really
fall significantly until after World War II when the United States
led the way.

In 1940, average tariffs in industrial countries averaged 40%.
By 1950 they had fallen to 24% and then to 12% by 1970. In 1990,
they were down to 5%, and if present trends continue, they will be
1.5% by century's end. Arguably, the present state of global free
trade is one of the greatest accomplishments of the post-war Pax
Americana.

Each of these drops reduced impediments to wealth creation,
resulting in more economic growth. As tariffs come down, GNPs
rise. Global trade, living standards, and overall economic activity
in much of the world have risen dramatically in the post-war era,
thanks in large part to U.S. free-trade leadership.

Currently, this tradition of bringing down barriers is develop-
ing a second wind. This is clearly seen in the expansion of the
European Union, the North American Free Trade Agreement
(NAFTA), Mercosur in South America (Argentina, Brazil,
Paraguay, Uruguay, and soon Chile and Bolivia), and proposed free
trade areas in Asia and in the Middle East.

In short, free trade is changing the meaning of sovereignty.
Increasingly, *it is not the nation-state which is sovereign, but the global
consumer.*

## From Place to People

Sometime in the last decade, we crossed the line separating the old
producer-driven economy from the new consumer-driven economy. The shift has been sudden and jolting, almost as if a final grain
of sand fell on one side of a scale, tipping the balance forever.

Political scientists long have maintained that a tyranny loses
power once the distribution of telephones achieves critical mass.
The same holds true for producer power in a world of global communications. With access to sufficient information, power shifts to
consumers.

With the right information, today's consumer can buy just about anything cheaper and faster, from someone, somewhere, without sacrificing quality. How many of today's young children will shop in a traditional "department store"? Instead, they are growing up in an era in which buyers increasingly are mobile bargain hunters who use the phone, computer, fax, and even the local newspaper, to ferret out the best merchandise for the lowest price.

With perhaps 30 million computer users roaming the Internet looking for a deal and 160,000 more said to be joining their ranks each month, the volume of inside information available to consumers is increasing exponentially. No wonder retailers and car manufacturers are abandoning "suggested retail prices" in favor of "everyday low prices."

In Europe and South America, telephone customers are phoning the United States on specially leased lines using "call back" services, then rerouting to a neighboring country they wish to call. Why? Because of the outrageous long-distance rates charged by local monopolies. Once these citizens discovered it was 20–50% cheaper to place a call to a neighboring country via the United States, they went ahead and did it.

Similarly, Japanese discounters now send planeloads of "professional shoppers" to the United States to bring back goods manufactured by Japanese companies for resale at home. Such goods are less expensive in America primarily because Japan's hierarchical and expensive distribution system drives up domestic prices. For similar reasons, Japanese shoppers are ordering by fax, mail and phone from U.S. mail order houses like L.L. Bean, Lands' End, and Eddie Bauer. Some of these direct mail companies are now hiring Japanese-speaking phone operators and printing catalogs and supplements in Japanese.

When Austria joined the European Union in 1995, Austrian consumers immediately poured across the border into Germany and Italy to buy cars. Why? Austria's highly protected and inefficient auto distribution system resulted in prices which were 40–50% higher than in neighboring countries.

People everywhere are learning to sidestep obsolete, expensive and cumbersome national arrangements which favor producers over consumers. They are using global communication and transportation systems to evade these restrictive economic environments. Even governments are not immune from this customer revolt. That's what Canada discovered when it raised excise taxes on cigarettes by more than 50%. Normally docile, law-abiding Canadians soon developed a passion for smuggling. At one point, Canadian officials believed fully a third of the cigarettes consumed in Canada were brought illegally from the United States, where a carton cost half as much. The Canadian government finally gave in and lowered the tax.

In addition to driving down prices, information is also lowering the barriers to entry for would-be participants in the New Economy. Many of today's knowledge-driven industries do not require vast resources. Bill Gates did not need to build a factory to get started in business. Nor did Steven Jobs, who built his first computer in a garage.

With knowledge as the key element of production, the start-up process for new information industries is quicker and takes less capital. The globalization of capital markets has also helped make money readily available to entrepreneurs around the world. Capital, like production before it, is becoming increasingly democratized and this "money" revolution is quickly spreading.

## From Low Knowledge-Added to High Knowledge-Added

The steel mill, the classic icon of the Industrial Revolution, consisted of a huge plant located near its raw materials, linked by roads and railways, and served by a mass of low-knowledge workers who needed a nearby city and its many services. Compare this massive arrangement to a single, creative mind, such as the bicycle manufacturer in Cambridge. He sits at a workstation with fax and computer access to brain trusts and databases around the world.

That, in microcosm, is a picture of the fundamental shift in the underpinnings of today's economy. Even tourism, the Third Wave sector which most resembles the steel mill in terms of capital and infrastructure, today differs markedly from its predecessor. While the old steel mill could be exploited by its owners, unions and governments at the expense of its customers, the tourist center cannot. Why? Because even though the hotel or theme park cannot move, the consumer can. If the owner's greed, the union's intransigence, or the government's taxes raise prices and lower the value for the customers, today's tourists, equipped with information and mobility, will simply go elsewhere.

The Industrial Revolution, as we saw earlier, raised the value of raw materials as an essential ingredient of production. Today the hierarchy of value is reversed. Raw materials are at the bottom of the list; people, the seed carriers of information, are on top.

## From Producers to Consumers

For business, this is perhaps the most important power shift of all. Consumers are now calling the shots and this shift is a *fait accompli*, a done deal. Consumers, not producers, are in control of today's economy and are using their power to drive down prices and raise quality standards.

To see the power of this new consumer in action, just look at the software industry and the Internet. While most software vendors were watching and waiting for Bill Gates' next move, millions of individuals signed up for access to the Internet without waiting for Microsoft to provide them with an interface. The next versions of operating systems software will support all the standard Internet services, yet none of the big vendors were directly involved in defining these new standards. The consumers effectively set the standards by going ahead and showing what they wanted from the Internet.

What we may be seeing here is a subtle but important shift in power away from software producers to individual computer users. History shows that once users take control, they never give it back. It happened in the transition from mainframes to minis and from minis to PCs. Now it appears to be happening again in software.

It was not always that way. In the days of the Agricultural Revolution and the Industrial Revolution, first the landed aristocracy and then the industrialists held sway over the economy. It was a seller's market. In those days, inventing a better mousetrap meant you could expect the world to beat a path to your door. Inventors and builders were the heroes of human progress, and the paragon of the Industrial Age was Henry Ford.

Ford was a revolutionary who set out to make affordable automobiles. His thinking was typical of the times. It did not begin with the *customer;* it began with the *product* Ford decided to make, the automobile.

Products, not consumers, were the center of Ford's economic universe. Consequently, Ford focused primarily on the means of production. His brainchild, the assembly line, changed the world as profoundly as any methodology ever invented. It allowed him, and others, to turn out large quantities of reliable, inexpensive goods.

The Model T was the marvel of its age, and more important for the long run, it democratized the process of production by increasing the availability and lowering the cost of manufacturing products. Today we think of mass production as old news, but during the age of the Model T the capacity to increase output and decrease costs mystified and astounded observers and dramatically raised living standards.

Nonetheless, demand in that era usually exceeded supply. Ford and other manufacturers could not make as many cars as could be sold. The factories were enormous and consumed huge amounts of raw materials and machinery, which often could not be provided quickly enough. It also took a long time to bring new capacity onstream.

Although production was democratized, capital was not. Few entrepreneurs outside the power elite had access to investment capital. Thus, leveraging debt was a strategy available to very few.

In the 1980s, as the Industrial Age waned, power shifted once again, passing from producers to consumers. Part of the reason for this shift was the democratization of capital. Another was the growing availability of proprietary information. Easy access to such data signaled some of the first stirrings of the new economy.

For many decades, restricted access to production information hobbled market activity. Even large producers lacked access to their competitors' costs, prices and performance. That began to change with the advent of the Information Revolution in the 1970s. For example, *Consumer Reports* became widely available and revealed the price and performance of just about every product and service. Suddenly, knowledge once restricted to a few insiders became widely dispersed. This changed people's perspective of worth.

From the perspective of today's savvy customer, it seems almost quaint that consumers once regarded, for example, one brand of gasoline or one kind of laundry soap as distinctly superior to another. Competition, like information, was limited. But, no longer. Today, value is the cornerstone of brand power.

## Trends to Watch For

As the economy transforms itself from one based primarily on analog technology to one based on digital technology, we can expect dramatic changes in the way business and government operate. Distribution, operations, production and support functions are being affected by the shift toward information as the key source of value. Some of the trends associated with this transition are already making themselves felt in the economy. These include disintermediation, integration, innovation and commoditization. Putting aside commoditization for the moment, something we'll discuss later in the book, let's examine the remaining three phenomena in detail:

▪ *Disintermediation.* New digital information systems amplify and accelerate normal market signals. This, in turn, facilitates the overhauling of value chains throughout the economy. Intermediaries, agents, brokers, wholesalers and middlemen, whose primary role is to boost market signals by moving information up, down or across the chain of value, can now be easily replaced with digital information. By way of example, consider how quickly Wal-Mart revolutionized retailing by linking stores directly to manufacturers using digital technology. In doing so, they eliminated the need for traditional warehousing, a classic middle-man function. This innovation provided Wal-Mart with a decisive cost advantage and soon forced other companies like Sears, to overhaul their own distribution system along similar lines.

So long as Wal-Mart can "control the customer," a prerequisite to success in today's economy, they will stay on top of the food chain. From this high ground, they can force manufacturers to accept razor-thin margins. But no advantage is permanent in today's fast-changing economic environment. If manufacturers can find a way to reach out to customers via new direct distribution channels, they could theoretically disintermediate retailers like

Wal-Mart. If this happens, it will have been made possible by the same digital technology which first enabled Wal-Mart's revolutionary retail system.

Disintermediation runs hand-in-hand with the advent of new distribution channels. Take, for example, Circuit City's move into automobile sales. Using their "CarMax" on-line operating system, Circuit City now distributes both used and new cars. Using "CarMax," customers can search computerized lists and descriptions of available automobiles and then make purchases on-line. By eliminating the "middle-man," CarMax offers consumers significant savings over traditional dealerships. CarMax is a classic example of digital disintermediation in action. CarMax also illustrates the phenomenon of *transmigration,* in which new competitors from entirely different industries enter a market via a new distribution channel.

The CarMax story also provides insights on potential antidotes for disintermediation. CarMax and the potential advent of "car superstores" are forcing automobile companies to rationalize their dealerships and weed out weak performers. Ford Motors CEO, Alex Trotman, candidly admits that while Ford's product quality has improved dramatically in recent years, "our biggest single problem is the averageness of some of our dealerships compared to other high-volume dealers." General Motors and Chrysler have exactly the same problem. Unless dealerships can find ways to add value with enhanced service and deeper product knowledge, they risk becoming an unnecessary and expensive layer in the overall distribution channel. To combat the threat of disintermediation, dealerships must find ways of adding value by increasing customer satisfaction and enhancing the overall buying and after-sales experience. This is one of the great lessons associated with disintermediation; it can be counteracted only by adding value to immediate customer relationships and this usually comes down to adding knowledge or customized service to the overall value proposition.

Another powerful example of digital disintermediation is found in the work of software developer, Middlegate, a new company, backed by three Silicon Valley venture capital funds. Middlegate is developing "intelligent agent" software which enables small businesses and educated "power travelers" to make their own bookings on the Internet. This process will save time and money but will also disintermediate the traditional travel agent. Interestingly, while the product is a threat to travel agents, it does not necessarily threaten travel agencies. By introducing this product to their small business clients, travel agencies can share in the profits from every transaction. In the Middlegate scenario, the transaction work is performed by the clients themselves, interacting with intelligent hardware, which "learns" preferences.

▪ *Integration* is another characteristic of the new economy made possible by digital information technology. These new information systems enable small companies to join large networks, thus gaining access to economies of scale previously available only to large corporations. As old value chains fracture and are digitally reconstructed, small corporations can insert themselves as suppliers to previously closed systems. For example, if you study the value chain associated with the new Boeing 777, or any North American–built airliner today, you will find a shifting landscape of suppliers moving into and out of the picture with each bid. Successful suppliers are linked to the assembler with advanced information systems. The aircraft is designed and tested using computer aided design programs. When the design is complete, specifications are downloaded to approved suppliers digitally. Parts are then manufactured, tested and sent to the manufacturer for final assembly.

Integration also allows manufacturers to involve suppliers in the design of parts. At its best, integration includes not only suppliers but also customers. Author and futurist Don Tapscott has referred to this process of involving customers in making the product as *prosumption*. Today, Levi's offers a service which allows customers to order jeans customized to their specific size, guaranteeing a perfect fit. Aircraft manufacturers have a long tradition of designing new products in close cooperation with important customers. Today, car manufacturers are moving in the same direction with customized models which can be delivered in two to three weeks. Parcel delivery operations like UPS equip customers to access their computer systems, so they can both ship and track their own packages.

To see the future, just look to the information superhighway, where every producer creating and sending information over the net becomes a consumer when accessing a bulletin board or other service. Today this integration and prosumption process is occurring on a global scale. As the price of telecommunications drops,

long distance rates will follow. Within a decade, a telephone conversation will cost next to nothing, regardless of the distance
involved. This means one of the most important limiting factors
imposed by geography on human activities will vanish.
Increasingly, the integration and prosumption process now being
experienced on a national scale will become a global phenomenon.
Many services will become internationally available and easier to
ship from country to country than hard goods are today.
Management will be able to control quality, production and after-
sale service, without regard to geography.

• *Speed and Innovation.* Faced with relentless competition,
along with the risk of commoditization and disintermediation,
companies will be forced to innovate or die. The pressure to find
new and better ways of doing business will lead to breakthrough
after breakthrough; we are already seeing this scenario played out
in high-tech electronics. For example, the Intel Pentium chip, a
technological marvel by any standard, was quickly commoditized
by Intel itself as it announced its new, more powerful P6 microprocessor. Everywhere, product lifecycles are collapsing. The auto
industry, which used to work on five- to seven-year cycles, is now
down to two-year cycles. Japanese electronic manufacturers, which
also used to work on multi-year cycles, now assume a three- to
four-month cycle before products are matched or superseded by
the competition. Last year, Sony introduced five thousand new
products. On Wall Street some financial products have lifecycles
measured in hours.

In this world of immediacy and innovation, tolerance for long
delays is fast disappearing. This explains, in part, the rising tide of
dissatisfaction with government, which seems interminably slow
at everything it does. Today, any institution, including government, which makes its customers line up and wait, is on the road
to extinction.

## What Does It All Mean?

Our economy is in the midst of a revolutionary transformation.
Economic power continues to shift both vertically and horizontally. Horizontally, we are moving from an economy based on the
nation-state to one based increasingly on global markets. Vertically,

we are moving at blazing speed from an analog, manufacturing-and-service economy to a digital economy based primarily on information and knowledge.

Emerging from the vortex of these two high pressure economic systems is the new consumer. Ready access to information and global competitive options has put the modern consumer at the center of the economic universe. Consumers are using their power to raise quality and drive down prices.

This relentless pressure from customers to improve performance and lower costs is forcing industry after industry to restructure, reengineer and rethink their business. In such an environment, leaders must extract the most value from their total production and distribution systems. Whatever seems to be adding the least amount of value to the customer must be squeezed out.

In some industries that boils down to ripping out the middle. In retailing, transportation and financial services, the "middleman" is being eliminated. In other cases such as health care, for example, health maintenance organizations (HMOs) are using their influence or control of the customer to force changes across the whole spectrum of their industry. They add value by forcing down prices, improving medical results, and simplifying distribution.

So, like a great kaleidoscope, the North American economy is remaking itself, taking on new shapes and hues each month, each week. In the course of this metamorphosis, the nature of value is changing and moving in new directions. It is an awesome process to behold.

# Part II
# Value
# in Motion

# 3

# What Causes Value to Shift?

*The universe begins to look more like a giant thought than like a great machine.*

*—James Jeans, astronomer*

Like a powerful river carving its own path across the landscape, economic value twists and turns as customers redefine what they need and expect. Modern leaders, much like the riverboat pilots of Mark Twain's day, need to keep a seasoned eye out for snags and fickle currents.

Sometimes the shifts in the stream of value are relatively slow and steady, allowing the perceptive organization time to prepare. Just as often, value veers abruptly, leaving the unprepared hard aground at a spot which a short while ago seemed so safe and serene.

Again and again, just when an industry thinks it has perfected a product to satisfy customers, consumers find a different way—faster, cheaper or both—to meet their needs. Consider Xerox's rude awakening.

As CEO David Kearns described in his book, *Prophets in the Dark*, the firm felt it was doing fairly well in the 1970s and early '80s. Xerox was profitable and productivity was growing by 7–8% a year, until new Japanese products began selling for less. That got Xerox's attention.

Kearns sent out teams to analyze the competition from top to bottom and was shocked at the results. The Japanese were able to carry six to eight times less inventory because they were so much more efficient at getting products out the door. While Xerox was proud that 95% of its incoming parts were error free, the Japanese figure was 99.5%. Xerox's overhead was double that of the Japanese as was its ratio of managers to workers. Worse yet, Xerox discovered that its industry was "targeted," meaning it was one of the sectors Japan, Inc., intended to dominate.

"There was no gap, there was a chasm" between Xerox and its rivals, Kearns said. Though Xerox had been getting feedback for years about the Japanese, the firm had been in denial. This startling wake-up call began Xerox's long road to competitive recovery.

## Caught by Surprise

Xerox's story is not unique. Value is shifting and reshaping itself so quickly these days, it can easily catch organizations by surprise, especially successful ones. Companies structured to excel in one situation find themselves at a serious disadvantage when a value shift occurs.

Airlines like Pan Am, Eastern and TWA thrived in a regulated environment, but were entirely unprepared to cope with the low cost, competitive world of deregulation. The U.S. machine tools and consumer electronics companies were utterly unprepared for the low price, high quality, build-share-at-any-cost onslaught of the Japanese in the 1970s. The larger U.S. television studios, which dominated the entertainment scene for decades, were good at catering to the "mass middle." However, when segmentation began eroding this constituency, the "Big Three" networks fell behind the value curve.

When Xerox dominated the copier market, during what Kearns called its "fat and stupid" days, it viewed value with an inward focus. Value, in effect, was what Xerox said it was. For example, Xerox provided outstanding service to clients. When something broke, Xerox was always there to fix it, and maintenance contracts became an important source of revenue. When design or production workers discovered glitches, there was a tendency to push the product out into the market anyway, secure in the knowledge the company could always fix it later. This is a classic example of being seduced by one's own strength.

Then along came Canon. Its strategy was to build copiers that did not break down and required little maintenance, and to sell them cheaper. Overnight, the value equation in the industry turned upside down. This new value reality caught Xerox completely by surprise and before long, the firm began a long, scary decline that took it to the brink of oblivion. It was at this moment of crisis that Xerox became open to learning again. That willingness to learn ultimately paved the way for a remarkable comeback under Kearns' leadership in the 1980s.

## Value = Quality/Price

Xerox got into trouble because the industry–wide perception of value shifted, and Xerox was not ready for it. The lesson here is an important one. The *customer*, not the corporation, determines value. Value is the subjective assessment which the consumer and the market make about the overall worth of a product or service. Value moves in new directions when a critical mass of customers redefine what they are willing to pay for. The customers' expectations change regarding the product, service, or even the entire industry, and these shifts can happen quickly.

For example, foreign cars, with their small size, stick shifts and fuel economy, were viewed as amusing by Detroit in 1970. Consumers believed otherwise, and by 1980, the foreign makes had stolen nearly 30% of the market. This switch was based not only on quality but on price as well.

Customers see value when their expectations are met or exceeded at a cost which appears reasonable. A great product at too high a price has little value; conversely, a poor product at a very reasonable price also has little or no value. Consider this tag line: "*Our product doesn't work but it's cheap.*" Would you buy it?

$$\text{VALUE} = \frac{\text{Quality}}{\text{Price}}$$

A successful product or service must meet both quality and price criteria if it is to provide value. With consumers increasingly in control, organizations must master both sides of the value equation. If they cannot, they are headed for trouble.

A short 20 years ago, the producer was in control and, in most industries, defined value. Many automakers were saying, in effect, "We know what is good for the American people. Choices and options are what they want and we will increase our prices for every new feature we offer in a vehicle."

Today, value is primarily defined by what the customer says it is. Those same automakers today listen attentively as American consumers describe what they want in a car, what they expect as standard features, and what they will pay.

This represents a major break with the past. Auto manufacturers, and others, are seeking what the consumer wants and is willing to pay, while producers adjust their costs accordingly. The days of cost-plus pricing are over.

## The "Black Hole" Effect: Commoditization in Action

Value is a moving target. As customers' expectations rise and their preferences shift year by year, they alter the definition of what constitutes value. What satisfied a majority of customers last season may not satisfy them now. Today's delight becomes tomorrow's expectation and the following day's commodity.

As expectations rise, innovations are drawn toward a "black hole" where they are soon regarded not as breakthroughs, but as bare minimums. The unique features of the first Apple computers, which made them so easy to use, are taken for granted today by most consumers. Anti-lock brakes and dual air bags, once considered expensive options on luxury cars, are becoming standard features on most automobiles. Shortly, auto buyers will expect side-impact air bags, too. Already, Mercedes-Benz is prototyping a vehicle which has no less than a dozen airbags.

## Commoditization: A Harbinger of Abundance

The fascinating thing about this black hole or commoditization phenomenon is that it signals abundance, not scarcity. Why? Because "availability" is the characteristic most closely associated with commoditization. When a product or feature becomes commoditized, it doesn't disappear; it simply becomes more available and affordable. Commoditization should not be confused with obsolescence; the commoditized feature or product retains value, but its "availability" reaches such proportions that it becomes a commodity . . . something which is "a given," and can no longer command a price premium.

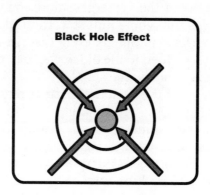

Even as the value of various features moves inward toward the "black hole," a second, even more profound shift can occur. Take computers, for example. Today the power, speed and versatility of computer hardware is increasing exponentially as prices continue to drop. This illustrates a classic "black hole" process in which old value erodes as performance improves.

However, this is not the only movement in value impacting the computer industry. Industry wide, value and margin are also shifting away from hardware altogether and moving toward software, indicating concurrent, multiple shifts in value.

Today, economic value is decided in the customer's mind and simultaneous shifts in value are becoming common. This means organizations, if they are to avoid being taken by surprise, must be actively looking and listening for hints of value on the move.

## Too Slow to React

Examples like the rise in popularity of foreign cars seem obvious to us now; however such shifts are less easy to see from close range. Today's market leaders are often slow to react to changing perceptions of value. Like IBM when value shifted away from the mainframe and toward the personal computer, these firms continue to maintain their primary investment in the old order, the old technology, the old corporate structure. They continue to lose vitality because they fail to recognize or understand the nature of the value shift that is happening before their eyes.

Sometimes organizations are so focused on combating the "black hole" effect, trying to protect a single product or category, they fail to take note of the far larger, more important secondary shift of value across the whole industry. Ironically, those who are not current market leaders may enjoy a distinct advantage when value shifts. Not as wedded to the old ways, they may be more able and willing to move when value shifts.

History shows that the customer base gravitates toward disequilibrium while business seeks equilibrium. In other words, the needs and wants of customers tend to change, while the companies naturally seek to stay the same. This can be a fatal dynamic when value shifts. Value bleeds out quickly when the link between the company's offering and the current customers' need is broken.

## The Whole Value Proposition

The bundle of value that an organization delivers to its customers is called the "value proposition." More than just the product itself, it includes price, service, selection, and intangibles such as image and brand equity. The value proposition, in short, is not just what the customer is buying but what he or she thinks she is buying. Thus, an American Express Gold Card is more than a charge card, and a Lexus is not just another luxury car.

Sometimes exceptionally strong brand and/or corporate equity can act as a bulwark against value erosion. But this rear guard protection can only stall the inevitable decline; it cannot stop it.

Harley Davidson offers a classic example. During the late 1970s and early '80s, when Harley was experiencing serious quality problems with its motorcycles, its distributors and customers grumbled, but stayed loyal. This loyalty, based on Harley's mystique, bought the company time to improve its quality and ultimately regain leadership in the industry.

If Harley's brand equity had been weaker when it entered the crisis, it would not have survived. Many companies do not have strong brand equity to fall back on in a crisis. A value shift can strike them quickly, fatally.

# What Causes Value to Shift?

Value shifts for many reasons. Sometimes the shifts are due to epic detonations, such as major technological breakthroughs, or even wars and natural disasters.

The great advances made in post-war aircraft were a by-product of the incredible investment made in aviation during World War II. The Cold War arms race accelerated space exploration and that, in turn, spurred electronic miniaturization. The discovery of printed circuits turned the vacuum tube into a museum piece in a matter of years. The combustion engine retired the horse as the chief means of transportation, a position it had held unchallenged for two millennia.

Not all shifts in value are so dramatic. More often, the change takes longer and is less obvious. But such shifts are no less powerful in their ultimate impact. Some of the most important and common causes of value shifts include the following.

## Demographics

Look at the impact an aging population is having on health care, travel, housing and even clothing styles. As the baby boomers age, push-up bras, fanny-lifting jeans and relaxed-fit pants are coming into fashion. In health care, the pre-World War II generation is causing a boom in home care, ambulatory and convalescent care. As that generation retires and moves to warmer climates, it also helps push down housing prices in the Northeast and raise them in the Sun Belt states.

The aging of the pre-war and baby boom generations will also have a profound impact on financial services. As the baby boomers inherit their parents' accumulated assets, we will witness the greatest generational transfer of wealth in history. This will create immense demand for financial planning services and new financial products. In fact, this has already begun.

## Technology

Technology has proved again and again that it can redefine what is possible in terms of performance and quality, as illustrated in the America's Cup race. An old sea chantey says of sailing ships that "sailor's dreams and wooden beams are what makes them go."

Today's high-tech matchups are as much a battle of super-computers as a race between boats.

The skill of the crew is still vitally important, but more and more, the margin of victory (*i.e.*, source of value) is determined by how information is brought to bear on the design and operation of the vessel. This is a microcosm of what is happening in our economy as a whole.

Closer to the average consumer's heart, examine today's new generation of semiconductors enabling computers to do things with sound and visuals undreamed of only a few years ago. This new capability is spawning powerful, innovative software. Computers have transformed information into a wealth-producing asset comparable to capital and energy.

Even the normally conservative industry of banking is being revolutionized by technology. Arguably, technology is now as important to banking as is capital. U.S. banks are consolidating at a furious pace in order to acquire the financial muscle to acquire the technology that, in turn, will improve their ability to reach the customer.

When the smoke clears, it is predicted there will be 20 or so big, technologically strong banks able to deliver a wide range of financial services to customers all across the country. The importance of branch banking will fall precipitously.

## New Materials

New materials present an entirely new way of doing things. As the price of wood goes up, for example, the use of cheaper and often stronger alternatives such as steel frames in construction is increasing. Fine ceramics are being used increasingly in engines and electronics. High-performance plastics and composites based on carbon fibers are transforming the auto and aerospace industries.

In 1979, the annual volume of plastic produced in the United States overtook steel for the first time. Plastics are often lighter and stronger than metals and can be made more cheaply. All-plastic cars and planes, held together by new superglues, could be common in the next century.

Better microchips made from gallium arsenide promise further leaps in computing power while fiber-optic and satellite advances are transforming telecommunications and medicine. Cement has even gone high tech and is being used to make bottle tops, brake shoes, and loudspeakers!

## Economic Cycles

Economic cycles can explosively shift value in new directions. During the Depression, value shifted away from private industry to government, especially the federal government.

The recession of the early 1990s fundamentally changed the value equation in many industries. Retail discounters and mass merchants like Sam's and Circuit City grew dramatically. Why? Their value proposition, based on large selection and low prices, was well matched to the times. One study looked at the commercialization of 112 major technological innovations and found that many were bunched in the middle of major world depressions.

## Regulation or Deregulation

Changes in the rules can completely change the definition of what constitutes value and what is acceptable in the marketplace. The United States leads the world in environmental technology because the government forced us to do it. Electric cars are coming. Air bags are here already, and now that they are a standard in all cars, watch how quickly manufacturers figure out ways to make them more effective, efficient and less expensive.

In the years following the deregulation of transportation, prices fell 29% in air travel, 20% in trucking and 40% in telecommunications. The increased competition brought on dramatic changes in what customers were prepared to pay for these services. In short, the value equation was fundamentally altered. The present bold deregulation of telecommunications will have a profound impact on value propositions within that industry. These shifts in value will in turn set off waves of restructuring and reengineering.

## Social Attitudes

Nuclear power is much cleaner than coal or oil and may be cheaper to produce. Yet, even such environmental and economic advantages could not save the industry from being buried beneath the public reaction to a single catastrophe. Since Three Mile Island, not a single nuclear power station has been built or commissioned in the United States. Such attitudinal shifts change what people expect in products and the prices they are willing to pay for them.

Another social preference, the desire to work at home rather than in an office, has changed the meaning of "going to work." This, in turn, has created a whole wave of new needs and caused value to move toward products and services (such as fax machines, modems and voicemail) to support home offices and attendant lifestyles.

When Americans travel to Europe today, they expect to use European cash machines. The public has come to expect seamless, highly convenient, global financial services as part of the overall value proposition—and they will get what they expect.

## New Methodologies

Like new technology, new methods can raise the bar on performance. Almost a century ago, mass production was a new methodology which changed the meaning of economic value. Total Quality Management and lean production are only two of the more recent methodologies which have altered the economic value equation.

A significant new methodology can rarely be exploited without changing the basic business model which surrounds it. If a company can, by reorganizing itself, produce a better product in less time and for less money, it has changed not only the name of the game, but the game itself. For Motorola in the radio business and IBM in the mainframe and punch-card business, it was not just technology that needed to change in order for them to follow the movement of value in their industries. They needed to organize themselves in a new way, configure their resources in a new way, and perceive their customers in new ways.

## Competition

Competition, perhaps more than anything else, can quickly trigger a value shift because some competitor, somewhere, is always ready to introduce new systems, products, offerings and very often, lower prices. Within the last decade, for example, two forms of inexpensive, almost instantaneous forms of mail service have appeared, fax and e-mail. They have changed the very concept of correspondence and made the traditional postal service seem like "U.S. Snail."

Now that we are increasingly part of a global economy, there are more competitors entering the market every day. Thus, there are more potential value shifts caused by competition. Thanks to global competition, automobile quality is largely an accepted given. Today, an American automaker cannot just say, "Buy my car because it's a high quality product." Quality is now expected, but this was not the case a few years ago. Until the early 1980s, American automakers could build shiny cars of mediocre quality and still easily make money. Global competition changed all that.

## Shifting Values in Action

Any number of factors can set a value shift in motion. Anything which changes the needs, wants or expectations of consumers can trigger the process. Probably no industry so clearly reflects the impact on value of demographics, changing social attitudes, and new technology as the automobile industry.

Despite a strong economy and relatively low interest rates in recent years, Americans have been slower to buy new cars than most industry experts expected. Sales are up, but not by as much as the industry might have hoped during an upturn in the business cycle. Why?

There is a whole range of reasons, beginning with demographics. Women are playing an increasingly important role in car shopping. Women very often select or strongly influence the purchase of the "family car," and because so many are working, they are also buying their own vehicles. This has tilted purchasing priorities toward safety and economy because women generally see cars more as tools than as toys.

Women are also shifting home expenditure priorities back to home improvements. Both men and women now see purchasing a computer as more important than purchasing a new car. Many things are now seen as more important than a new car, including entertainment systems, new kitchens, and vacations. Owning a new car has dropped from third on the list of household priorities in 1984 to 11th in 1994.

Social attitudes also have changed. Having the latest model is not the status symbol it once was. Many people consider keeping a car and getting the most out of it as a sign of being a smart consumer.

Technology is also influencing this behavioral shift. Today's cars are better and last longer. There are also, thanks to a boom in leasing, lots of good second-hand autos on the market. Finally, the price of automobiles has crept ahead of household incomes. Contrast this with the price of electronics, which have fallen relative to incomes. With the average car costing twenty thousand dollars or more, people are taking their time before making a decision to purchase.

All in all, this is a potentially important change in perceived value. Priorities are shifting and so is purchasing power. Arguably, value has been shifting out of the auto industry for years. Automobile manufacturing is no longer as important to the economy as it was 30 years ago, and the change in consumer priorities seems part of a long-term trend.

This example highlights the paradox which often accompanies changes in value. Even as the perceived importance of owning a new car declines, U.S. auto manufacturers are doing fine. Companies like Chrysler and Ford, having lowered costs, raised productivity and improved quality, experienced record profits in the mid-1990s. This was accomplished not by selling more cars, but by selling better cars, which cost less to build.

## Technology vs. Methodology

Technology is the most visible factor that can kick off a value shift. Interestingly, technology tends to follow value shifts as often as it initiates them. It usually lags rather than leads the movement of value.

Very often, when you look at the big picture, the "revolutionary" new technology cited as the catalyst for change is usually not so new. More often than not, it has been around for a long time, but no one has figured out how to use it to add value for society. The electric motor and the steam engine existed well before Henry Ford's mass production system finally gave us the means of exploiting them.

Having the capability to do something new does not necessarily mean the world is ready and willing to do it. Federal Express' "Zap" mail failed, not because the methodology was weak, but because the demand was weak. There simply were not enough people who perceived value in the product.

If technology is not a primary detonator, what is? Often, it is the methodology that organizes the technology, although the incubation period for new methodologies can be long. Total Quality Management, for example, needed 10 to 15 years, and a lot of economic pain, before the methodology took hold in North American business. Computers have been around for more than 40 years, but we are only learning now to really combine them with expert systems to dramatically raise productivity and service. Consider the value shift to home health care just beginning to blossom. Much of the medical equipment needed for home care has been available on Kmart shelves or in mail order catalogs for a long time.

Now that the shift to home health care is finally underway, money and brain power will flow into this sector along with more and better technology to support remote health care. When this new technology arrives on the scene, it will add further to home health care's value. But this new technology will be in response to the fundamental shift in value rather than a cause of it.

# 4

# What's So Different About Today's Value Shifts?

*The new source of power is not money in the hands of a few, but information in the hands of many.*

—*John Naisbitt*

## Value Shifting in Real Time

In his wonderfully insightful book, *Digital Economy*, Don Tapscott shows how new value is turning our definition of what customers will pay for upside down. Tapscott points out that "telephones used to cost money, but after a monthly charge, their local use was free. Today, cellular phones are mostly free, but cost a lot to use locally. In the old economy, computer hardware was the big cost driver and source of profits. Today, general purpose hardware is becoming dirt cheap. Cost and profits have shifted to software and services." In industry after industry, we are seeing economic value move in new directions and take on new form. Here are just a few examples of shifts in value we are seeing today:

- **Financial Services**
  Transacting → Lending → Storing/Investing

- **Car Rentals**
  Automobile/Location → Speed and Convenience

- **Entertainment**
  Distribution → Programming

- **Computers**
  Hardware → Software
         ↓
  Individual → Groupware

- **Travel**
  General Purpose Agents → Specialists → Travel Management

- **Banking**
  Retail Distribution → Remote Digital Access

- **Transportation**
  Trucks and Planes → Integrated Logistics

- **Airlines**
  Plane → Reservation Systems → Ticketless Access

- **Roofing**
  Replacement → Preservation

- **Health Care**
  High Cost Settings → Low Cost Settings

- **Clothing**
  Manufacturing → Distribution → Fashion & Brand Management

The movement of value is not unique to the 1990s. Value shifts occurred at the time of the Crusades, with the building of cathedrals in the Middle Ages and the rise of urban centers in Europe, with Christopher Columbus and the great age of exploration, with the invention of Gutenberg's printing press and the Protestant Reformation, with the American Civil War and with the arrival of mass production. All of these events, and hundreds of others like them, marked the beginnings of value shifts in economic history as society's needs and wants changed.

What is different today is the speed with which value shifts occur. Velocity is clearly increasing. Why? Chalk it up to two things—*information* and *competition*. There is more of both at work in today's economy.

Added competition means customer expectations are constantly being raised with new offerings. Access to information means customers quickly find out about these new possibilities. Information and competition combine to make shifts in value quick and inevitable.

Consider the case of Fidelity, an aggressive investment company, which pioneered "no load" funds and helped revolutionize investing. Fidelity outmaneuvered many of the old market leaders by offering a new value proposition based on cutting or reducing brokerage fees. Fidelity was not bashful about advertising its funds, which tended to perform extremely well. Fidelity demystified investing and to some extent democratized what had once been a "high brow" business, catering largely to the wealthy.

Now, Fidelity itself is subject to the scrutiny of an army of well-informed consumers. For example, Mutual Fund Investors Alert (MFIA) publishes a Fidelity Profit Alert under the banner "Find Out What Fidelity Doesn't Want You To Know." This means any perceived weakness in a Fidelity fund is instantly communicated to the marketplace. Fidelity is now racing to stay ahead of the very consumer revolution it helped create.

## A Nuclear Chain Reaction

Value shifts come in waves. Think about what's happening today in transportation, telecommunications, entertainment, health care or tourism. They are all undergoing massive waves of change. The pattern is clear. New expectations and needs bring on new technology, methodologies, product offerings and a host of new competitors. These factors feed off one another, igniting yet more value shifts. Taken together, the whole process resembles a chain reaction, releasing enormous intellectual energy.

The sudden shift in power from producers to consumers has unleashed forces around the world, rapidly altering value equations and causing industries to collide as they drift into each other in pursuit of value. Telecommunications, for instance, is getting involved in the cable business, and cable in the telecommunications business. Together they are venturing into the entertainment business, even as electric utilities toy with the idea of becoming information carriers.

Value is moving in a number of new directions all at once. This makes it doubly difficult, but doubly *important*, to stay ahead of the curve.

## Productivity Paradox

To fail to stay ahead of a value shift is to risk becoming irrelevant. Because margins shift along with value, those organizations which catch this wave can profit handsomely. Some are so well positioned vis-à-vis the new value equation, they can make money in spite of themselves. Arguably, this is what happens in the early days of most new industries.

The new value proposition is always more efficient and more compelling than the model it replaces, and with such an advantage, profits are nearly unavoidable. For example, in health care today, value is shifting rapidly toward "integration" and "lower cost settings." This means that HMOs and home care operations are well positioned to make money.

However, these profits hide an inherent paradox. Despite their profits, these early winners are not necessarily efficient, at least when compared to the potential efficiency of the new paradigm. Take, for example, the first transoceanic jetliners. They were much more efficient and many times faster than the passenger ships they replaced. Their cost and convenience were so superior that they swept the great fleets of ocean liners off the seas in a matter of a few years.

But were the Boeing 707 or DC8 really efficient aircraft? By yesterday's standards, yes, but not by today's. Loved by the pilots who flew them, these old jets were nevertheless noisy, smoky gas guzzlers. Today's profitable HMOs and home care operations are health care's equivalent of the DC8, better than what they are replacing, but not nearly as good as they are going to become.

This "productivity paradox" is typical of industries experiencing an influx of value. They make lots of money, not because they are efficient compared to what is possible, but because they are efficient compared to what exists. In ironic contrast, industries experiencing value deterioration and its inevitable by-product, margin pressure, are usually very efficient. These mature industries have learned to squeeze every last ounce of efficiency from the old paradigm as a matter of survival. The only way to hold capital in the old industry, while margins are declining, is to become very efficient.

# Falling Into Place

Once a value shift clearly begins, vast amounts of resources follow. Look at how fast value is shifting toward home health care and how much access to money there is for companies involved in that business. When you look at that value shift in retrospect, you wonder why it took so long for it to happen.

First, home is where people prefer to be, especially when they are sick. Most people consider even the best hospitals as awful places. Second, it is so much less expensive to lie in your own bed. Third, as any nurse will tell you, you are safer at home than in a hospital. You are much less apt to develop infection or be otherwise injured in your own home than in a hospital.

There are limitations to home care, but most of them are technological. Some procedures performed in hospitals cannot be done at home. Over time, the inflow of resources chasing value will bring on an arsenal of home health care products that will change our view about what can be done at home versus what must be done in hospitals. It was, after all, only a few years ago that testing for pregnancy required a visit to the doctor.

When a value shift like this seems so clear, one can imagine medical equipment manufacturers thinking of all the hospital products that could be repositioned for home use. (If they are not, they *should* be!)

The value shift to home care does not mean hospitals are going to disappear, nor does it mean there is no need for improved equipment or that hospitals will stop ordering equipment. But there will be an increasingly higher margin in home care and pressure for medical manufacturers to create equipment to support this shift in value. As mentioned earlier, technology more often follows than leads.

# Closest to the Customer

In an information-driven economy, power moves downstream toward the customer, so those who are closest to the customer are best positioned to win. This is precisely what is happening in the pharmaceutical industry today. Not long ago, the real value in pharmaceuticals came out of research and development labs. While new products are still vitally important, power has shifted toward those with information on the client. Managed care companies (HMOs) began collecting information on what drugs individual patients were using, knowledge formerly held by doctors and druggists and not readily available.

Companies like Medco used this information to press doctors to use less expensive but equally effective alternative drugs. Their knowledge of the customers overtook the pharmaceutical company's knowledge of chemistry. This triumph is evident in margins which shifted toward managed care companies. In 1987, HMOs, using the services of Medco and similar firms, commanded discounts of 11.3% versus 1% for traditional buyers. By 1992, HMO discounts were up to nearly 27%. Along with this shift in power came a massive shift in market share. Managed care grew from 25.5% in 1987 to 55% in 1992 and is still growing.

Recognizing the importance of this shift, Merck & Company bought Medco in 1993. Merck's intent was not to vertically integrate (Medco does not push Merck products) but to gain access to Medco's database. In short, it was pursuing knowledge-driven margins, which had already started to shift toward customer information.

Once value shifts, everything else begins to fall into place. A mad dash ensues to see who can capture the most value in the new domain. This is true of all value shifts, not just in health care. Why do you think IBM so aggressively pursued its $3.3-billion-purchase of Lotus? It was pursuing value, which is shifting toward software.

All in all, the process might be messy, but it works, and is fascinating to watch.

## A Microshift in Value: The House Call

An excellent example of a microshift in value is to be found in the electronics industry where CompUSA, Office Max and Tandy's Computer City are piling up profits by reintroducing an old fashioned concept, the house call. It seems customers are willing to pay $80 to $140 per visit for assistance in installing, adjusting or repairing computers or other home electronic systems. In retrospect, it all makes sense. With more and more people operating home offices and with home electronics becoming ever more powerful and sophisticated, a shift in the locus of technical support was inevitable. More and more consumers and small business owners find themselves stranded when the expensive technology they have purchased underperforms or stops working. Anyone who has ever tried to take apart a complex home theater system because the CD sub-component didn't work will understand the problem. A friend of ours likened the experience to trying to reverse-engineer the space shuttle.

Category killers who sell equipment expecting busy consumers to stop their lives and "bring it in" when it breaks down are missing an important opportunity to add value. In contrast, those responding to the rising need for on-site technical support are being handsomely rewarded. CompUSA says that profit margins on house calls can be as high as 20%, much higher than on merchandise. At Microcomputer Publishing, a high-end retailer in New York, 50 of its 90 employees are now technicians. Computer City says that home service (which customers pay for) and free installation of upgrades have significantly reduced expensive returns. Responding to such an obvious shift in value is not just a sound profit making strategy, it also creates a barrier to disintermediation.

## Double Shifts in Value

Value often moves in more than one direction simultaneously. Such double shifts in value can sometimes act as a smoke screen, making it difficult for executives to isolate and understand the importance of events taking place around them. In the mid-1960s, passenger shipping companies, for example, were battling a shift in transportation value from ships to jet planes. When crossing the Atlantic or the Pacific, people increasingly preferred the speed of air travel (10 to 20 hours) versus the luxury of sea travel (5 to 10 days). Steamship marketing executives wracked their brains to find ways to fill berths. They lowered prices, added new shipboard activities and even tried painting the ships different colors, but nothing worked.

Meanwhile, value on a larger, industry-wide scale was shifting toward cruising. Not many people wanted to cross the Atlantic by ship; but they did want to take vacations in sunny locations, and going by ship was increasingly popular. Cruising, which would eventually become the fastest-growing segment of the tourism industry, was born. This birth went unnoticed by most of the traditional steamship companies because their best brains were absorbed in trying to get people back on the North Atlantic. It was left to outsiders, like Carnival Cruise Line's Mickey Arison, to lead the new industry toward the 21st century.

IBM was also taken by surprise by a double shift in value. In the late 1970s and early '80s, much of its energy was focused on the value movement from the mainframe business toward the PC business. IBM was well positioned in both businesses, but its historical roots and its chief source of revenue came from mainframes. To push aggressively ahead with PCs would threaten the old business. While wrestling with this dilemma (unsuccessfully, as it turned out), it failed to recognize the far more fundamental shift in value toward software and away from hardware altogether.

As Ross Perot likes to point out, when he started EDS, software and related services represented only 10 percent of the total revenue of the multi-billion-dollar computer industry: Hardware accounted for the rest. To IBM, which dominated the hardware sector, software looked like a side show. Yet to Perot, with a thousand dollars in investment capital, and a dream, 10 percent looked pretty good. IBM eventually got the message but not until later in the game. Then it had to buy its way in back into the market.

## Getting Closer to the Customer

Nearly all of the value movement we see today is toward global service and value-added information. If an organization does not head in the same direction, it risks being left behind, caught in the wrong economic quadrant when the smoke clears.

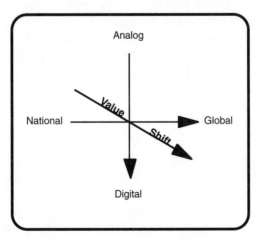

In the mid-1990s, Ross Perot's old company, EDS, now one of the world's largest systems integrators, began buying consulting firms. Why would a firm whose role is to manage a client's computer hardware and software want or need to buy a business consulting firm? One answer is to get closer to its customers.

Applying computer technology has become a key part of strategic planning and decision making. The line between consulting firms which provide strategic support services and system integrators which provide information technology services is blurring. Consultants traditionally help executives address fundamental business issues, and increasingly, information technology is one of those issues. By acquiring consulting expertise, the system integrator gets closer to the vital need driving the purchase of information technology services. It is a classic knowledge-driven strategy.

Using retail shopping as an example, in half a century, value has shifted from the small local store, to the large downtown department store, to large superstores in the malls, to today's highly segmented retail market of discounters, specialists and superstores. Where will merchandising's value shift to next? It is already happening in home shopping, which combines merchandising with the telecommunications, cable and entertainment industries.

This is similar to what is happening to personal computers for the home. Not long ago, most industry experts believed businesses would be the market for powerful PCs. Yet, the home computer is emerging as the "muscle machine" of the 1990s. Today's multimedia entertainment and educational software require lots of computing power. As a result, a typical multimedia home PC now comes with a 500-megabyte hard drive. In 1994, nearly 18% of home computers were sold with Intel's most powerful chip, the Pentium, compared to 15.6% of business machines. Nearly 70% of home computers sold in 1994 had CD-ROM capability. Home PC sales are expected to surpass total business sales in 1996. This shift in raw computing power to the home, combined with the increasing importance of networks like the Internet, will only accelerate the underlying economic shift in power from producers to consumers.

Transportation is another area where knowledge-added value is bringing businesses closer to the consumer. The deregulation of transportation in the 1980s triggered a competitive free-for-all which produced a new definition of transportation value, requiring answers to three questions: How fast? How reliable? How affordable? For people on the road or in the air, travel schedules had to become instantly available. For those wanting to ship goods or documents, it did not matter if the items went by land, sea or air as long as the process was quick, reliable and affordable.

Suddenly, information became the key to adding value. For package and document transportation, customers demanded to know, "Where is my package right now and when will it arrive?" Today, any shipping company which cannot track a customer's parcel is dead. Next-day, or two-day, delivery anywhere in the country is now something we have come to expect. Rapid delivery is no longer a value-added element, or a "*wow!*" factor. The value-added element of logistics now lies in simplifying the process for customers and in dramatically reducing the costs. (Global transportation costs per pound have dropped, yet shipping bills in many cases have gone up because our expectations have risen, and we opt to pay for expedited delivery.)

Transportation companies are no longer calling the shots as much as they are heeding the wishes of their clients. In a sense, they are leaving the business of transportation and becoming consultants—purveyors of knowledge, expertise and most importantly, information.

## The Value Chains

While executives understandably tend to focus on reconfiguring their own firms, they often overlook how the industry-wide chain of value is changing. What is a chain of value? At the corporate level, it is the series of steps taken to add value for the customer, such as raw materials, items added by the assembler and the distributor, and after-sale service. Taken together, these all make up the corporate chain of value.

It is important to understand that when value shifts, it often does so on an industry-wide basis. For example, the end of the

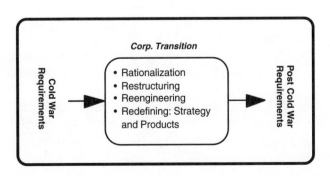

Cold War altered the value equation in the aerospace industry. There was a significant drop in demand for military aircraft. This forced dramatic changes in the way McDonnell-Douglas, Boeing, Hughes, Lockheed and Martin Marietta operated. The firms slashed costs, reduced defect rates, simplified operations, contracted-out peripheral functions, and trimmed product lines.

Those changes occurred within the context of individual corporations—makers of aluminum, composite materials, landing gear, simulators, windows, seats, storage bins and a thousand other items were required to reengineer their operations to stay in tandem with their largest customers. This, in turn, affected their suppliers, and the process cascaded down through the industry.

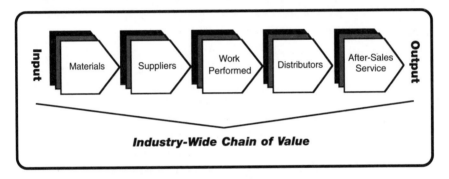

**Industry-Wide Chain of Value**

The tumult did not end there. It was not long before the big players in the aerospace industry began to merge operations to further cut costs. The coming together of Lockheed and Martin Marietta is a classic example, as was the merger of Grumman and Northrop. Before long, the whole industry-wide chain of value, from suppliers to manufacturers to distributors, was again overhauled.

## Integrating the Chain of Value

Such large-scale revolutions include the merging and integrating of strategic work flows across the entire chain of value. Reengineering and integrating the "total" value chain can reveal enormous waste and redundancy.

Consider what has happened to the auto industry's chain of value over the past 15 years. First, there were rising customer expectations of quality and the introduction of lean production and

TQM. As a result, the Big Three slimmed down and systematized operations. People were laid off, contracts renegotiated, and inefficient or redundant facilities closed. Next, billions were spent on new technology, new plants and state-of-the-art equipment. Huge investments were made also to train employees and more importantly to teach employees to play critical roles as partners in a total quality process. All of this took place at the corporate level.

Meanwhile, industry wide, the Big Three entered into alliances with competitors, such as Ford with Mazda. Chrysler absorbed American Motors and its Jeep operations. Lean production and TQM meant being more efficient by, among other things, shrinking inventory. Shrinking inventory meant forcing suppliers to ship parts just-in-time, and with dramatically higher levels of quality and reliability.

That, in turn, forced suppliers to overhaul and reengineer their own operations to meet these demanding new criteria, who ended up putting pressure on their own suppliers.

Thus, the shift in value in auto manufacturing in the 1980s worked its way into related industries, such as transportation. Just-in-time manufacturing created a wave of demand for reliable, expedited transportation. UPS and Federal Express found themselves as critical links in this new, faster, leaner chain of value, because unless the goods arrived in time, the whole process broke down.

Viewed from the perspective of the total chain of value, much of this improvement was focused on the middle of the chain on *production*. And it worked! The quality of U.S. automobiles shot up. Efficiency improved, in some cases dramatically. Suddenly, Chrysler emerged as the lowest-cost car producer in the world.

What about the front and back of the chain? The next stage of the improvement process requires auto executives to look downstream at distribution, which accounts for 30% of costs. It is no accident that GM set out in the mid-1990s to overhaul what was called its "large, unwieldy dealership and distribution network." This process is now under way and will result in a distribution system that is cheaper, faster and more customer focused.

W. Edwards Deming was right: "The system will do what the system will do." To effect change, we must alter the system. This rule is as true today as when Deming first enunciated it 50 years ago. What has changed is our view of what constitutes the system. Increasingly, competitive advantage is derived by rationalizing and improving the total industry-wide value chain. If you look

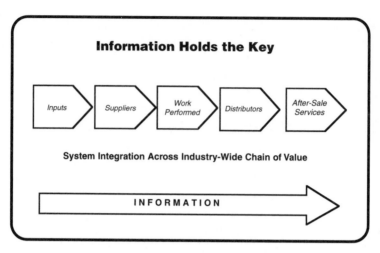

carefully, you will see that this is precisely what price and quality leaders like Wal-Mart, Ford and Motorola are doing today.

Again, the key is to integrate with suppliers and share information and procedures to make the value chain transparent and seamless. Linked by common information systems and procedures, the various partners in the chain begin acting organically, as if they were one entity rather than separate companies. The result is that huge chunks of work flow are exposed as redundant and thus, expendable. It is not unusual for these reengineered value chains to be 30–40% cheaper, faster and more reliable than the fragmented systems they replace.

## Top of the Food Chain

The two reengineering efforts, corporate and industry, often start simultaneously. Again, most people understand the corporate shift but not the larger one. Think of it this way: *as value shifts, so does the process by which it is delivered*. In fact, it is hard to think of a value shift which does not impact the value chain in some way.

As we have seen, large-scale restructuring is taking place across whole industries. Retailing, telecommunications, entertainment, transportation, health care, pharmaceuticals and utilities are all undergoing massive changes in response to value moving in new directions. Weak players and underperforming components are being eliminated, and industries reconfigured to provide more value, quicker, and at less cost. As non-value-added components and redundant steps are replaced, the need for inventory, working capital and personnel services drop, often dramatically. Those most at risk, whether organizations or individuals, are those farthest from the customer. Those closest to the customer and the customer's need for information are most likely to be at the top of the food chain. All this movement, from the restructuring of an entire industry to the reshaping, creation or elimination of individual jobs, is set in motion by a shift in customer perceived value . . . a very small explosion leading to a very big bang.

# *Part III*

# Coming to Grips With Shifting Value in Business

# 5

# Why Even Smart Companies Sometimes Act Dumb

*When faced with a choice between changing and proving there's*
*no need to change, most people get busy on the proof.*

*—John Kenneth Galbraith*

People, organizations, products, services and value propositions . . .
all have a beginning, a middle and an end. Most companies last
only a single generation, and only a handful make it beyond two
generations. Of the 1925 Fortune 500 list, almost all are gone. Even
the Fortune 500 list of 1970 has lost more than half its members.
Death, as we are so often reminded, is part of life.

Although nothing lasts forever, organizations can extend life
by continually adding value. Arguably, this is the only way to
extend life in a free market system. Of course, this means continually adapting and changing. Unfortunately, most organizations,
when faced with the need to change, choose instead to perish.

Value often shifts in one direction as the firm moves in another,
much like a drowning person who, becoming confused, swims away
from the lifeboat. To understand this pathology, we must first understand the lifecycles of organizations. Such cycles bear a remarkable

resemblance to lifecycles in nature. Natural scientists tell us that life follows a predictable pattern, resembling a great S-curve.

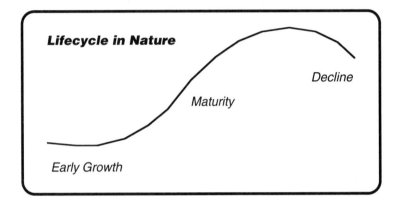

Under a microscope, these large lifecycles actually appear as multiple S-curves.

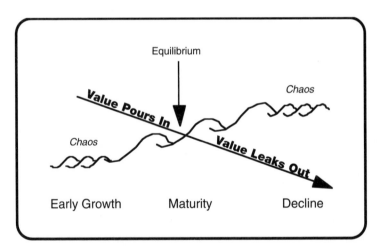

At the beginning, the short, choppy S-curves represent the pain, exhilaration and chaos of birth. The beginning of each corporate lifecycle is also shown by short, choppy S-curves. At this stage, value is pouring into the industry. From a distance, these short S-curves appear symmetrical, even aesthetically pleasing, but the truth is far more brutal. These little curves represent chaos.

Living through such periods of change brings to mind the Chinese curse, "*May you live in interesting times.*" At the beginning of the growth curve, value is pouring into the industry like a torrent.

Everyone is trying to capture as much of this value as possible, but no one is sure what will work best. Consequently, multiple models, technologies and methodologies battle for supremacy. You may remember when 30 brands of personal computers and several incompatible operating systems were on the market. That is what this chaotic start-up period is like. Today, the Internet and its supporting industries are well into this chaotic start-up phase of growth.

In this early stage, as the industry searches desperately for the right value proposition, each new corporate offering brings a market response. Winning and losing can be affected by even the smallest variables. Picking the winners and losers in such a melee is a risky business. History tells us the best technology or concept may not always win out. Witness the video battle between VHS and Beta, in which the latter was considered by technophiles to be superior, but the former emerged the victor.

This early chaos reflects the heroic, entrepreneurial age of the corporation or the technology. In these heady years, anything is possible. "Try it, do it, fix it" becomes the order of the day. Everyone feels the adrenaline. This heady start-up phase, though, is usually brought to an end with a bloody shakeout, followed by industry consolidation.

During the second stage, winners emerge, the long lifecycle S-curves take over and the environment becomes more stable. Value is more or less in equilibrium. The shakeout leaves a handful of players still standing, all intent on recouping their investment.

## Repeating the Pattern of Success

The age of experimentation ends, and the age of implementation begins. Industries shift from tumult to stability. During this stage, success belongs to those who can master, improve and then repeat most efficiently the winning pattern or formula. The whole organization structure, way of operating, and culture is geared to repeating the pattern of success. Continual improvement becomes a central goal. Every effort is focused on refining and making more efficient the existing model. During this period, those threatening the pattern, including intrapreneurs, entrepreneurs and other champions of new models, are shunned, perhaps even exorcised. This stability can last for years, even decades. Things move merrily along until value shifts again. This next shift brings on maturity, decay and finally, lost value.

This last stage is signaled by a crisis. But within the whirling, clanking apparatus designed to repeat the corporation's successful pattern, the level of concentration and noise is so great, no one may notice the movement of value. Financial results by their very nature are lagging indicators, and thus, often remain strong well into the downturn. As we previously pointed out, dissenting opinions often are not welcome.

## Old Order in Decline

As value moves from one business model to another, it slowly unhinges the old order. Whatever the causes of the value shift, such as demographics, economic cycles, deregulation, or social attitudes, the business environment changes dramatically. Profit margins head south, and in time, investment capital flows out. Slowly, imperceptibly, the old, successful model of the past becomes less and less functional. At this point the short, choppy S-curves, so familiar at the beginning, start to reappear.

Organizations with forward-looking sensors, and these are few, may pick up distant signals of trouble ahead. Most are too busy perfecting the old pattern to notice. Eventually, indicators such as customer satisfaction, market share, market valuation, and brand equity start to erode, and value visibly deteriorates. Now, the short, choppy S-curves of chaos and the resulting discomfort are evident to almost everyone. There is a nagging feeling that something is wrong, but few can articulate the problem. This is the moment of truth for the institution and its leadership. If the organization is to survive, it must now move in bold, new directions. Unfortunately, if history is any guide, most fail this important test.

## A Story of Failed Change

If you go out looking for it, you will find value in the most unlikely of places. The key is to recognize it when you see it. New value often comes in forms that are often very different from the old. Take, for example, a company called Slamco, Inc., which is actually a composite of several companies.

Slamco was an industrial manufacturing firm whose core products consisted of high-grade construction materials. More than a century old, this firm had a long tradition of success, but found itself under increasing competitive pressure as market share shrank and margins eroded. The traditional market leader, Slamco had propelled itself to success using a simple, but powerful formula. It sold top quality products and supported clients with well trained representatives who inspected large construction projects and wrote "free" specifications.

These specifications were very exacting and so tended to favor Slamco's high quality, premium priced products. Because these products were among the best on the market, the client was usually well served. All in all, the formula worked well. The company experienced decade after decade of growth and achieved revenues of nearly one billion dollars.

However, by the late 1980s, this value proposition was weakening. The quality of products throughout the industry had improved greatly during the decade. Slamco no longer enjoyed an absolute product-quality advantage. Still worse, the value added by its "reps" was also eroding. Increasingly, they found themselves in competition with independent construction consultants.

Thanks to new information technology, these independent consultants provided more detailed reports and specifications than Slamco's reps. Although the independents charged for this service, their reports were perceived as being technically superior and, more importantly, unbiased. In short, the value-added provided by both Slamco's core products and its network of reps was eroding. Value was moving away from the old success formula in a classic way. Independent consultants were using superior information technology to disintermediate Slamco's traditional relationship with its customers.

The first people to recognize the seriousness of the situation were the reps themselves. They complained bitterly to the company about having to work harder and harder just to stay even with the competition. However, the company turned a deaf ear to their concerns. "Salespeople are always complaining," some executives said as they blocked investment in the updated technology that would allow its reps to compete with the independents.

Ironically, while unwilling to invest in technology to support their sales and service representatives, Slamco did invest heavily in new construction products, even though such products were quickly becoming a commodity in the industry. Why? Investing in construction materials was something Slamco understood and was familiar with. Investing in information technology was alien and appeared risky.

The company had always operated on the assumption that its superior products were at the root of its success. This theory was flawed. Although high quality products were indeed part of the success formula, what really made the formula work was the network of sales reps. They provided the added value which differentiated the company from its competitors.

If Slamco had bothered to look, it would have seen this truth in the numbers. During the 1980s, as the competition closed the product-quality gap, the company managed to stay ahead of the pack. Why? Because it had a superb sales force. It was only when the value-added provided by the sales force went into decline by the late 1980s that the company found itself in real trouble. Even then, its first response was to invest more and more money in construction materials.

Amidst this melee, a small band of discontented sales reps developed a new information system for managing large materials inventories. These renegades believed future value-added would come in the form of information rather than products. They began marketing their inventory management system to large national and international clients who were responsible for managing dozens and sometimes hundreds of building projects. These clients were desperate for help and welcomed the innovation. Overnight, the demand for the product skyrocketed as sales doubled and then tripled. More importantly, for every dollar of inventory management sold, the company also sold ten to twenty dollars in core construction materials.

News of the new inventory management system spread quickly through the sales force. It was the first good news for the reps in a long time, but rather than celebrate, senior management was horrified. The response of the executives was sullen and uncooperative. They were reluctant to invest in the product, and at sales meetings, they were uncommunicative and even testy when questioned about the new system. They did not like the new product because it turned everything they had ever learned about the construction business upside down. In the end, they starved the new inventory system of funding.

In despair, the renegades began jumping ship. They took their concepts, enthusiasm and expertise to the competition. Within five years, Slamco had lost several hundred million dollars in market valuation and was sold to a competitor which had embraced the "information value-added" concept. It was a sad ending for a fine firm, slain by its own aversion to learning.

# The Doom Cycle

As the Slamco example shows, both birth and renewal call for vision, courage and a capacity to undertake lots of risk. However, what is clearly different between the beginning and the end is the business environment where these skills will be applied. The chaotic environment during the early growth years is very different from the comfort and certainty which prevail just before the final crisis. At the beginning, resources are few, but so are constraints. Companies, often with empty coffers and burdened by debt, feed off their dreams.

At the other end of the lifecycle, resources abound, but so do constraints. Stock analysts, boards of directors, stockholders, unions, existing strategies, investments in product lines and old technology, politicians, community considerations—all these, and more, get in the way of change. Those who feel threatened by the proposed change resist mightily. Even those not threatened, like the investment community, are likely to be skeptical.

In most corporations, when a value shift occurs and the organization attempts to respond, vested interests will try to slow or even stop the process. They will perceive it, and probably argue against it, as a risky leap into the dark. These vested interests can include shareholders, who will hesitate gambling on a new, unproven product or service, and market analysts, who may criticize management if it appears to be drifting away from its core competency. An underlying company-wide commitment to employees, customers and existing investment can also block the transition. It is all these factors, more than outright stupidity or stubbornness, which keep organizations from adequately responding to value shifts.

Efforts to introduce new, disturbing market information is resisted. The dangerous data is suppressed or ignored because if it were dispensed and believed, it would require changing the organization's structure. This explains why mature organizations have such difficulty launching new businesses. The old organization imposes itself on the new business and kills it off before it can disrupt the status quo. In doing so, it dooms itself.

In their book, *Discontinuous Change,* David Nadler and Robert Shaw refer to this as the "doom cycle." Circumstances change, but the organization does not. In fact, the doomed organization openly fights change by disregarding or suppressing data which points to new opportunities or requirements. Blinded by past success, doomed organizations become cautious, risk averse, unforgiving of errors and intolerant of those who would rock the boat.

By this point in the cycle, confidence has mutated into arrogance. The middle of the organization, in particular, tends to disdain outsiders and outside ideas. This makes it difficult, if not impossible, to introduce new concepts of any sort.

In summary, the entrepreneur risks all, and consults few; the CEO of a mature organization affects all and answers to many. The need to limit risk and gain consensus narrows the established leader's scope for action. Sometimes, it prevents action from being taken altogether. Often the best which can be obtained is permission to play at the margin of the problem, to dabble without taking decisive action. This explains, in part, the inertia which causes organizations to freeze and subsequently perish in the face of large-scale shifts in value and new customer requirements.

## Another Transition Under Way

Eastman Kodak Company has been a phenomenal 20th century success story, but by the mid-1990s, value was on the move. Kodak had "dabbled" with digital applications, but had not made a full-fledged effort, fearful it would make the company's traditional film and chemical products obsolete.

Recognizing the seriousness of the situation, the board of directors turned to George Fisher. The former CEO of Motorola was a hard driver, famous for setting stretch goals for improvement. It was Fisher who pushed Motorola toward Six Sigma (3.4 errors per million), then thought to be an impossible goal. In his early encounters with Kodak's manufacturing executives, he was promised five-fold improvements in certain processes. In classic Fisher style, he responded, "Why not 10 times?"

Upon taking control, Fisher quickly tightened costs by simplifying some segments of the business, but he did not undertake the kind of bloodletting eagerly anticipated on Wall Street. He viewed cutting costs as an important but secondary goal. Fisher is a builder, not a cutter. Instead, the focus of Fisher's value-added strategy called for growing the company by moving into the digital era. He discovered that digital technology within Kodak was dispersed and isolated in pockets throughout the firm. He even uncovered memos from past executives censuring Kodak's investments in digital businesses and technology.

In moving toward digital technology, Fisher faced a classic dilemma met by those who would effect change in mature organizations: the new technology tends to jeopardize existing investments and customers. As Fisher pushed Kodak in new digital directions, he alienated old line "film" employees. These hard working, loyal employees produced 90% of the company's revenue and felt slighted and ignored, given Fisher's preoccupation with digital technology. Fisher did his best to make amends by championing strategies to also expand film sales, but this was perceived as an afterthought by old line film employees.

Fisher also upset people by breaking the tradition of promoting from within and, instead, going outside for executive talent. Furthermore, he had to deal with protests from some of Kodak's bread-and-butter customers. Professional portrait photographers, for example, threatened to boycott Kodak films after the company demonstrated new products that made instant digital copies of photographs, without mentioning the importance of copyright laws. One of Fisher's new "outsiders" admitted this was an error and promised to include copyright warnings in the future.

Overall, Fisher's strategy was sound—hold on to and expand the old business while growing the new digital business. The question is, will the internal Kodak system allow him to succeed? Existing employees, customers and shareholders all have something to gain or lose in this bold effort to move Kodak into the 21st century as a leader in digital technology.

## Disruptive Technology

Professional photographers, Kodak's most loyal customers, were threatened by the proposed changes. Just as often, it is disinterest, not outright opposition, which slows the introduction of new technology. That is what happened to IBM when it considered moving into minicomputers, but its large business and government customers were not interested. This demonstrates another reason mar-

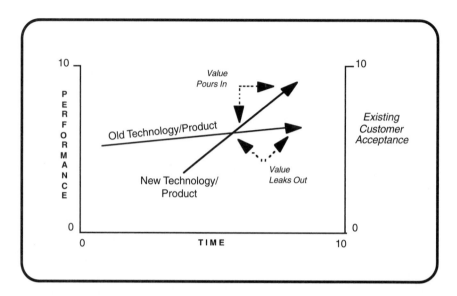

ket leaders usually are not very good at championing entirely new technologies. They are too busy serving existing clients, battling competitors, and looking to expand the core product to pay much attention to tomorrow's breakthrough products and services.

There is an economic disincentive, too, for big companies to be on the cutting edge. New technologies usually underperform compared to the dominant technology in their early stages of development. However, they have a way of catching up and ultimately surpassing the old technology. By the time the market leader recognizes the seriousness of the situation, the new technology or methodology has overtaken the old, and the leader is forced to play catch up.

However, if you stay alert and track the movement of value, as explained in the next chapter, you should be able to pinpoint the sector of your industry that is most likely to grow. Then you have two choices: (1) become a fast follower, acquiring the needed core competencies to make the transition or, (2) buy your way in through alliances or acquisitions of smaller, nimbler competitors. On balance, the latter seems to offer the best prospects. Small firms with low overhead and a "feel" for the emerging market and technology are more likely to be successful in championing new products or technology than old line firms. Whatever strategy is adopted, it is important to protect the new entity from the old, nurturing it and allowing it to be different, so it is not smothered by existing norms and procedures.

## Encyclopedia Britannica

To see a company blindsided by new disruptive technology, we need look no further than Encyclopedia Britannica. This story contains important lessons regarding the burden of past success and the power of internal vested interest opposed to change. It also offers important lessons regarding shifting value, commoditization and disintermediation.

For two centuries, Encyclopedia Britannica published the best-selling encyclopedia in the world. They completely dominated the industry. However, by the early 1990s, it was becoming evident that new CD-ROM technology enabled the world's summary of knowledge to be stored on compact disks in a form cheaper and easier to access than traditional encyclopedias. At first, Encyclopedia Britannica didn't pay much attention to these developments because it was too busy watching its traditional competitors like Colliers and World Book. In hindsight it's clear they should have been watching Microsoft and Grolier, who were busy producing and selling encyclopedias for CD-ROM applications.

If Encyclopedia Britannica had been paying any attention at all to its customer base, it would have noticed that the same people who buy encyclopedias were now investing in CD-ROMs and computers—and for the very same reasons; they were concerned about their children's education. In short, the basic buying motivation was unchanged, but the perception of value was clearly shifting away from Encyclopedia Britannica's old analog offering. By the early 1990s, new competitors were already disintermediating Encyclopedia Britannica from its traditional customers. By 1994, Encyclopedia Britannica had slipped from first to third in market share.

One of the reasons Encyclopedia Britannica was slow to react was because of its past success. A large part of this success had been based on its superb sales force. Sales people and their concerns were at the center of Encyclopedia Britannica's universe. The organization's culture, structure and compensation system were all designed to support and incent its sales force. So long as the old value proposition contained equity, this formula worked well. But once value shifted in new directions, the sales force became a stumbling block to change . . . and it's not hard to figure out why. It all comes down to basic math. You can earn a lot more commission on a $2,000 set of books than on a $100 CD-ROM program. As a result, Encyclopedia Britannica's sales force acted like a drag-chute, slowing up the organization as it searched for a new strategy to regain its competitive edge.

Fortunately, the shock of falling to third place in the industry galvanized Encyclopedia Britannica into action. The company finally took steps to reshape its business strategy. Interestingly, by this point, CD-ROM encyclopedias were themselves being commoditized, as hardware manufacturers gave them away with the purchase of new personal computers. This forced Encyclopedia Britannica to look toward the next technological leap in search of a breakout strategy This led to the development of Encyclopedia Britannica's on-line encyclopedia service. This new product targeted primarily educational institutions rather than individual families. The advantage of Britannica's new service is that its digital encyclopedia is updated daily with new knowledge and is available instantaneously on a global basis. It soon became the company's fastest-growing new product. In essence, Encyclopedia Britannica had changed its product from a published set of hard cover books (a 19th century analog product) to a digital directory targeted at an entirely new market. In undertaking this bold strategy, Encyclopedia Britannica stepped back from the brink and established a new path to the future.

## The Courage to Abandon the Old

Commercial history offers countless examples of organizations which stayed too long with an old technology or old model. By the time they realized the need to change, it was too late. Fortunately, there are also examples, although fewer, of well led companies which had the courage to abandon old certainties and move into the future.

Motorola, for instance, moved away from car radios as a core offering while the business was still strong. As Chairman Robert Galvin likes to point out, those competitors from the 1940s who stayed in the car radio business are now long gone. Motorola survived and prospered because it moved away from old businesses in time.

Northern Telecom also moved away from its core offering while it still contained considerable equity. In the 1950s and '60s, Northern Telecom was one of the world's best manufacturers of electromechanical telephone switches. Beginning in the '60s, Northern decided to go digital and develop a whole new product line based on this advanced technology. This was viewed as a "bet the company" move and opposed by many within the organization.

Although clearly a high-risk maneuver, it worked. In the 1970s, Northern emerged with the DMS100, arguably the world's first affordable, fully functioning digital switch. This established Northern as a leader in digital switching and propelled the company toward two decades of extraordinary growth. As for electromechanic switches, they are historical curiosities, today found mostly in museums. If Northern had stayed with this technology, in which it had so much equity and expertise, it might have become a historical curiosity itself.

Another example of abandoning old technology at its height is to be found in Zebra Technologies, which in 1982, was the market leader in the paper tape-punching machines industry. That same year, the company's co-founders made a decision to enter the business of making industrial bar code label printers at a time when sales of their paper punch machines were at an all time high. In 1994, the company earned $21 million on sales of $107 million, with operating margins of 29%, largely as a result of its bar-coding products. Not surprisingly, competitors are quickly appearing on the scene. In 1991, the company went public and its stock has since appreciated fourfold. Today, technological change is again transforming the bar code business. The question now is whether Zebra Technologies, as a larger, publicly owned company, can adapt to the next wave of technological change as quickly as it did when it was a smaller, privately owned company.

## Yin and Yang of Change

In the late 19th century, American Express was a successful freight forwarder, expanding with the railways across the country. Toward the end of the century, American Express changed its core business from freight forwarding to processing money orders for immigrants. This dramatic shift was resisted fiercely by the "old railroaders." Later, the company went global when it transitioned from money orders to Travelers Cheques, a uniquely innovative product which contributed mightily to the growth of travel and tourism around the world. Again, the move was resisted by powerful insiders, including many in American Express' New York headquarters.

In the late 1950s, the company again transitioned to a new paradigm by introducing its now famous charge card. It did so despite dire warnings that consumers would never give up cash for plastic. Later in the 1980s, the company again defied conventional wisdom and expanded its business to include a broad range of financial services.

This last diversification effort offers a classic example of the yin and yang associated with pursuing new value propositions. In the late 1970s, American Express Chairman and CEO, James D. Robinson III, recognized the need to move the business away from dependence on transacting money through charge cards and Travelers Cheques. He and others inside the firm recognized a subtle but important value shift toward storing or investing money, and to a lesser extent, toward lending money.

Given American Express' strong brand image, global presence, and affluent clients, the company was well positioned to provide additional financial services. In pursuit of this strategy, the company purchased a number of financial institutions, including Shearson, Lehman and IDS, a Minneapolis-based financial planning firm which targeted primarily Middle America. American Express also launched the Optima Card, its first revolving-credit card, in 1987.

## Timing and Execution

Looking back, it is hard to argue with the logic. The value shifts were real, and the status quo was undesirable, if not unsustainable. Despite the soundness of the assumptions, the strategy was, in the end, less than successful.

The failure had as much to do with timing and execution as it did with flawed strategy. The purchase of Shearson Lehman took place just before the downturn in the North American economy. This, combined with the speculative excesses of the 1980s, caused the market to swoon, and the bottom fell out from under Wall Street in 1990–1991. Suddenly, diversification into the brokerage business did not look like such a great idea anymore, and Shearson Lehman became a millstone around American Express' neck at a time when its Optima credit card rang up huge losses.

This all led to a transition in leadership within American Express as Harvey Golub became chairman and CEO. His approach was to aggressively pursue the existing strategy of selling off non-performing assets, such as Shearson, and consolidate the company to a core of travel-related service, IDS, and the American Express Bank. He also reengineered $1 billion out of the cost base. This done, Golub launched a host of new products, including the American Express Purchasing Card and a revitalized revolving credit product, the True Grace Card. He also rebranded IDS as American Express Financial Advisors.

By the mid-1990s, American Express again was experiencing record profits. But a careful look at the numbers showed that the fastest-growing profit center in the American Express empire was American Express Financial Advisors, formerly IDS and a relic of the original diversification strategy. (IDS has been a profit maker for American Express from the beginning, experiencing after-tax earnings of 21% throughout the 1980s.) At its present rate of growth, American Express Financial Advisors could soon be generating more profits than any other component of the business.

## Lessons Learned

Was American Express right to diversify in the late 1980s and early '90s as value shifted toward storing (*i.e.*, investing) money and away from transacting money? Almost certainly, yes. Remember, the worst thing an organization can do when value shifts is nothing.

American Express' longevity has been rooted in its ability to build brand strength even as it transitioned toward new businesses. The timing of this shift was clearly off and, arguably, so was the execution, but the "instinct" to move in new directions was sound. This story provides a classic example of the risks associated with large-scale change: the assumptions behind the strategy, even the strategy itself, can be sound and you can *still* get into trouble.

So Harvey Golub finds himself back at the beginning. He has record profits, cash and one of the world's great brands in his corner. Yet, he faces the same dilemma Robinson faced—a mature business whose core offering is under pressure. His initial response of launching a host of new card offerings, including a revolving credit product, has clearly paid off but looks suspiciously like opening moves in a larger game. Perhaps another shoe will drop at some point in the future.

In today's economy, the status quo can never be comforting for long. As President John Kennedy liked to remind his cabinet, "The dangers associated with bold actions are, in the end, usually less than those which accompany comfortable inaction."

## Getting Unstuck Is Not Easy

It is one thing to see value shifting, but entirely another to turn this perception into an immediate, decisive and correct action. Focusing a large, complex organization on the need for change is not easy, even for the ablest of leaders.

The movement of value appears self-evident, seen from the perspective of economic history. Given enough time, distance and data, everything becomes clear. The same is true when historians dissect a long-ago battle and the necessary decisions appear obvious. However, for those involved in the real struggle, whether in the marketplace or on the battlefield, the "fog of war" is ever present.

Leaders in the midst of the fray rarely perceive "the beginning," the position from which historians later contemplate events. The great Russian writer Count Lev Nikolayevich Tolstoy described this reality in his 19th century classic *War And Peace*. In discussing Field Marshal Mikhail Illarionovich Kutuzov's decision to defend Moscow at Borodino, and later his controversial decision to abandon the city, Tolstoy provides us with what may be the best and most graphic description ever written of the chaotic circumstances in which executive decisions are made.

Tolstoy introduces us to the general as he prepares to confront the French army. He is flooded with mutually exclusive recommendations from his staff. At the same time, he cannot pinpoint the exact location of the French army and possesses only fragmentary information about the locations and movements of his own divisions. When he calls for more information, what he receives is confusing and contradictory, forcing him to use intuition to separate rumor from fact.

His adjutants, his generals, the czar, even civilians with petty gripes take up his time. All the while, Kutuzov's army continues its retreat toward Moscow on half a dozen different roads. Eventually, perhaps accidentally, the army collides with the French, and the great battle begins. Later, historians will describe Kutuzov's decision to fight at Borodino as "brilliant, courageous, an act of genius." Tolstoy knew better, and so does any CEO who has ever been involved in making decisions under pressure. Sometimes we stumble our way to success.

Leaders dealing with today's value shifts can sympathize with Kutuzov. They, too, must make decisions, often with inadequate, conflicting information amid a welter of concurrent activities. The source of the new value often poses a potentially mortal threat to the old value proposition. The leaders may intuitively sense that their old business formula is losing power, but are unsure why. Even if they do know why, the massive investment in the old system is a bar to quick action.

## The Overriding Instinct

Faced with a shift in value, the overriding instinct of most leaders is to circle the wagons. The urge is to protect what already exists—brand equity, physical assets, people, products and customers. While perhaps understandable, such action can make the transition to a new value proposition very difficult. It is not unusual for executives to have a blind spot, especially in tracking the movement of value within their old core business. Data indicating a newly sprouting value can be easily denied, quietly suppressed, or sometimes unconsciously smothered to prevent it from growing and threatening the status quo.

For instance, paper manufacturers completely missed the value shift to lighter, more heat resistant styrofoam cups. When styrofoam first came onto the scene, it was expensive . . . $24 per thousand versus $20 for paper cups. It was also bulky to ship and suffered from quality problems. The paper manufacturers considered it a passing fad. They were wrong.

Within a few years, the foam cup manufacturers solved their quality and transportation problems and improved their manufacturing process to the point where they could make cups for $4 per thousand. This spelled the end for paper cups.

Years later, the foam cup manufacturers resisted innovation in the face of new environmental concerns. One industry executive remembers hiding money in his budget to fund research and development for edible cups made from soybeans. When headquarters found out, they put a stop to it. "We're in the paper and plastic business; what has that got to do with soybeans?" And so the pattern repeats itself.

## Blind to the New

A company we know was for years the dominant player in the business of making steel shafts for golf clubs. They were the market leader because they made the best steel shafts in the world, and invested heavily in steel shaft technology. Unfortunately, that heavy investment blinded them to the importance of new composite materials.

Graphite and composite material shafts were considered amusing by company executives, who ignored the performance advantage of these new shafts. This denial continued even as composite shafts began to eat into their market share. Value deterioration was clearly under way, but everyone denied this reality and tried to whistle their way past the graveyard.

By this point, the company had waited too long. Almost overnight demand shifted, and composite materials took over the high end of the market. Now the company found itself faced with the unenviable task of rebuilding its manufacturing facilities and acquiring new core competencies while hemorrhaging market share and profits. With sufficient time, money and effort, the company ultimately made the transition to composite material technology, but the process was painful and costly. It would have been better to have paid attention to this shift in value toward composite in the first place.

## Paradox of Change: The Problem Is Often the Solution

Change management is ladened with paradox. When a value shift brings on a crisis, such as that which the North Atlantic steamship companies experienced in the 1960s (discussed in the previous chapter), the source of the threat is often as not also the source of the solution. In this case, it was the jet airplane which drove the great liners from the North Atlantic but it was also the jet plane which ultimately made possible the birth of today's modern cruise industry. After all, it's airplanes which fly millions of passengers to Miami, Ft. Lauderdale, San Juan, New York and Vancouver to board their ships.

The same pattern repeats itself again and again in commercial history. For example, the movie studios regarded the VCR as a mortal threat when it first came on the scene. They fought this new technology at every turn. Fortunately for them, they failed, because today videos provide movie studios with their single largest source of profits.

When American Express first brought out its charge cards, the travel community regarded them with great suspicion. They thought American Express would use the card to disintermediate travel agents from their customers and dominate the industry. Of course just the opposite happened. The charge card and later credit cards became a boon to the travel industry by making the payment process more secure, as well as more convenient.

So if you are faced with a shift in value, remember this paradox: *the source of the threat is often the source of the solution.* After all, what is a paradox but a truth standing on its head to get attention.

## The Importance of Change Mastery

Very often, organizations do not initially recognize value decline as the source of their problem. The symptoms can make themselves felt in a number of areas throughout the organization. In medicine, this phenomenon is known as "referred pain." A kidney problem can manifest itself as lower back pain or a high fever. It takes time, testing and experience for the medical practitioner to determine the real source of the problem.

The same is true of organizational maladies. For example, many Fortune 500 companies undertook large-scale reengineering efforts in the early 1990s. They did so on the assumption they had a cost problem, but a number of those firms had an epiphany of sorts in the course of their reengineering efforts. For some, even while costs declined, market share and market valuation did not always improve, or improved only marginally. Why?

The market knew something the reengineers did not—that more was at work here than just a cost problem. Beneath the focus on high costs lay a fundamental erosion of value, and until this was addressed, all the cost cutting in the world would not make a difference.

The real payoff from reengineering, the firms found, came not from cutting costs, but from finding new ways to add value for customers. While paring expenses was useful and necessary, it was not sufficient to win back the marketplace. The key to victory lay in finding ways to grow value for customers and ultimately for shareholders.

Confronted with value erosion, the worst thing an organization can do is nothing. The initial response may be off the mark, but at least the organization is responding. The capacity to change and adapt to new market conditions and rising customer expectations is becoming an indispensable ingredient for success in today's economy. When value shifts, you *must* shift with it . . . quickly. Change mastery is emerging as a meta-competency for the next millennium.

# 6

# Recognizing and Tracking the Movement of Value in Your Industry

*Information has to be organized so it questions and challenges a company's strategy.*

*— Peter Drucker*

Value is dynamic. Proactive organizations must dedicate themselves to staying ahead of it. Just as Wayne Gretzky's success as a hockey player comes from his ability to anticipate where the puck is going, business success will increasingly depend on management's ability to anticipate where value is going. No one can afford to fall behind the value curve in today's competitive environment. When value shifts, you must shift with it and quickly.

Executives who don't monitor and track value and respond to shifts with new strategies set themselves up for disaster down the road. Those who use only "lagging" indicators to assess progress are, in fact, behind the curve already. By the time they realize they have a value problem, the value shift has already happened.

Recognizing and responding to the movement of value on an ongoing basis requires a commitment to learning. You must learn new ways to understand customers and abandon old ways of delivering value to them. You must be obsessively attentive to customers' needs, their changing perception of value and how your competitors affect that perception. Learning holds the key to survival in tomorrow's economy, and we'll discuss that topic in more detail in Chapter 8.

## A Focus on Tomorrow

The most successful organizations will look over the horizon at how tomorrow's customers will define value. In short, they will accurately predict where value is *going to be*. Although the movement of value will vary from industry to industry, an overall pattern is now clear, and it cuts across all industry lines.

Knowledge-intensive work is the new cornerstone of our economy. The shift to knowledge intensity is unmistakable in almost every key economic statistic: overall growth, exports, productivity, employment, profits and salaries. Wherever you look, the numbers tell the same story—knowledge is power.

If you watch where margins are going, you can map the movement of value toward information and knowledge. Industries that have the highest ratios of knowledge workers and employ the most knowledge-intensive systems are usually the value leaders. Jobs, salaries and profits are growing most rapidly in categories like software design, interactive advertising, management consulting, home care nursing and data security—all of which are knowledge intensive. In contrast, jobs and salaries are shrinking in areas of low or modest knowledge intensity.

The patterns which reveal the movement of value *within* a specific industry or sector aren't always as obvious however, particularly for managers closest to the old value proposition. Unless the shift is seismic, it's easy to miss. Outsiders, not trapped by existing assumptions and models, often have an easier time recognizing a value shift, than do insiders close to the status quo. For insiders who want to know where value is going—and *wanting to know* is the key— it's not really difficult. But you must be on the lookout. Given enough data, you can begin to draw a complete picture of value and its movement in your industry or sector.

# The First 15%—It Must Be Right

Recognizing, measuring and tracking shifts in economic value in an industry gives a company a crucial strategic advantage. It starts with inputs. W. Edwards Deming and Joseph Juran, founders of the modern quality movement, spent years convincing executives that the first 15% of the inputs to a process had a disproportionate impact on the outcome. Get these inputs right, and the remaining 85% of the process falls into place.

When it comes to strategic planning, the first 15% consists primarily of "knowledge labor"—figuring out where value is going and what needs to be done to successfully deliver on this new value proposition. It's both an information game and a thinking game. Once you know what needs to be done, the remaining 85% consists of executing the plan effectively and efficiently. Both ends are important, but again, the first 15% has a disproportionate impact on the overall outcome.

How do you get this up-front effort right? By perpetually asking these questions:

- What key factors drive customer purchase decisions and customer perception of value in your industry? How are they changing?
- How are old and new competitors affecting key customer purchase drivers and customer perception of value?

Also, ask where your organization is saying "no" to customers and find out why. Although this is usually a more isolated symptom and is often ignored, the answers may tell you a lot about where value is headed in your industry. In fact, frontline employees, particularly sales and customer service people, can be critical sources of information. They are often the first to sense the initial, faint signals of changes in customers' perceived value, although they usually do not express it that way. What they see are dissatisfied customers or declining sales.

Finding the answers to the above questions is not always easy, but you can do it if you use the right information-gathering tools. That information will become the source of your company's economic life and vitality. Armed with this data, you'll know what customers are really willing to pay for and what will increase their willingness to make repeat purchases and recommend your product or service to others. You'll know how you stack up against competitors vis-à-vis the customer's perception of value and why. You'll know what you can sell, what you cannot, and why. You'll know which products and services customers will demand in the future. In short, you'll have the guidance system you need for superior strategic planning.

# Value Landscaping™

Value Landscaping™, a tool developed by our colleagues at the Atlanta Consulting Group, graphically represents the movement, direction and future position of value in a given industry. Value Landscaping produces a much deeper understanding of customers than traditional market research techniques do. In fact, it turns much of traditional market research on its ear.

The results of applying classical market research have been less than stellar and almost never identify key areas of differentiation. A survey conducted in 1992 by Group EFO, a London-based consulting firm specializing in new product development, revealed that 86% of all new product launches fail. The surprising aspect of this fact is not, in our opinion, the rate of new product failure, but rather the fact that we have come to accept the failure rate as if it were carved in stone and immutable. Meanwhile, evidence continues to grow that traditional market research is inept at predicting how complex customers' value perceptions really are.

Approximately 90% of all U.S. firms trumpet their commitment to "customer focus" in advertising, public relations and corporate mission statements. Yet customers continue to catch them by surprise. Recently, Ford Motor Co. concluded only some 30% of prospective minivan customers would purchase a four-door model, so they didn't build one. Today, over 70% of all new Chrysler minivans sold are four-door versions and the discounts and rebates for Ford's minivans have now begun.

Whirlpool recently misjudged the European consumer's perception of value for household appliances. As a result, since 1992, its average selling price has dropped 15%. The company is now rolling out new European products armed with a new, albeit costly, understanding of the European consumer.

A large U.S. bank made a substantial investment to create the fastest letter-of-credit operation in the world, yet customers consistently rated the bank's performance in the bottom ten. Traditional customer research techniques couldn't identify the gap between the customer's perception of value and the bank's perception of value. After applying Value Landscaping, the bank discovered customers were neither looking at nor evaluating the operation from the bank's perspective. The bank was providing 48-hour paper turnaround, when all the customers wanted was a letter-of-credit *number*, which any bank could provide in two hours.

In these examples, what customers would value or be willing to pay for was not accurately identified. Decisions were based on false assumptions about customers, assumptions that produced no competitive advantage.

Value Landscaping transcends a good deal of what other customer research methods miss. It supplements the normal demographic aspects of market research with data that identifies what customers believe, or are willing to believe, and how they feel about a company, brand, product or service. The influence of what customers believe or are prepared to believe and how they really feel, is much greater than traditional research methodology has recognized. But in fact, these variables correlate more closely to actual sales and actual consumer behavior in the marketplace than anything else.

An executive team at a company that manufactures and markets laser printers came up with what they believed was the "ideal" printer for a new target market. When they used Value Landscaping to check their ideal against customers' perceived "ideal,"they were astonished by what they learned. The customer's ideal laser printer wasn't even a printer! It was a multi-functional system that combined phone, fax, copier, and printer in one machine. Following value in this case required the organization to scout unfamiliar technological terrain. This meant change on a scale that none of the top executives had anticipated. In the end, they chose to take the leap and become one of the first companies to introduce multi-functional systems in the marketplace.

It's not unusual to find executives harboring a vision of the ideal company, product, or service that's at odds with the customer's perspective. Why? Because executives continue to rely on traditional research to form their vision. Look at the number of experiments that have failed to meet expectations in the arena of interactive television. Customers continue to say one thing in focus groups, then do something entirely different. They say they want educational programming, but play along with game show hosts when their trial service gets connected.

The blurring of boundaries between telecommunications, computing, cable, entertainment and software has caused a scramble to figure out the combination of features, programs, services, reliability, and price consumers will flock to. The giants in these industries, even after making significant investments in customer research, are still trying to determine what consumers will really pay for. Those who find the keys that unlock consumers' true priorities will surely leap ahead of the pack.

## A Different View

If we want to really understand how customers perceive value, we'll need to apply less familiar approaches. Traditional anatomy textbooks explicitly stated that heads should be dissected from the side. Ignoring this longstanding practice, a small team of surgeons and medical students recently decided to anatomize the head from the front instead. By doing so, they discovered a new muscle which begins behind the eye and extends to the lower jaw. Executives, like physicians, have been looking at customers from the side for too long. This doesn't mean traditional customer research techniques should be abandoned, but it does mean that their shortcomings need to be overcome.

For example, if you ask customers why they buy $200,000 sports cars, they probably won't say, "I bought the car because I can't drive my 5-million-dollar house around," even though that may be precisely the psychological tendency that motivates most people to buy expensive sports cars. This type of psychographic information is at the root of nearly every purchase decision we and our customers make. Resemblance to truth is not the same thing as truth. The *true* perception of value and the discovery of latent customer needs lie at the subconscious level and are largely unexplored. The Value Landscaping tool was specifically designed to work at this subconscious level.

## Customer Satisfaction and Perception of Value

The breakthrough invention of X-ray photography eliminated the surgeon's tools as the primary method for diagnosing complicated ailments. Today, traditional X-ray technology now appears crude when compared to second and third generation imaging tools such as computed axial tomography (CAT) and magnetic resonance imaging (MRI). However, these advancements were only made possible because we continued learning from the initial X-ray breakthrough.

The quality movement spawned the importance of measuring customer satisfaction nearly two decades ago. Since then, more than 15,000 academic and trade journal articles have been published on the topic, mostly under the banner of TQM. This is one reason why firms with comprehensive Total Quality Management systems are generally more responsive to customer and market requirements. In short, they have learned to listen to their customers. Thus, they are more likely to detect the movement of value and less likely to be ambushed by shifts in customer sentiment. For example, the steel golf club shaft manufacturer mentioned earlier was considered a laggard in implementing its parent company's TQM process.

We've learned a lot in the two decades since organizations started caring about customer satisfaction measures, however. One key revelation is that *customer satisfaction* and *customer loyalty* are different. Traditional quality management systems have focused on measuring customers' satisfaction with existing products or services, which provides important data. But beyond "satisfaction," it's also important to measure "customer perceived value" and "customer loyalty" as determined by willingness to make repeat purchases.

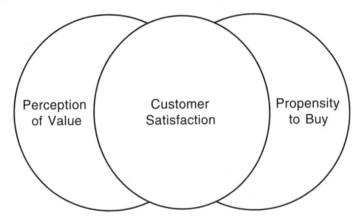

Customers may be satisfied with a product or service and still not buy it again. Why? Because they perceive some decrease in value, as measured by the ratio of perceived quality over price.

In the late 1980s, Digital Equipment Corporation's mini-computer business was on a downward slope, yet in survey after survey customers rated DEC their top vendor. Similarly, in the early 1990s, 85–90% of customers who drove American-made cars claimed they were satisfied. Yet, the average repurchase rate held steady at just below 50%. In both cases, the information on satisfaction provided very few clues about repurchase decisions and little information about customers' value perceptions.

Why would a customer claim satisfaction but still not be prone to repurchase? For openers, price-cutting competitors may be altering the value equation. Perhaps the product's brand or corporate equity may be in decline, which reduces its perceived value. The product may also have fallen out of fashion or lack utility or certain features that customers believe are important. There are any number of reasons why customers may not repurchase, even though they are nominally satisfied. This is why it's vitally important to track customer satisfaction *and* perception of value.

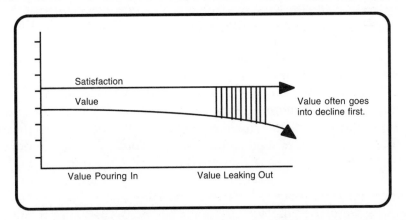

During a company's halcyon days of growth and strong earnings, customer satisfaction and value usually move in tandem. At the beginning of an obsolescence cycle, customer satisfaction can remain amazingly high even as value begins to decline and customer loyalty erodes. If a decline in value goes unchecked, it eventually impacts satisfaction. But this can take time, and in the interim, you may be dangerously exposed. By the time the dropping "satisfaction" indicators come across your desk, market share is most likely also in decline, and the damage is done.

Compaq Computer offered superb quality and service in the early 1990s, but competitors cut prices aggressively, causing Compaq to lose market share. By the time it woke up to the problem, its value proposition and profits were in decline. Compaq adjusted quickly. Because of its high perceived quality and brand equity, the company eventually won back the lost share, but at a cost. It would have been better not to have fallen behind in the first place.

Customer perception of value is the bedrock of any value assessment. Unless customers perceive high value, your value equation is probably in decline. Customer satisfaction is a legitimate measure of value, but it can also act as a sedative, lulling you into thinking everything is fine. Physicians now reach for second and third generation imaging tools to show them what's really going on with a patient whose ailment persists. Exercise the same caution if you rely upon customer satisfaction, a first generation tool, as the sole indicator of your position on the value curve.

## Competitive Scoping

Successful businesses keep a watchful eye on their competitors as well as their customers. Airline employees, for example, continually monitor the prices other airlines charge for common routes. If a competitor comes out with a new discount package, they don't want to read about it in *USA Today*.

It is important to note that any competitive assessment should be done first and foremost to determine how competitors affect the customer's perception of value. Remember, value doesn't just disappear; it simply moves somewhere else or to someone else. Moreover, it's usually not the well-known competitor who finds a way to change the value equation in a given industry. Often times such a competitor emerges from the periphery. Emerging or marginal competitors are companies which "don't belong." They appear out of place, as if they accidentally drifted into your business.

Don't be fooled by these strange-looking characters. They may look odd, but they can be deadly. They are probably not lost. In fact, they likely know exactly what they're doing. They plan to smile a lot while stealing as much of the market from you as they can, hoping you're too stupid to notice. And guess what? History shows that this is a pretty good strategy. Market leaders tend to ignore newcomers until they're at their throats. Taiwan's Formosa Plastics is now the world's largest maker of PVC, but even in the late 1980s, the industry's major players took little notice of this company.

Where do these intruders come from and how do they get in? *Something* changes. Sometimes, it's new technology that opens the door. Perhaps some change in distribution strategy creates a channel of entropy. Regulations may have eased, thinning the traditional walls that separate industries. Or, maybe there is a new pattern of alliances in your industry that the interloper takes advantage of. If any or all of these things occur, businesses can move into new territory.

For example, titanium is now used in mountain bike and racing bike frames instead of steel. Meanwhile, metal alloys, having reached their temperature and durability limits, are being replaced by more moldable plastics and composite materials in product after product. Many cars now have plastic body parts. A ceramic turbo engine is used in Nissan's 300ZX sports cars, and chobham ceramic armor is displacing steel on all modern tanks.

Thirty years ago, no one in the steel industry regarded plastics or composites as competitors. They didn't even show up on the industry's competitive radar screen until well into the 1980s. Yet today's composite materials are competing with steel everywhere, especially in high-profit sectors of the industry. From golf club shafts to precision tools, composite materials are becoming dominant

A similar sneak attack occurred in banking when a host of financial service companies were allowed to establish banking-like relationships with their customers. This is classic disintermediation in action. After ignoring this phenomenon for years, banks finally recognized it as a serious threat—and not a moment too soon. Today, banks are being outflanked by these non-bank competitors who are offering investment, checking, money transfers, and loans to customers.

Non-bank competitors have also established beachheads in a number of important sectors, including venture capital markets. Banks appear especially inept at finding and funding growth companies. It is no accident that traditional banks, the chief source of capital to the old Second Wave economy, now account for only a small fraction of the money raised by corporations and individuals in the United States. Why? Because growth companies are usually knowledge-intensive. The assets are intellectual, which look suspiciously intangible to traditional bankers, who much prefer to loan on fixed assets such as machinery, inventory, bricks and mortar.

The arrival of cyberspace and "e-cash" will only accelerate the move away from traditional banks. How serious is the threat? The truth is that banking is required, even in a cyberspace world, but banks, as we know them, are not.

The same process is at work today in transportation. Airborne Express is competing with Federal Express, and both compete with the U.S. Postal Service. Meanwhile, new integrated logistics companies like Ryder are establishing alliances with key industrial customers like GM's Saturn car division. Ryder's mandate is to keep parts, people and trucks in nearly constant motion, and it uses information technology to pull this off.

As a logistics integrator, Ryder becomes *part* of the host company's operation because both parties have done a great deal of technology integration and programming. This means that Ryder, now close to the customer, gains ascendancy over the total transportation and logistics chain of value, including the trucks and planes.

Ryder's role is similar to that of a systems integrator in the computer industry. Systems integrators ask for bids on hardware or software on behalf of their clients, which forces prices down. Ryder does the same thing with trucks and planes, which also forces prices down. In a sense, trucks and planes are becoming commodities now that their purveyors are a step removed from the customer. In time, relationships like those that Ryder is building may allow integrated logistics companies to disintermediate the traditional relationship Airborne or Federal Express has with their largest customers.

## Are You Being Invaded?

Are there any strange newcomers drifting into your market? Before saying no, think about it carefully! Is there anyone meeting a similar need, or providing a similar service, but in a way that changes the customer's perception of value? Remember, these odd characters can be lethal. You don't want to wake up one night to the sound of a little voice telling you, "They're *here*." Now is the time to pay attention.

Start by drawing up a competitive radar screen. Begin by drawing a simple circle on a page. Divide the circle into two sectors, one for well-known competitors and one for strange newcomers. Next, put in the names of competitors which fall into either category.

Once your radar screen is done, draw a red circle around competitors in both sectors whose market share or revenue is growing. Make a list of those competitors that are growing and those that are not. What's the difference between these lists in terms of strategy, economics and value proposition? Do you see any patterns?

Chances are you'll see some very distinct patterns indeed. For example, one growth sector in the domestic-airline industry is characterized by short haul, point-to-point carriers which are usually non-unionized and have significantly lower costs (i.e., Southwest Airlines and its clones). Internationally, companies like

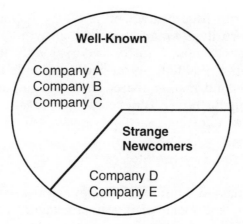

British Airways are increasing market share and profits by taking advantage of their huge economies of scale, vast network, high service levels, lower costs and immense brand equity. Caught between the two, old line domestic carriers are weighed down with expensive hubs, high labor costs, and huge capital costs.

Again, value rarely sits still for long. How is the value landscape changing in your industry? Where is it headed today? A mosaic of patterns will start to take shape once you discover how customer purchase drivers are changing and how competitive alternatives are affecting the customer's perception of value. Without such insights, strategic decisions are like misguided missiles.

# Other Tracking Tools

*Margin Analysis*

If you watch where margin is going, you will find it is usually chasing value. Margin is a surrogate for value; when value shifts, margin follows. Thus, tracking the margins of your firm and competing firms can point you to where value is headed. By tracking margin, you can actually "see" the movement of value in the numbers. If a product commands 20% margins in an industry whose overall margins are 5% or 6%, then something is up. The perceived value of this product is clearly higher than its competitors.

For example, one large systems integrator noticed a small blip on its revenue screen: its information security business had profits five to six times greater than its core business. The firm quickly responded to this nascent demand and now happily reports that information security is a major source of growth.

Unfortunately, most industry leaders don't watch where margin is going. They tend to focus on traditional indicators of success, such as profits and market share. Those are important measures but they're only historical. They tell what's already happened, not what the future holds.

## Growth Analysis

Who is growing and who is not? Forget about size and profitability for a minute and look exclusively at growth. Tomorrow's winners start small, but they grow fast. The key is to find them.

When the American auto industry was heading for trouble in the late 1960s, General Motors, Ford and Chrysler nervously watched each other, while Toyota, Honda and Nissan were busily changing the customer's perception of value by dramatically improving quality. When demand for dedicated word processing machines began to level off in the early- to mid-1980s, Wang, CPT, NBI and other industry leaders were competing by adding new features to their hardware. Meanwhile, the DOS standard for personal computers liberated entrepreneurial programmers to develop word processing software applications that were no longer hardware dependent. More recently, another standard, TAPI (technology applications programming interface) now poses a threat to the dedicated PBX switchboard—personal computers equipped with circuit boards and software can now perform many PBX functions. Suddenly, relatively unknown firms like Dialogic, Mediatrends and Brooktrout are stepping into the ring with NEC, AT&T, and Northern Telecom.

## Market Valuation

While it may seem irrational at times, the market is still one of the best barometers of value. In its own crazy way, the market tends to discount today's profits and look toward tomorrow's profits and/or growth. If a company's market valuation is low, it's because the market senses trouble ahead. It might be, for example, intensified or even self-destructive competition, such as the airlines have engaged in; aging technology; a decline in capital investment; or a poorly focused corporate mission or goals. Whatever the perceived problem, such numbers could signal value deterioration, and they should be taken seriously.

It's simple to calculate the market valuation of your own company and its competitors. Just divide the stock's market value by revenue. Add debt to revenue if possible, because the money was borrowed to add value, and this is one way to determine whether or not it is doing so. If you run the numbers on yourself and your competitors, some interesting patterns regarding the movement of value will likely emerge.

The implications for organizations that are losing value can be profound for everyone: stockholders, suppliers, employees and the community in which they operate. It's important to note, of course, that a company whose market valuation is falling isn't necessarily losing money. Many businesses in value decline are very profitable, but chances are they are not growing.

### Brand and Corporate Equity

What is the state of your corporate and/or brand(s) equity? Is this equity strengthening or weakening? What do customers believe about your company and its brands of products and services? More importantly, what are they *willing* to believe? As significant as the brand issue is today, few firms can clearly define where their brand equity lies. This makes it difficult for them to clearly define the qualities or identity that makes them unique.

Very often, a product's inherent value is rooted in its brand equity. When customers buy a Compaq computer or a Harley Davidson motorcycle or use an American Express Gold Card, they acquire more than just a raw product or service. There is something about the brand itself that adds additional value to the relationship. When corporate or brand equity declines, the perceived value of the product or service invariably follows.

## Freeing Up Resources to Pursue Value

When value moves, management's first challenge is to find out where it has gone and what shape it is taking. But even after this investigative work is done, organizations may find it hard to pursue the new value proposition aggressively. Why? Because the bulk of the organization's resources, especially money, is tied up in the old value proposition, and liberating that money is not easy. "Old" products and services whose value has declined may remain profitable nevertheless. They often represent the core of the old business and are integral to brand equity and corporate history.

Trying to squeeze money out of these old products and services to pay for new and more valuable ventures can be very difficult. There are always a thousand reasons why the money and resources should stay put. The hardest argument to resist involves aggressive growth plans for expanding the old value proposition. It is hard to say no to people who want to grow the business. However, you should be asking, "Is this the right business to grow?" That is where a cost-of-capital analysis can come in handy.

Assessing performance against the cost of capital is not a new idea. It was used by Alfred Sloan at GM before World War II and later by General Electric, until the market began to focus more on earnings. The concept remains a powerful one and has been successfully reintroduced as Economic Value Added or EVA® by the consulting firm of Stern, Stewart & Company. This important management tool is being widely used by such companies as AT&T, Coca-Cola, CSX and Quaker Oats.

By using EVA, an organization can identify which products, services, operations or activities are exceptionally productive and add unusually high value—and which ones do not. EVA is a compass that points to capital that can be freed to chase a value shift.

EVA is a technique that can show if you are earning enough to justify the capital being expended in a business, division or product line. In other words, is a certain venture paying for the capital it employs? The formula for EVA is based on operating earnings less taxes and cost of capital.

---

**Sales − Operating Expenses − Taxes − Cost of Capital = EVA®**

**Debt or Equity**

EVA® (trademarked to Stern, Stewart & Company, New York.)
Proponents of EVA® believe that investments in quality and training should be treated as capital expenditures and expensed over 3–5 years.

A company or subsidiary may be profitable but still provide low economic value. In short, it may not earn its keep by paying for the capital it uses. Alternatively, a small unit with modest profits may have high returns relative to the cost of capital invested.

One financial services firm we worked with had a core product that was synonymous with the company's brand image, but market share and profit margins were shrinking. Nevertheless, the company still had a huge chunk of its invested capital tied up in the old business.

Meanwhile, a small, fast-growing segment of the company seemed to spring up out of nowhere, selling new products and services to existing customers mostly through on-line services. Insurance, telephone services, travel specials . . . whatever products or services customers said they wanted were sold through this new arm of the firm. Financed with only a $10-million investment, and run by a staff of 20 employees, it returned revenues of $100 million in its second year. The small business was "virtual"; the company neither owned nor built any of the items it sold. In essence, it was leveraging other people's research and development investments. Next to the old giant, this new virtual business looked tiny and inconsequential, but it represented the future.

An EVA or similar cost of capital analysis would have revealed the need to shift capital from the old and dying (but still profitable) business to this new, growing sector of the company. Properly used, EVA can highlight areas that are tying up resources that might be employed more efficiently in the quest for value.

## When the Value Landscape Changes, Everything Else Changes

The entire global economic apparatus is now driven by value. Consumer power, combined with increased competition and information, is a catalyst behind the movement of value. In most industries, it's no longer a question of *whether* value is moving in new directions, but where and how fast.

Once a value shift within the landscape is recognized, the next step is to prepare the organization to pursue this new value proposition. That might require making changes to existing *strategies, structure, core competencies, core processes, product and service offerings, human resource systems, advertising programs, brand management programs,* and *customer loyalty programs.* Such changes cannot be made easily or quickly, but the sooner an organization responds, the better. Organizations that are blinded by a value shift may find themselves too far behind to catch up.

To keep from falling behind, management must establish, at the very least, first-rate monitoring systems for tracking such factors as customer satisfaction; customer perception of quality and value compared to competitors; corporate and/or brand equity; and customer loyalty as measured by the tendency to recommend and/or make repeat purchases.

Anything less than this constitutes a case of "flying blind" with no instruments, maps, or compass, just the wind in your hair. That can be invigorating for a while, but it can also turn deadly.

## Is There Life After a Value Shift?

Do companies or industries experiencing serious value decline ever move themselves back up the curve to value prosperity? Sometimes they do. Remember our discussion about the value crisis that steamship lines found themselves in during the 1960s? One of the oldest and most traditional of these companies, Holland America Line, made the transition from crossing to cruising very successfully. It shifted its ship registration from Amsterdam to the Dutch Antilles, decreased costs, purchased new ships, and pioneered new routes, including one to Alaska.

By the 1980s, its ships were fully booked and HAL, as it is called in the industry, was viewed as one of the most successful cruise lines in the world. Interestingly, it made this transition while preserving the best of its "Old World" traditions, including luxury, superior service, cleanliness, and superb food. HAL even advertised that particular style with the tag line "Ocean Liner Service," which made a big hit with modern travelers.

## The Lesson of "Enigma"

With customer expectations growing and value on the move, figuring out what needs to be done is more important today than ever. Those hoping to muddle through without planning or preparation are headed for trouble. Strategic intelligence about customers and competitors is absolutely vital in today's environment. The payoff from having the right information and knowing how to use it is enormous. The cost of not having the right information or acting upon the wrong information can be catastrophic.

By way of analogy, one of the most important factors in the Allied victory during World War II was the breaking of the German "Enigma" and Japanese "Purple" codes. Breaking these codes was an incredible technological achievement. To pull it off, British and American counterintelligence units worked for years and actually designed and built the world's first computer in the process. Thanks to this remarkable feat, the Allies knew much of what the Axis powers were planning to do and when they planned to do it early in the war. The importance of this information cannot be exaggerated.

Great victories, like Midway and D-day, were made possible by the availability of vital strategic intelligence. The cost of obtaining this crucial data was insignificant compared to its impact, and even more insignificant when compared to the cost of the total war effort.

By war's end, the United States alone had spent more than $400 billion to achieve victory, an incredible amount of money in uninflated 1940s currency. The United States would also spend another $100 billion on aid to its allies and former enemies through the Marshall Plan and other programs. In comparison, breaking the Enigma code, which made victory possible, was financed with a budget of a few million dollars.

These figures reveal why the cost of getting the right information up front is infinitesimal compared to the ultimate cost of executing the plan or strategy. Investing in intelligence is the best way to ensure a successful outcome. And while few executives would argue with that, when push comes to shove, a great many are reluctant to make even a small investment in their intelligence gathering systems. Perhaps this is because the intelligence gathering and planning stage of the business process is intangible and a little abstract, while the execution phase applies real resources—people, buildings, technology, marketing and advertising. These are forces executives understand.

Whatever the source of this blind spot we would all do well to remember the Enigma's enduring lesson: *those with the best information win.*

# 7

# Using Old Tools to Get a Handle on New Value

*Man is a tool-using animal. . . . Without tools he is nothing, with tools he is all.*

*—Thomas Carlyle*

Because the economy and, indeed the world, is changing so fast, it is essential to keep our feet firmly on the ground as we plan for the future. The movement of value is an issue best addressed with coolness and common sense. The last thing we need is another onslaught of hype such as accompanied the debut of reengineering in the early 1990s.

Americans are our own worst enemy when it comes to new business concepts. We love novelty and newness. We become so enamored with new ideas, we burn through them the way a child rips through toys on Christmas morning—squeals of delight, followed by three or four minutes of interest, then onto the next new plaything. That is our pattern with new management techniques, too.

We fall in and out of love very quickly. We adopt each new methodology without making sufficient intellectual investment to understand the underlying concept. Then we are disappointed when the new miracle tool turns out to be useful, but not a panacea. Not having really mastered the idea makes it all the easier to abandon as we move on in search of the next Holy Grail. That is why management fads are almost uniquely an American phenomenon.

We also tend to be inherently impatient and hunger for instant gratification. This weakness is exploited by fast-talking consultants and a news media desperate for a new angle on a story. As the former Fox network CEO Barry Diller pointed out, we have a tendency to "spin subjects to unsustainable heights and then let them fall. We want everything there before the fact and when it doesn't materialize instantly, we dismiss the whole thing as impossible or a failure." In short, we set ourselves up for disappointment from the beginning.

In truth, the incubation period for new ideas takes much longer than we might like to think. The press, for example, can move the "information super highway" from concept to reality in a matter of weeks, but the real thing will take years to pull off.

## Oscillating Between Extremes

New ideas and concepts take a long time to germinate. For instance, installing quality improvement concepts within U.S. industry took more than a decade. And even then, it only took hold in those sectors which were subject to intense and relentless competitive pressure.

There is no better place to view our fickleness than Business Process Redesign, or "reengineering," as it has come to be called. Reengineering is a useful, powerful process for radically redesigning strategic work processes. Unfortunately, it was shamefully oversold and, in many cases, poorly implemented. As the inevitable reengineering failures make their way to the front pages of the business press, a predictable reaction will set in. Reengineering will go from "hero" to "bum" overnight as process redesign and breakthrough thinking falls into disfavor.

Our propensity to oscillate between extremes, to view management techniques as either perfect or useless, is silly and gets in the way of learning. In the real world, things are rarely tidy. Strategies and tools do not always work as planned, and even when they do, the results are rarely neat and clean. In truth, the whole process of applying new techniques and tools is messy and involves a lot of trial and error.

No management tool is omnipotent. Value Landscaping™, described in Chapter 6, is a useful tool for tracking the movement and transformation of value. That's all it is . . . a *tool*. And no management concept or tool is a substitute for getting the basics right.

If the core product you offer is broken, there is no point attempting to realign your business around a new value proposition. If the work flows in your organization are riddled with waste and service failures, it makes no sense undertaking an arcane reengineering strategy. If customer satisfaction monitoring systems do not work, or worse, do not even exist, there is no logic in setting up elegant systems for tracking brand equity or the movement of value. The improvement process must start at the beginning, with the business plan and the basic product or service.

Getting the basics right really does matter and is certainly a prerequisite to adopting more sophisticated or advanced improvement strategies. It's time to move beyond the hype and let common sense play a bigger role in our thinking and planning.

## The Importance of Need

Before all else comes the need to change and stay abreast of shifting customer requirements. This may sound pretty elemental, but you would be surprised how often this is overlooked or slighted. To better understand the change process, we undertook a study of a number of large, successful reengineering efforts in the early 1990s. These large scale efforts each involved targeted improvements of several hundred million to over a billion dollars. We sought to learn what patterns and methodologies worked. As consultants, we wanted to find out what change methodologies were most successful, and then, of course, replicate them for sale. Imagine our horror when we discovered that implementation methodologies were *not* central to success!

While we did find a number of characteristics common to successful change efforts (such as a clear aim, superb communications, and a focus on concrete results), these were not the primary determinants of success. The real driver of change was *need*.

In this survey of reengineering and corporate change efforts, the most important finding was contained in a single line: "*Having a compelling need to change is a better predictor of success than any given methodology chosen to drive the change.*" As we probed more deeply, it became clear that the cornerstone of change was understanding what needed to be done and believing it was necessary to do.

IBM's problems in the early 1990s, for example, were rooted in the firm's unwillingness to see the need to make the kind of painful, large scale change that new CEO Lou Gerstner ultimately had to force on the corporation. Even as late as 1994, 40% of IBM's middle managers did not perceive a need for radical change. With such a "frozen middle," it's a small wonder that previous CEOs were not able to move the organization toward reform.

Without a clearly perceived need, real or induced, it's unlikely any organization will undertake painful but necessary changes. As our survey showed, if the need was clear and the leadership present, most organizations found a way to make change happen, even if they had to grope and crawl their way through the process. Having a superb implementation process made the process easier and reduced the pain and expense, but that was not the critical factor for success.

Out of this study we developed our Primal Change Model, which contains four elements:

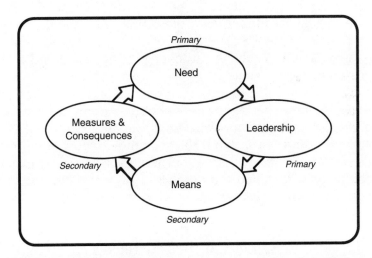

The basis of successful change begins and ends with having a clear, compelling need to move away from the status quo. Unless you recognize that where you are is not a good place, there is no perceived need for change.

Next comes determined leadership. It is hard to do much about the need without leadership. A high need, low leadership combination can be deadly. Without leadership, an organization which knows it must change becomes dysfunctional, or even hysterical with anxiety.

An organization in trouble, which is offered no way out by its leadership, goes "nuts," as one of our clients succinctly put it. Turf battles break out as every sector and every individual seek to protect themselves. Common purpose and customer focus are quickly buried beneath an avalanche of self-interest. No organization can survive long in this state.

When both need and leadership are present, the next prerequisite is having the right measures and consequences. That is, the organization must be able to define where it wants to go and how it will quantitatively know when it gets there.

These quantitative measures describe what will be different after the change has been successfully made. These outcomes must then be tied to appropriate consequences. If the organization must boost customer satisfaction from 94–99%, or reduce cycle time from one day to one hour, those measures must be built into corporate plans and cascaded down through the organization. This planning only works, though, if backed by appropriate consequences. Those who achieve their goals and assist the organization in achieving its goals must be rewarded. Those who fail to make their goals or inhibit the organization in achieving its goals must be subject to some consequences. This is why most successful change usually results in turnover at the top or middle of the organization.

Only when all these elements are in place—need, leadership, measurements and consequences—should the organization focus on its change methodology. Once the foundations are in place, the organization can then seek out the best, most robust blueprint for change that it can find. But be warned, even the most exquisite methodology will fail in the absence of a compelling need and focused, determined leadership.

## A Look at the Old Tools

In the spirit of exercising common sense, let us look at some of the tools required to manage in this new knowledge-driven economy. Value may be taking on new forms, but the tools required to manage in this new economy are not necessarily new. In fact, the most important ones have been around for a long time. We just have to learn to use them in different ways.

## Forcing Mechanisms

Creating a need for change is not easy if the crisis has not arrived yet, or the employees do not recognize it. Most people and organizations would prefer to wait for a crisis to clearly arrive before acting. By then it may be too late or many of the best options may be gone.

Great leaders throughout history have always understood the power and symbolism of forcing mechanisms. When Cortez landed in Mexico, he ordered his troops to burn the boats so there could be no turning back. Now *that* is a forcing mechanism! When a Roman legion appeared in danger of giving way to the enemy, the legionary commander would sometimes resort to a strategy known as "throwing the standard." This meant throwing the legion's standard, the equivalent of its regimental colors, amongst the enemy. For a legion to lose its standard was the ultimate disgrace. Those not killed in the battle would be subject upon their return to Rome to extreme censure. So "throwing the standard" was one way of immediately focusing everyone's attention on the *need* to improve performance. Nothing quite so drastic as "throwing the standard" is required in modern business to focus people's attention on improvement. Most employees want to do better and require only a little direction, encouragement and leadership.

Unfortunately, history also shows that successful organizations easily fall into a state of entropy, where the impetus to improve disappears. When this happens, a forcing mechanism can jolt the organization into action.

When Jack Welch took over as CEO of General Electric in 1981, the company had backlogged orders of over 28 billion dollars, sure to provide a rich stream of revenue for several years to come. Many GE executives thought that was good enough. What Welch saw, though, was a paucity of orders for steam turbines and nuclear power equipment that augured ill farther down the road.

Welch adamantly declared that any GE business which could not sustain a number one or two position in its industry would be sold. That was a forcing mechanism that had the effect of bringing sometimes reluctant managers on board.

Far-sighted leaders can use the measures and consequences component of the change model to force the organization in new directions. These forcing mechanisms constitute ambitious, strategic goals which are linked to appropriate consequences. Motorola's

Six Sigma, GE's "One, Two or You're Out," American Express' one-billion-dollar reengineering target are all examples of successful forcing mechanisms. For organizations suffering from complacency or market-leader syndrome, forcing mechanisms can be a powerful tool for eliciting change.

One of the most effective forcing mechanisms is to set stretch targets for improvement, such as moving from 99% accuracy (about 10,000 errors per million) to 99.999% accuracy. Or, as Motorola did, aim for Six Sigma, or about 3.4 errors per million.

However, setting stretch goals will only create a compelling need for action if everyone believes the leaders are serious about achieving these aggressive targets. Forcing mechanisms must be backed by the credibility of the organization's leaders. They must make it clear these targets are real and that people will be held accountable for achieving them.

## *Emphasis on Quality*

We see headlines in the business press these days which ask, *"Does Quality Still Count?"* What utter nonsense! Despite America's impressive quality and productivity comeback, a chasm exists between where we are and where we need to be regarding quality.

Just look around. Are you satisfied with the output of public education? If quality is not a problem anymore, how is it that aircraft companies build, and the FAA approves, planes that crash when they have too much ice on their wings? Why do trains derail and spill toxic wastes, all because work processes failed or in some cases did not even exist? What about the man who entered a Tampa hospital to have a leg removed, and woke up the next day to find they had removed the wrong one? How's *that* for a quality failure?

Or, how about the airline's hub-and-spoke system? Does it work? If you think so, try getting from New York to Savannah through Atlanta or Charlotte on a Friday afternoon. Why is it the technical manuals for your VCR cannot be understood by anyone who's not an electrical engineer? How about those 1-800 "Help" numbers which always ring busy? Have you ever stayed in a hotel where the soap dish in the shower won't hold the soap, or the water turns scalding when someone flushes the toilet eight blocks away?

Quality as a discipline has only had a short run in this country. While we have made significant progress, we should not take our eye off the quality ball now. There is still plenty of work to do. If a product or service is poor, then quality management is still not an integral part of that organization's modus operandi. In fact, each year American business and government waste between 20–30% or more of their revenue through errors and rework stemming from poor quality. That's 20–30% of $6.5 trillion. Does quality still count? You *bet* it does.

Interestingly, most of the talk about quality being yesterday's news comes not from the boardroom, but from the pressroom. The press, in its relentless search for a new angle, has become bored with quality. And no wonder—it's been in the headlines for a decade or more.

The business press played a vital role in awakening North American executives to the importance of quality improvement in the 1980s. Documentaries like NBC's "If Japan Can, Why Can't We?" helped detonate America's quality comeback. Today, the concepts of process redesign and Total Quality Management are no longer mysteries requiring interpretation and explanation. In fact, David Glass, the CEO of Wal-Mart and one of the country's most important business leaders, lists *The Deming Management Method* as his favorite book. Fifteen years ago, most Fortune 500 executives did not know who W. Edwards Deming was.

While quality may no longer be a novelty and no longer news, that does not mean it is no longer important. In truth, after years of hard work by both business and government, America still has a long way to go in the quality revolution. Less than 40% of major U.S. corporations have launched organized quality improvement efforts. The challenge is to get the rest of corporate America to focus on quality.

Those firms which do, such as Intel, Motorola, Ford, Xerox, Black & Decker, UPS, American Express, and Milliken, need no encouragement from the press to stay the course. They can see the results for themselves. As survivors of the 1980s quality wars, they know what happens when you take your eye off the quality ball. Having fallen behind once and sweated blood to catch up, they don't intend to make the same mistake again.

So we should not worry too much about press disinterest in quality improvement. The thing to worry about is the level of business interest in the subject, and here there is still work to be done.

## The New Dimensions of Quality

Quality remains the single most important component in determining value, yet the definition of quality (*i.e.*, what matters to the customer) is changing. The days are gone when having a product that merely "worked" could separate you from the competition. Compliance quality is still important, but it hardly constitutes a competitive advantage. Workability has come to be expected. So you need to find ways to add value to your workable core product or service. In today's economy, this means adding information and knowledge. At its best, this value-added knowledge enables you to partner with the customer and become an extension of the customer's business or lifestyle. This partnering is sometimes referred to as prosumption.

Levi Strauss, for example, uses technology to custom-fit jeans for women. The customer is measured as she tries on sample jeans in the store, then the data is forwarded to a computerized fabric-cutting machine at the factory. The custom-ordered jeans cost only $10 more than the mass-produced versions.

Similarly, the transportation industry adds value by tracking products and speeding up delivery times. Integrated logistics firms add value by remaking the host company's logistics chain and dramatically reducing costs. Charge card companies add value by providing customers with travel management services and the capacity to extract discounts by bundling purchases. Software producers add value by enhancing the capacity of the customer's hardware. What is your company's strategy for adding value and partnering with your customer?

## Continuous Improvement and Innovation

There is a lot of talk these days about the importance of product innovation and process breakthroughs. This debate reflects one of our periodic swings in sentiment away from continuous improvement, toward innovation and breakthrough thinking. But just wait, the mood will swing back again. Not so long ago, innovation and rampant individualism were out of style. We were in the throes of rediscovering the importance of standardization and the power of eliminating redundancies. We found that by straightening out the kinks in work flows, we could produce dramatic improvements in productivity. When done properly, the results were amazing . . . speed rose, costs dropped, productivity improved, and so did safety. It was like a miracle; people could hardly believe it.

Then along came the reengineers with their focus on "discontinuous improvement" and the pendulum swung back toward innovation. Soon, Continuous Process Improvement (CPI) appeared rather dull and pedestrian. The reengineers took advantage of this sentiment to label CPI as slow, unimaginative and mechanical. None of this was true of course, but the message suited the marketing needs of the moment. Today, with the benefit of hindsight, we can clearly see this was a false quarrel. The marketers of reengineering picked this fight because it helped differentiate them from the total quality movement, and many of us fell for it.

Reengineering and CPI are just different points along the same continuum. To start one is to begin the other. The polarization caused by the reengineering vs. CPI debate was harmful and distracting. The whole fuss was about as relevant to the real economy as the annual fashion debates about hemlines. The overblown rhetoric surrounding such tools as reengineering creates an obstacle to learning. The supposed dichotomy between CPI and innovation was never real, at least as it applies to existing business processes. For an organization seeking to improve, it is not a case of choosing one over the other, but of pursuing one or both when they make sense. Teams which set out to incrementally improve processes very often break through and achieve dramatic results. Inversely, breakthrough teams searching for dramatic improvement often fall short and only achieve incremental results. Either way, things get better.

Both reengineering and continuous process improvement operate along the same continuum, only they have different starting points. Reengineering starts with innovation and moves to standardization, while CPI starts at standardization and moves to innovation.

At the core of our understanding of quality improvement is the basic product or service. This core, although successful today, must be continually replenished and renewed to meet rising customer expectations. The core offering begins to decay from the moment it is born. The minute a product or service is introduced, competitors try to match or better it. Even where the competition is slow to respond, the product ages by virtue of its own longevity. Disneyland today offers a host of new experiences that were not available when the first Disney theme park opened. If Disney, content with success, had rested upon its laurels and not added attractions, the company's overall value perception would have long since declined.

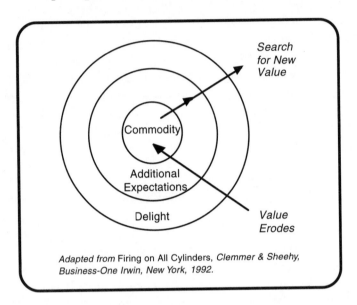

Adapted from Firing on All Cylinders, *Clemmer & Sheehy,* Business-One Irwin, New York, 1992.

In highly competitive markets like electronics and telecommunications, these waves of rising expectations can crest very quickly. Today, households are throwing away obsolete computers which contain 10 times the digital power Apollo 11 took to the moon. We are now discarding five million computers a year globally. Television viewers already take for granted big screen TVs and digital sound, as well as home theater systems with access to 100 channels. For those of us brought up with *Howdy Doody* and two channels, the pace of obsolescence is mind-boggling.

How do you stay ahead in such a fast-moving environment? You pay attention to customers. Where else are you likely to find out what customers want and where the market is going? This explains why organizations with first class customer-listening systems tend to stay ahead in their markets.

## Managing the Customer Base as an Asset

Some customers can tell you how to improve your *existing* products and services and how to make them better, faster, cheaper or more convenient. Other customers, a troublesome minority which is never satisfied, can provide insights into *tomorrow's* requirements and expectations. These tough, hard-to-handle customers hold the key to the future. They stretch suppliers to the limit with outrageous demands.

These unreasonable customers make a point of challenging the status quo. They are not satisfied with what you currently offer or how you offer it. They want more, and in demanding "better" or "different" outcomes, they very often take you to the limits of your existing paradigm and point the way to the future. If you don't listen to them, someone else will.

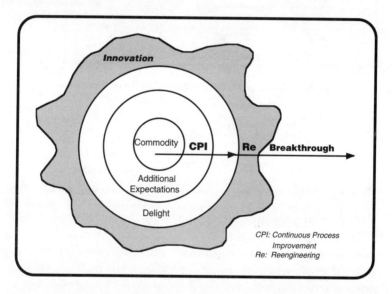

It is no accident that Michael Porter in his authoritative work, *The Competitive Advantage of Nations,* listed "demanding customers" as critical assets in building a world class industry. For example, American aerospace owes part of its success to the demands of its toughest customer, the U.S. Air Force. In its relentless search for lighter and stronger materials, better engines, and improved avionics, the Air Force pushed suppliers to the limit by continually upping the specifications. As a result, U.S. aircraft makers became the world's technical leaders in the industry, and this edge spilled over into the manufacture of commercial aircraft as well.

In his autobiography, test pilot Chuck Yeager described how high altitude aircraft can come right to the edge of space. At altitudes near 100,000 feet, the stars of outer space are visible beyond the earth's atmosphere, even at mid-day. Pilots who have flown to such heights have been "to the edge." This is what tough, demanding customers do for a supplier; they take you "to the edge." If you stay with them and don't falter, they will show you the future in the form of tomorrow's value. This brings you into the fourth ring of innovation where reengineering was born.

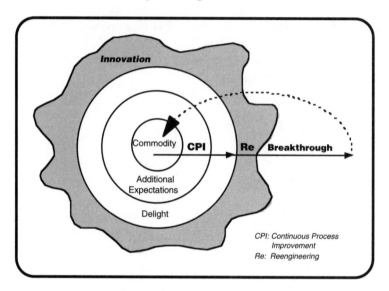

However, if you go beyond this point, you leave the realm of continuous improvement and innovation and enter the heroic landscape of the innovator or inventor. At this end of the spectrum you encounter the scientists, inventors, entrepreneurs and eccentrics who will bring us tomorrow's ideas and technology. These people are not interested in improving things; they want to *create* things. Once the new technology or innovation is created and in place, its value immediately begins to erode. You start again trying to improve the new core offering, and the whole improvement cycle begins anew.

## Tough Customers as Assets

Successful companies staying abreast of the movement of value almost always have access to a core of tough, demanding customers. These customers do more than just keep you on your toes; they force you to improve. Often, they will even point the way to the future in terms of new product and service offerings. Take the case of the transportation industry. Its toughest customers are most likely to be found in the area of integrated logistics, where customers become outright partners. This explains why having a successful, growing logistics business is essential to any large scale transportation company today. Integrated logistics becomes that industry's window on the future.

Twenty years ago, Japanese auto manufacturers were winning over large numbers of the U.S. auto industry's toughest customers. These customers were more concerned with finding value than helping preserve the Big Three carmakers' dominance of the U.S. market. They wanted "quality" and were unwilling to take anything else. It was these demanding customers who ultimately brought the Big Three around and set the stage for the U.S. auto recovery in the 1980s.

The term "learning organization" has been used to describe so much that it runs the risk of losing its meaning. Yet, if you hang around with tough customers long enough, you'll soon discover what it means to learn. Tough customers force you to learn. If you don't keep up, they dump you. The key is to constantly seek out these customers, and then once you have them, do everything you can to hang on to them.

## Impacting the Bottom Line

Proper management of the "customer asset" can have a greater impact on the bottom line than almost any other form of asset management. Invariably, there is a dramatic impact on net earnings if you can increase by even a few percentage points this group's propensity to buy. This explains why quality theory has always maintained that keeping rather than getting customers is the key to business success.

Frederick F. Reichheld and W. Earl Sasser, Jr., in their groundbreaking *Harvard Business Review* article "Zero Defections," showed how a 5% increase in customer loyalty can produce a profit increase of 25–85%. A later study in *Fortune* showed that Reichheld and Sasser's estimates were probably conservative.

Although all customers are important, some are clearly more profitable than others. The most loyal customers are usually the most profitable of all. Companies that take the time to analyze the figures are likely to find their most loyal customers (i.e., the top 20% in terms of spending and longevity) account for most of their profits. In some cases, these loyal customers account for 120% of profits (in short, they account not only for all profits but they pay

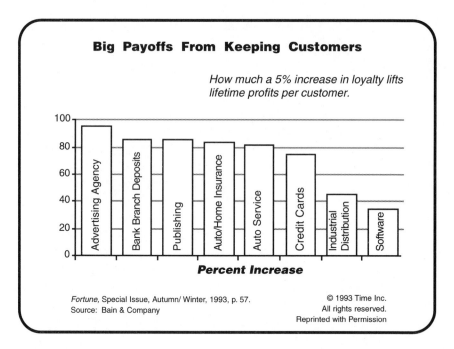

**Big Payoffs From Keeping Customers**

*How much a 5% increase in loyalty lifts lifetime profits per customer.*

*Percent Increase*

for much of your losses on other areas). Take these customers away and many corporations would find their business no longer viable.

The economics of customer loyalty was demonstrated to one financial services firm when it experienced an astounding 16% spending increase after implementing a customer loyalty program aimed specifically at long-time customers. More importantly, this new spending by existing customers came in an industry where the cost of getting new customers runs seven times higher than maintaining old customers. The cost of the loyalty program, which consisted of offering incentives and frequent flier mileage points for using the product, was significant, yet it was small compared to the cost of trying to raise 16% more revenue by attracting new customers.

Customer loyalty programs can include special discounts, parties, premiums and other rewards. For example, General Motors, by launching a co-branded credit card that put 5% of spending toward the purchase or lease of a new car, was able to offer a savings to its loyal customers while helping boost its own sales.

Surprisingly, few companies monitor customers on a regular basis, and fewer still make special efforts to enhance their relationship with their most loyal and profitable customers. Sadly, many firms *do not even know* who these customers are because the companies lack a system for tracking them.

Sensitive customer tracking systems identify not just (a) customer satisfaction, but also (b) customer perceived value, and (c) propensity to buy. While these three categories are closely related, there can be subtle but important differences. A customer may be satisfied and still not have a high propensity to buy again. Understanding what drives customer behavior is essential to building loyalty and managing the long-term relationship.

## Calculating Customer Asset "Yield"

In an environment of margin pressures and increasing competition, organizations must learn to manage all their assets, including the most important one, customers. Firms must think in terms of improving the "yield" on their existing customer base. This will not happen by accident. It will require a disciplined strategy aimed at enhancing loyalty and increasing the propensity to buy.

Most often, organizations do not know what the customer is really worth, except in the very gross sense of total revenue. One way of personalizing this learning is to assess the lifetime asset value of a single customer in your top 20% category, using the formula in the table on page 120.

One client in the medical field, after completing this formula, was astonished to find that its customers were worth several million dollars apiece. Yet another client, in the capital goods industry, discovered customers whose total lifetime value was several hundred million dollars. In the consulting business, few clients have a lifetime asset value of less than $750,000. Even in low margin industries, such as home products or cosmetics sold directly to households (such as Avon or Shaklee), the lifetime asset value of a customer can be tens of thousands of dollars. The formula is in the table on page 120.

Having customer-contact employees and executives complete this net asset value exercise is an extremely effective training tool. It brings on a gestalt that forever changes one's view of the customer across the counter or on the phone.

While it is important to know what the customer is worth, it is even more important to know how to drive up this net worth. How do you go about doing this?

Go back to the formula and ask yourself at which points you could increase the value of this customer. There are several points of leverage. For example, you could:

1. Increase average amount of purchase.
2. Increase frequency of spending.
3. Extend the relationship over more years.
4. Increase the propensity to recommend or refer.

Each of these represents a point of leverage where you could increase the yield on your existing customer base. After all, you have already paid good marketing money to get these customers into your system, so the cost advantages of this strategy are enormous.

# Intimate Knowledge

The key to leveraging your company's relationship with customers is intimate knowledge of them. What sort of knowledge? Well, for example:

- What drives spending frequency and amounts?
- What actions could be taken to increase frequency or deepen spending?

---

Average Purchase

_____

Multiply by the Average Number of
Purchases per Year _____     X          _____

Total Annual Asset Value per Year               _____

Multiplied by the Number of Years Customer
Stays With Organization     X                  _____

Multiplied by the Capacity of This Customer
to Influence at Least One Other
Person to Purchase      2  X                   _____

Lifetime Asset Value                           _____

Derived from Clemmer and Sheehy, *Firing on All
Cylinders*, Business-One Irwin, 1991.

---

- What additional value will be needed to enhance loyalty or increase propensity to spend?
- What could we do to deepen and/or broaden our relationship with the customer?
- What could we do to increase their propensity to refer and recommend?
- What additional needs or requirements does the customer have which are presently not met?
- Are there additional products or services which could be sold to this customer through our existing distribution system?

This information is readily available, given the right tracking system. Once armed with this data, it is possible to design a loyalty program which adds value in the eyes of the customer and drives the kind of buying behavior you want. The cornerstone of this strategy is knowing where and how to add value.

The right array of employee, customer and brand equity sensors, when cross referenced, will provide a wealth of data for strategic business planning. This will tell you specifically what to do more and less of, while highlighting those actions, features, offerings or strategies which provide the greatest leverage with customers. There is no way to over-estimate the importance of this information. It holds the key to quality improvement.

## Making the Most of Brand Equity

Brand management is not the sexy topic it was a decade ago, but it is likely to make a comeback over the next few years. Early in the 1990s, recession and deflation put pressure on overpriced brands, taking away some of their panache, along with their fat margins. Well-educated customers insisted on knowing what additional value premium brands brought to the party. Those not able to provide a convincing answer found customers shifting to no-name brands.

However, it is likely premium brands (at least those which learned from their mistakes) are going to make a comeback as the global economy recovers and expands. Underpinning the global expansion will be a focus on value as a by-product of quality over price. Within this formula, we can expect a subtle but important shift in emphasis *away* from price and *toward* quality. As global growth absorbs excess capacity, power will shift ever so slightly back in favor of quality in the customer's mind.

Although the consumer will remain very much in control and will not allow price gouging, buying decisions will be subtly influenced by perceived quality. A shift of a few degrees in the value equation, one way or the other, can make an enormous difference. After all, markets are made at the margin. The difference between a buyer's and seller's market can be as little as a few percentage points either way.

## Renewed Emphasis on Growth

This subtle but important shift back toward quality will be accompanied by increased emphasis on growth as a vital business strategy. Having spent a decade restructuring and cost cutting, many corporations are ready to again focus on customer service, quality and growth. While market leaders would argue they never lost interest in these subjects, evidence shows that much of the corporate world has been absorbed recently with cost-related issues.

Corporations will also have learned the hard way that once prices are reduced, the market does not allow you to raise them again quickly. A drop of 5% in price can have a huge impact on the bottom line. In fact, in many industries a 5% drop in price, without accompanying cost reduction, can cut profits anywhere from 20–50%.

As growth once more becomes the focus of corporate strategy, brand power will loom large, and for good reason. In a global economy, strong brands have tremendous reach. Like information and capital, premium brands reach across borders. They constitute a sort of global language of their own. The brand equity in Coca-Cola, Nike, Compaq or American Express is not confined to any single country. A consumer buying these products or services in New Delhi, Singapore or New York understands what they are buying. These common expectations are based on an unstated promise communicated without words even being spoken.

Another reason premium brands grow in importance is because they are perceived to provide quality, and people are willing to pay a premium for them. Those with strong market positions invariably are perceived as being high-quality providers of goods and services by their customers. Firms such as Dupont, Intel, Corning, American Express, 3M, Disney, UPS, Toyota, Sony,

Mercedes-Benz, Caterpillar, AT&T, Motorola, British Airways, Xerox, and Hewlett-Packard have established market leadership based on perceived quality. If questioned, these companies will, without exception, point to quality management as a key ingredient in both their brand and business success.

Brands with superior perceived quality earn net margins that are nearly four times as high as those perceived to be inferior. The work of author Bradley Gale reveals that quality is a more important driver of competitive position and business results than any other single factor tracked, including market share, cost and total growth of the market.

The PIMS database, one of the largest of its kind anywhere, has shown that over a 20-year period perceived quality is the best indicator of business success. Even firms with commanding market share at the beginning of the period showed steady erosion if perceived quality did not improve. Conversely, those with high perceived quality but low share saw their market share increase.

Firms with higher relative perceived quality and larger market share are able to charge a higher price. Interestingly, research shows these high quality firms have costs which are no higher, and often lower, than their lower quality competitors. Brands which are established market leaders because of perceived quality can also afford to spend more on advertising. They are under less pressure to offer special promotions and price discounts. The tilt back toward quality in the years ahead will work in favor of these premium brands, at least those which are properly managed.

However, a quality reputation must be earned. Even brands with a commanding market share cannot raise their relative prices beyond a given threshold without convincing customers they are also expanding the quality of their offering. That's why leading brands tend to lose share if they are not also quality leaders. This loss of share can happen even when the affected firms do not raise their relative prices.

In short, if one raises prices without also increasing relative perceived quality, the overall value equation goes into decline. At this point, market share can erode dramatically. Both premium brands and no-name brands must provide value in order to survive. The difference between the two is that premium brands are under less pressure to reduce price in order to meet the customer's value requirements. They avoid this price trap by growing the perceived quality of their offerings as a means of offsetting a somewhat higher price. No-name brands, on the other hand, having relatively low perceived quality, must close the gap by reducing price in the form of promotions, discounts or everyday low pricing. Given a choice, which game would you rather play?

## Avoid Being Trapped by Success

Using forcing mechanisms, stressing quality, making continuous improvements, taking advantage of brand equity, and perhaps most of all, managing the customer as an asset are all tried-and-true tools for helping you keep up with shifting value. The task of guarding against the dominance of the *business* by the *organization* is endless, and one from which mature firms must never shirk or tire of.

Having been successful for so long, it is easy for those inside the organization to think their success is the result of their structure and culture. They begin to believe their own press. They forget that all success ultimately comes from adding value for customers.

The internal apparatus, while important, plays only a supporting role in success. It is the customer, not the organization, who is the star of the show and who makes the company successful. In the best of cases, the company and the customer are knit together with trust, common purpose, and shared vision and values.

# 8

# Learning Drives the Quest for Value

*No problem can be solved within the same consciousness which caused it.*

—*Albert Einstein*

Nothing is more difficult than trying to teach smart people to learn. Market leaders have a particularly difficult time learning because they have been successful based on what they know and *knowing* always interferes with *learning*. However, in times of value decline, what you know can become a serious impediment to action.

In an economy increasingly driven by knowledge, learning has become a prerequisite to growth. Not only must people continually learn, but so must organizations. Companies and organizations which learn quickly are able to add value quickly and stay ahead, or at least abreast, of the movement of value. Those unable to learn quickly will fall behind.

So, the age of the learning organization is here. But what *is* a learning organization? It is one which readily absorbs information from its environment, such as market conditions, shifting consumer tastes, rising customer expectations, new competitive threats, regulatory trends, technological shifts, and changes in distribution channels. It then digests and uses this information to create new sources of value. In doing so, it creates yet more information which it sends back into the environment—via internal memos, articles, books, case studies, and other means—thus, further contributing to society.

We sometimes confuse the learning organization with the "perfect" organization and this is a mistake. Learning organizations are not perfect—they do not do everything right, but *they do learn from their mistakes.* When something doesn't work, they correct the error quickly.

When American Express, for example, fumbled its first revolving credit product, the Optima Card, it went back to the drawing board and started again from scratch. When Ford first launched the Taurus and had quality problems with the hoods of the cars, it rejected these inferior components and went to work with suppliers to fix the problem. (In the old days, it would have just repainted the hoods and shipped the product anyway!) Similarly, when a friend of ours bought a Toyota Previa van that turned out to be a lemon (not something which happens very often with a Toyota product), the company was horrified. Not only did Toyota provide a new one, they took the old one back to the factory in order to reverse-engineer the van and find out what had gone wrong.

The big difference between learning and non-learning organizations is not measured in their capacity for error but in their capacity to respond to error. Persistence in error is a sure sign of an organization which, in today's politically correct parlance, is "learning-challenged." That's why people are so infuriated with government these days. It refuses to stop doing things which clearly don't work.

But don't be fooled. Dumb organizations are not necessarily staffed by dumb people. In fact, there may be a lot of very smart people in a dumb organization. They are trapped there by a brain-dead organizational apparatus and are often very frustrated. The learning disability usually lies at the organizational level, not with the individual.

For instance, Mikhail Gorbachev, one of the great world figures in the second half of the 20th century, was a smart man trapped in a dumb system. The Soviet bureaucracy was incapable of learning or adapting. Gorbachev recognized that unless the system was reformed, it was doomed. His answer: *perestroika,* opening the Soviet system to new information.

It was a brilliant, daring gamble, yet it didn't work. In the end, the old order could not be saved. The new information brought on by perestroika quickly overwhelmed the slow moving, inflexible Soviet system. But in his attempt to save the old order, Gorbachev made way for the new. He and Eduard Shevardnadze made history by freeing Eastern Europe, ending the Cold War, and bringing democracy to the Russian people.

## Characteristics of a Learning Organization

*1. It possesses a learning ethic.* All learning organizations share a learning ethic. They want to learn, and they enjoy it. If something doesn't work, they are obsessed with finding out why, so they can fix it. Strategic information is an exciting asset to be shared and nurtured. Individuals are encouraged to improve themselves, enhance their skills, and learn as much as they can.

What creates learning organizations? We know that leadership, supporting values, and trust all play a role, as well as incentives. *The best incentive for learning is competition.* A recent Canadian Conference Board study of innovation discovered that new technologies and methodologies were most likely to be employed by industries facing intense competition. Protected industries or those facing little competition showed no interest or enthusiasm for innovation. They had little incentive to learn, so they didn't. All their energy went into finding ways to raise prices.

*2. It pays attention.* Remember your third-grade teacher admonishing you to "pay attention"? Well, she was right. We must be alert to what is going on around us. Information is the primary propellant of renewal. So, successful organizations take in a lot of information.

What kinds of information? *All* kinds—happenings in the field, sales promotions which work or do not, suppliers' recommendations, uses for new technology, competitors' ideas, perceptions by satisfied customers, perceptions by unsatisfied customers, what "renegades" on the firm's periphery are thinking, feelings of rank-and-file employees. The list is endless.

In a world transitioning from one economic era to another, the capacity to pay attention to what's happening around you is a prerequisite to survival. Only by taking in and synthesizing information can an organization hope to adapt to fast-changing circumstances.

Organizations that cannot absorb information quickly are certain to fall behind. In some industries, the definition of value is shifting so quickly that the penalty for failing to pay attention is almost immediate. The wake-up call comes in the form of lost market share or declining margins.

In *Taurus, the Car That Saved Ford*, author Eric Taub described how in the late '70s and early '80s, Ford designers were cut off from much of the information they needed to redesign cars for a new era. Isolated behind locked doors and armed guards, Ford's designers were working to perfect the soft, mushy "boulevard" ride which insulated the driver from the driving environment—even though customer requirements were moving in entirely the opposite direction.

Ford's market research teams returning from California could literally see foreign cars taking over the road. Foreign car ownership already was over 25% in many California cities and would grow to 40% by decade's end. Consumers opting for Mercedes-Benz, BMWs, and Mazda RX-7s were clearly looking for something more than the Crown Victoria had to offer. Numerous studies were done on what this new breed of driver was seeking. Unfortunately, little of this information reached the hermetically sealed environment of the Ford design labs.

How does an organization pay attention to what's happening in its environment? By actively listening and seeking out new sources of information. These sources can include market research, brand equity analysis, customer satisfaction surveys, focus groups, employee satisfaction surveys, benchmarking data, quality-improvement team data, and interviews with salespeople and front line employees. Information can also come from alliances, mergers, or the hiring of professionals who bring to the organization varying experiences. The key is to systematically seek out this information and inject it regularly into the organization.

The process cannot be left to chance. Obtaining customer and employee views, brand analysis, market trends, and benchmarking data, for example, must be disciplined and regular. Yet surprisingly few organizations collect such data on a regular basis.

But collecting data by itself is not enough. It must be transmitted throughout the organization loudly enough to be heard and to force change where needed. There is no point having just one sector of the organization undergoing important learning if the rest of the organization is denied access to this information.

For example, field people—those closest to the customer—usually see competitors' moves first or sense a change in customers' preferences. Too often, they cannot get the attention of higher-ups. For data to really have an effect, it must be noticed, then translated into operational objectives, with consequences spelled out.

Vital information, as we have seen, can come from any number of sources. The key is knowing what to do with it. Doomed institutions are often awash in data regarding the need to change. Pan Am, Eastern Airlines, and Wang had plenty of data telling them they needed to do things differently; so did Sears, GM, and IBM before the fall. It's not lack of data, but rather the propensity to ignore it, which determines an organization's fate.

3. *It's led by the enlightened.* In the old industrial model, the leader's role was primarily to exercise control. In an economy now driven increasingly by information, the leader's role has changed. Successful leaders must now focus on building organizations which can take in and create new information.

Today's post-modern leaders intuitively know there is a danger in the comfort zone. Very often, a dose of discomforting information is just what is needed to get the organization focused and moving. If the uncomfortable information is fed back to the organization repeatedly and in such a way that it cannot be ignored, it will force the organization off center. This will cause it to oscillate, slowly at first but eventually in wider and wider sweeps away from the status quo. With destabilization, the learning process begins.

If you think about it, this is precisely what occurs when an organization undergoes a crisis. Lost market share, layoffs, mergers, or the prospect of outright closure all cause the organization to veer wildly away from the status quo. People become unnerved, morale drops, irrational behavior occurs, and the organization may even appear at times in danger of becoming dysfunctional. A leader's first instinct in a crisis may be to stabilize the situation, slow the oscillation, and generally "put a lid on it." However, there are times when that is the very worst thing to do.

One client of ours, for example, wanted to know how well it was tracking and delivering its products. What it found was shocking. The firm was mishandling 20% of its deliveries and was completely outperformed by its main competitor.

At first, this benchmarking data was denied and rejected. The CEO kept forcing it back into the system by setting performance goals based on the data. Reluctantly, the company took up the challenge. It set out to reduce shipping errors by 98%. This audacious improvement target could only be achieved by overhauling the entire shipping process. So the company contracted with an integrated logistics firm to reengineer its shipping process, using the latest bar-coding technology. The reengineered process was so success-ful it became an industry benchmark.

The detonator of this change clearly was the introduction of new information—the data which showed the firm to be bungling 20% of its deliveries. The information would not have been acted upon if the CEO had not forced the data into the system by tying it to compen-sation and management objectives. Setting the goal of 98% improve-ment forced the organization out of its comfort zone. As it moved up the learning curve with its new bar-coding and shipping system, the organization acquired a new and powerful core competency in the ex-pedited delivery of products. Ultimately, this was shared in the indus-try, setting off a new round of learning. Everyone benefited.

Thus, in cases where significant change is needed, it may be in everyone's best interest to keep the organization off balance. In this game of brinkmanship, the key is to bring the organization right to the edge without pushing it over. For instance, when Motorola set its first 10-times-improvement goal, no one believed it was possible to achieve. The reasons given for why it could not be done were legion. At the root of this resistance was the implicit recognition that even *aiming* for such a target would be destabilizing. And achieving it would be traumatic. If Galvin and Fisher, the leaders of the organi-zation, had blinked at that moment, Motorola's quality improve-ment process would have instantly stalled. Instead, they made it clear that the goal was non-negotiable. In the end, it was the organi-zation which blinked, not its leaders. It is good it turned out that way: the "10-times crisis" set Motorola on the road to world-class quality performance and industry leadership.

Another valuable function of a leader is to protect internal sources of information from bureaucratic assault, but he or she must also inject this information into the larger organization. While pock-ets of new information must be protected, they cannot be so com-pletely cut off that there is no cross-fertilization. This balance can be achieved, for example, by coupling teams from larger and smaller systems, or assigning one or two key individuals from the larger sys-tem to act as partners on teams grappling with new concepts. A third is to arrange for a long integration period overseen by a special liai-son. In any case, the wise leader manages sources of internal infor-mation as valuable assets in the same way one would manage valu-able external information.

One of the things which separate human beings from animals and machines is our capacity for introspection. We can look inward and ask ourselves *why*. We are even capable of grappling with paradox, although not always gracefully. *Star Trek* fans will recall that troublesome computers in the show's script were made to self-destruct with little more than a command: "Prove that your prime directive is not your prime directive." In trying to ponder the imponderable, the computer implodes.

Not so with mankind—we are at our best when probing beyond our realm of certainty. The challenge for today's leader is to create organizations which more resemble human beings than machines. We must develop organizations capable of introspection—able to take in information, synthesize and create new information. In other words, organizations capable of managing paradox. Such organizations learn daily, and thus they adapt, evolve and thrive.

## What Makes an Organization Learning-Disabled?

Conversely, organizations which cannot learn are learning-disabled. How do you identify them? Well, first of all, when they make mistakes, they keep on doing them, no matter how awful the results. In *The March Of Folly*, Barbara Tuchman cites Philip II, the 16th century monarch of Spain, as a classic example of a slow learner. Even after the disaster of the Armada, in which he lost his whole fleet and nearly bankrupted the country, Philip remained convinced of the "absolute excellence" of his policies.

In World War I, thick headed generals on both sides insisted on employing frontal assaults with massed infantry against entrenched machine guns. Persisting in using 19th century tactics against 20th century weapons, they sent a whole generation of Europe's youth to their deaths. After four bloody years, casualties numbered in the millions.

In more recent history, North American car manufacturers suffered the same problem in the 1970s. Study after study indicated the desire of consumers for higher quality, more fuel efficient automobiles. Yet the car makers simply refused to hear the message. They changed their advertising, altered logos and jingles, added hood ornaments, installed velour seats and fake wood dashboards—anything but do what customers wanted. Not only were they resistant to change, they did not even want to hear about it.

The auto makers were downright hostile to information which pointed to their deficiencies. Quality guru W. Edwards Deming was not welcomed in Detroit for nearly 20 years. J.D. Powers, who instituted annual comparative quality assessments of automobiles, was once booed from the stage by a combined audience of United Auto Workers leaders and Big Three management. It was not until the 1980s that these companies engaged in the kind of serious Total Quality Management effort necessary to win back their customers.

## No Incoming Data

Another characteristic of slow learning organizations is that there is usually little or no external data coming into the organization regarding customers, competition, market conditions, technological trends, or anything else. It is hard to learn when there is nothing to learn with.

Occasionally a dumb organization will find itself with access to good sources of external data, but this information is rarely fed back to the organization in a systematic way. It just goes into a void. Learning-disabled organizations consistently underexploit the information they have. They sometimes even suppress sources of new information. Internal information, such as that which comes from salespeople, technical service reps, and customer service operators, is rarely leveraged.

In the 1970s, GM entered the NUMMI (New United Motor Manufacturing, Inc.) joint venture with Toyota to produce a new generation of small cars in Fremont, California. The purpose of the joint venture was to discover the "secret formula" behind the success of Japan's car manufacturer. General Motors selected some of its best and brightest engineers and managers for the NUMMI project.

Within a few years, NUMMI saw amazing gains in quality and productivity as it produced a superb line of new small cars under the Nova brand name. While designing and building the Nova, the GM staff assigned to the project learned there was no "secret" to producing high-quality small cars—it was just a question of getting the basics right. These GM staffers were now seed carriers of what W. Edwards Deming would call "profound knowledge."

So what did GM do with this profound knowledge? The company buried it and its "carriers" as deep and far away as it could. The NUMMI graduates were treated as pariahs. No one inside GM wanted anything to do with them. Why? Because their knowledge represented a mortal threat to the status quo at General Motors. It was only years later, with the building of the new Saturn division, that GM cycled back to exploit this insider knowledge.

## Paradigm Paralysis

Why do organizations choose to perish rather than take in and respond to new information? Largely because, in effect, the central nervous system of the institution has been damaged. This loss of capacity to absorb information occurs over time and is usually caused by an overabundance of wealth. Cushioned by success, layers of hierarchy build up throughout the organization. To preserve the status quo, these calcified layers invariably block or attenuate market signals.

Sometimes organizations even structure themselves to be dumb and to stay dumb. They set up barriers and buffers to the flow of new data. Early on, for example, it is not unusual for sales personnel to feel a shift in customer requirements, but often they do not have a means of communicating this to the people designing the product.

In a highly fragmented organization, information easily becomes trapped in narrow, functional "silos" or disparate regional units. In this way, vital data can be bottled up at lower levels or among certain groups but cannot be shared with those who need it. For instance, market research, sales, or customer service staffers often have access to mountains of invaluable data which never leaves their department, thus not getting into the hands of decision makers.

Sometimes bureaucracies armed with rules and regulations are structured precisely to keep organizations from learning. Picture this—a real life organization of several thousand people processing hundreds of millions of dollars a year in transactions, isolates itself from the outside world by taking in no external market data. It is flying blind—and *likes it that way*. The many layers of management filter signals moving up the organization. As the signal passes through each layer, it weakens. What little gets to the top is carefully screened, controlled and sanitized.

It is no accident that since the time of Caesar, generals have insisted that frontline reconnaissance units report *directly to them*. This structure is rooted in two thousand years of bitter experience. No sanitation or attenuation of data is permitted. No intermediate layers of command are allowed to get into the way of the truth.

How many business executives have similar access to raw, uncontaminated data? How many know what is *really* going on out there?

To prevent data moving horizontally across the organization, thick "membranes" sometimes develop between the vertical silos. Marketing does not talk to Sales, and neither would think of communicating with Design or Manufacturing. In such environments, it's not unusual to find outdated information technology and primitive information support systems; e-mail and networking systems are often regarded as unnecessary fluff. No one communicates with anyone else, and that is the way everyone likes it.

Surely, you may say, such organizations don't exist in this day and age. You *bet* they do! Government is full of them, and the private sector certainly has its share. These organizations erect structures which trap information and blunt opportunity.

Take the case of one financial services firm presented with an immense global marketing opportunity involving a joint venture with a large medical association. The financial services firm was organized along regional and product lines while the opportunity spanned the globe and transcended any individual product. As a result, the company had difficulty forming a team to champion the venture.

The client repeatedly found itself dealing with regional or product line executives whose interests and focus were narrower than the new idea. The client wanted to talk about global opportunities, but the firm's executives were only interested in how this impacted "Canada" or "Mexico," or how it affected a particular product line.

The marketing executives who had stumbled across this opportunity in the first place could see that the medical association was becoming impatient, but the marketers had no place to take their pleas for help. There was no person or group within the company responsible for pursuing global opportunities or trans-product lines. In the end, not surprisingly, the medical association took the opportunity to a competitor better organized to meet its global needs.

The kind of self-destructive behavior shown by that firm is almost always rooted in past success. People cling to today's failed paradigm precisely because it was yesterday's successful innovation. Whatever the cause, the result is paradigm paralysis. The organization stops learning.

Sometimes organizations are so busy being successful, they don't have time to learn. And because they are so successful, they can afford to be dumb . . . for a while. In the course of our work, we have seen organizations which, because they are in the right place, at the right time, catch a value "wave" which carries them to success, despite their best efforts to prevent it. Soon, though, this success becomes a burden because it provides an excuse for not learning.

Organizations unable to learn are unable to adapt and, as a result, perish. This culling process goes on all the time in free market economies—companies falter or even go bankrupt while new ones are born every day. However, the morbidity rate increases exponentially during times of economic transition. This is precisely what's happening today, as the rate of turnover in the Fortune 500 increases with each passing year.

## Resisting Information

Resistance to new information is not a phenomenon restricted to large, unhealthy organizations, although it is more pronounced in them. Even healthy organizations can resist new information. Why? Because information on rising customer expectations, or a competitor's superior performance, or erosion of brand equity is almost always painful and disruptive. Even information generally known or suspected by insiders can be disruptive, when given tangible form.

That's why consultants often are useful. They feed back information that already exists inside the organization. It is illustrative of the problem that organizations must go outside to learn what they already know. They do so because their internal culture and systems prevent them from hearing it from inside. To be heard, it is packaged and transmitted from outside.

But outsiders cannot force an organization to change, and the mere fact of calling in external help does not guarantee a willingness to change. A firm we know regularly calls in consultants, at considerable expense, to help shift the organizational culture toward greater customer focus. What follows is a predictable and elaborate step dance, in which the external consultant is slowly enculturated and captured by the "middle" of the organization, whose unconscious role is to protect the status quo. The first step in this process calls for the external change agents to be surrounded and bombarded with busy work. The list of activities to be performed grows and grows, as the pace increases. Targets set for years must now be accomplished in a quarter or a month. Everybody is so busy "doing" things, there is no possibility of learning. Energy displaces reflection, activity crowds out results. The outsiders are soon run off their feet and then the whispering begins in the hallways. "These guys aren't that good . . . why are we paying so much? We can do this ourselves." Access to the executive floor becomes harder and harder to get. Soon it becomes clear this latest set of consultants is on its way out. The organization has once again dodged the bullet. The need to change having been obviated, everything goes back to normal. Pockets of people within the organization may still recognize the need for change, but this "prescient few" now duck for cover. The change effort is now over, until the next unsuspecting set of outside consultants is brought in to begin the dance again.

All organizations seek homeostasis, an equilibrium in which everything is predictable. Information, especially discordant information, challenges the status quo and makes homeostasis impossible to achieve. This is precisely why it is resisted. Ironically, what organizations most seek, stability and predictability, usually signal the beginning of death. Organizations too comfortable with the status quo are almost always headed for trouble.

## How to Escape Entropy

How does an organization escape this bureaucratic trap and keep itself open to information?

1. *Put the right systems in place.* As we have mentioned before, the first thing to do is ensure processes are in place for gathering information such as customer satisfaction, employee satisfaction, market research, benchmarking, and brand analysis. Quality and process improvement teams are also excellent sources of new information. In fact, it can be argued that where quality improvement processes have been most successful, it is because they generated vital new information for the organization to synthesize and act upon.

2. *Protect insider information.* When sources of new information come from inside the organization, through alliances, specialty teams, reengineering teams, or quality improvement teams, these sources must be protected from the larger bureaucratic amoeba. Just as external information can be ignored, internal information can be

suppressed. This suppression takes many forms, the most effective of which are subtle.

For example, the agents of change are often broken up to better "integrate" them into the larger organization, or they are drawn into a mass of "coordinating meetings." Sometimes suppression takes the form of limiting resources to the new entity or smothering it in bureaucratic busywork. It is hard to engineer a revolution when most of your waking hours are absorbed in trying to understand and complete a host of forms.

It is also a mistake to allow rigid norms, procedures and instructions to be imposed on a team whose aim is to create new information. In life, it is information (DNA) which gives shape to living entities, not the other way around. So it should be in organizations. New information may dictate entirely new structures, organizations and procedures. To allow form to dominate knowledge is a travesty of logic, which guarantees the triumph of sloth and bureaucracy.

*3. Instill trust and knowledge-driven value.* Companies are complex mechanisms with moving parts. They are increasingly information driven and dependent on the expertise of knowledge workers. This combination of complexity, information and value-added knowledge does not lend itself to the old command-and-control environment. These new organizations cannot be "ordered" to perform. They succeed only by virtue of their common purpose and cohesion.

In the new economy, wealth comes from taking in knowledge and synthesizing it, and then creating new value-added knowledge with it. Trust, teamwork and cohesion are essential to this process. This commercialization of knowledge requires sharing. No one can create knowledge-driven value alone in today's work environment. It must be a collaborative effort, but how can there be collaboration without trust?

Today's organizations are increasingly disparate and virtual. Loose-knit groups of knowledge workers, networked together electronically, must have a high degree of trust and common purpose in order to perform. In fact, such trust may be all that holds them together. We will take an in-depth look at that in the next chapter.

# 9

# Something Gained
# ... Something Lost

*Use what words you will, you can never say anything but what you are.*

—*Ralph Waldo Emerson*

The great English land owners of the 18th century concluded they could make more money by replacing farmers with sheep. Historians now view the great land clearances of that period as inevitable because the economics of the old order simply no longer added up. Nevertheless, it was a sad day highland chieftains turned their own kinsmen out of their homes and sent them packing to Nova Scotia just to make room for animals.

Today, our largest corporations have begun the modern equivalent of the "great clearances." Suddenly, loyalty and corporate affiliation does not count for much, nor do old, obsolete skills. Today, the same sad drama is being played out at IBM, Mobil, Xerox, BellSouth, AT&T and other large corporations. These changes, too, are inevitable, but as the whole economy becomes increasingly absorbed in reducing costs and displacing labor, a note of caution is in order. What if, in our lunge to reduce costs, we destroy our capacity to produce wealth? In a number of cases, as we will show, this is precisely what has happened.

A main theme of this book has been that, given today's new

value requirements, change is necessary, even desirable. But we must be careful in undertaking this change; otherwise, we risk creating a wasteland—an empty, purposeless, and joyless work environment. Organizations operating in such an atmosphere become brittle and break at the first sign of stress.

Indeed, many corporations have damaged the very systems they set out to improve. The modern firm is a delicate machine made up of work process, technology and people. You cannot drop the equivalent of a neutron bomb on the human infrastructure of an organization and expect the machine to go on functioning smoothly.

## Painful and Protracted Process

The highland chieftains, too, were richer after the clearances but something irreplaceable had been lost. The system of clan loyalty, which had stood for two millennia or more, was gone forever. The relationship between the chieftain and his followers had become purely economic.

Something is gained and lost in every change. Today, America is in the process of losing its old, Second Wave economy. Although it will gain much in return, the process is proving painful and protracted. Any other society would have already reacted to the level of disruption now being visited upon the U.S. economy. No society anywhere, except perhaps the nations of the Pacific Rim and Eastern Europe, have undergone such dramatic changes within the last 15 years. And there is more to come.

Wise leadership will be required if we are to avoid a reaction to the bloodletting of recent years. Rather than viewing employees as a liability to get rid of, perhaps it's time we concentrated more attention on their value as an asset. Instead of cutting our way to success, we should be focusing on creating wealth and adding value. Instead of shrinking companies, maybe we should be thinking about growing them again.

We might even try to reassure employees that they are still needed and have important work to do. But that's not the message we're sending when business magazine photos show Mike Hammer, the original reengineering guru, standing on the shores of Lake Ontario brandishing a crowbar over his head. Workers are painfully aware that their bosses are eagerly lining up to attend Hammer's reengineering seminars.

The dilemma confronting today's leaders is that Hammer is half right. Significant change in our corporate structures and business designs is clearly needed. The economy has changed and so must business. If we do nothing, we will fall behind, our competitive position will deteriorate, productivity will decline, and living standards will drop. So ignoring the problem is not an answer. As Shakespeare reminds us, "Nothing comes from doing nothing."

However, if we must act, we should do so with skill and vision. This is not a sentimental wish but a pragmatic assessment. If we do not learn to better manage today's historic transition, the process could well backfire.

The downtrodden crofters forced off their land in the 18th century had little recourse and few options. The New World offered their only way out and served as a social safety valve. Had this option not existed, violence would almost certainly have followed. Today's displaced workers do have options. In a democracy, there is always recourse to the ballot box. If the critical mass of voting citizens decide events are moving too fast, they will simply slow them down politically. As in the 1930s, people could again begin to blame the "market mechanism" itself for their troubles.

## An Underlying Moral Question

Beneath today's trauma lies an underlying moral question regarding the very purpose of business and markets. *Why do they exist?* Is it to make profits, create wealth, serve shareholders, or create jobs for employees? The answer is: all of these and more. Corporations exist to serve the interests of shareholders, employees and customers. However, they should exist to also serve the interests of society, to make life better. If firms perform well, they are rewarded with profits. Business should be an instrument of social progress, with profits, dividends, salaries and rising share values as by-products of meeting this larger requirement.

By adding value, corporations serve society. In the course of adding value, the best interests of all stakeholders are also served— so long as these interests are kept in balance. But any time the balance of interest between shareholders, customers and employees swings too far in one direction or the other, value suffers and so does society.

For instance, in the late 1970s and 1980s shareholders perceived that some management teams were putting their own interests ahead of owners. This brought on a wave of shareholder revolts, corporate raiding, leveraged buyouts, and a renewed focus on corporate governance. Or, take the auto industry in the 1950s, '60s and '70s. While prices went up, quality went down. In Detroit, it was arrogantly assumed no one would mind or even notice being fleeced. The United Auto Workers and management of the Big Three met regularly to carve up the pie and yell at one another. Completely self-absorbed, they lost sight of the customer. Then one day, they looked up and found their customers were gone—they had moved on in search of better quality and service.

Losing customers is a sobering experience and it shocked the auto industry out of its complacency. That was the beginning of the U.S. auto recovery. From that moment of awakening, it took Detroit more than a decade to catch up with its customers. Recovering was hard, tough work. Had the industry been afforded the protection from competition which it sought, it would almost certainly have faltered long before the course was run. The auto industry learned to add value again only because it was forced to; this recovery was driven by pain, not virtue.

Now our society is again grappling with whether corporate America is being wise. It is a matter of perception. Just look at the organizations which have each laid off tens of thousands of employees since 1992: IBM, 122,000; AT&T, 125,000; GM, 74,000; U.S. Postal Service, 55,000; Sears, 50,000; Boeing, 31,000; Hughes Aircraft, 25,000; McDonnell-Douglas, 21,000; BellSouth, 21,000; Digital Equipment, 20,000.

Will these layoffs result in long-term improvements? In some cases, yes. But we are starting to learn that not all layoffs improve value for shareholders or society. Dominance by any one stakeholder group usually results in a loss of focus on value, the true purpose of commerce. Is the balance out of whack today? Perhaps, but we're too close to these events to say for sure. A decade from now, historians will be better able to pass judgment.

However, what's clear is that employees in large corporations are being pulled through a keyhole. In the rush to chase value and to restructure, employees have suddenly become expendable and are no longer "our greatest asset," as firms used to boast. Now they have become "our greatest liability," or at least that's the message we are sending to them.

## Reengineers Run Amok

During the reengineering craze of the 1990s, we smashed hierarchies, dismantled work processes, shredded relationships, shattered confidence, denigrated old loyalties, and turned middle managers into an endangered species. In short, we put the American economy through a meat grinder and buried forever the 20th century concept of corporate loyalty.

Large corporations have been restructuring and laying off workers at unprecedented rates for a decade now. This wave of restructuring has moved beyond manufacturing into services and will soon be impacting the public sector. No one is immune.

At first, restructuring was prompted by offshore competition which forced American manufacturers to get serious about quality and productivity. Later, in the early 1990s, downsizing was driven by global deflationary pressure. The end of the Cold War also had an impact as it rendered huge chunks of our military industrial complex redundant.

But the root cause of all of this restructuring is the emergence of a global, knowledge-driven economy. This is forcing the overhaul of our old analog economic structures. The forces behind this transition are immensely powerful, and the adjustments required are large and painful.

In 1990, 316,000 jobs were eliminated, with the figure increasing to 555,000 jobs in 1991. In 1993, the figure was again at the half-million mark and by 1994, it was 516,000. Job losses in 1995 again topped half a million. Although more new jobs are being created than are being lost, this is cold comfort to those displaced in this process.

By amplifying the downsizing phenomenon, the press makes things worse. After all, bad news is "news." The closing of a plant or the reduction of a workforce is the sort of dramatic stuff which lends itself to catchy headlines. On the other hand, wealth creation is subtle and less visible. While local newspapers and TV newscasts focus on plant closings, they fail to see the opening or expansion of a business across the street; it is invisible to them. Why? Because one is "news" and the other is not. This might explain why as things got better in the 1980s, the headlines got worse.

## The Dark Side of Reengineering

It is no accident that reengineering became popular during the early 1990s, a time of recession and deflation. In many industries, the disinflation of the 1980s had given way to outright deflation by the 1990s. This created a "cost" crisis which forced organizations to reexamine their cost structures. Business Process Reengineering fit well with this cost-sensitive environment. Promises of quick, dramatic improvements struck home with executives desperate to reduce costs. As a result, right-sizing, downsizing, rationalization, and most of all reengineering, became the order of the day. In the end, it all came down to cutting costs, especially headcount.

This focus on reducing headcount and driving down costs soon overwhelmed the original purpose of reengineering, which aims to radically redesign strategic work processes. At its worst, this led to corporate anorexia, as businesses permanently reduced their capacity to grow, add value, expand market share and sustain long-term competitiveness.

This tilt toward cost control and away from adding value was driven in part by the tone and language of many of the reengineering gurus. As the poet Walt Whitman reminds us, "Use what words you will, you can only say what you are." As author Don Tapscott pointed out in his insightful work, *Digital Economy*, the words employed by the reengineers in the early 1990s contained an inherent undertone of "violence." They spoke of "shooting dissenters," "nuking the existing structure," and "breaking legs." Unleashing this violence on the human infrastructure of an organization was bound to do damage. Battered, downsized organizations emerged from their reengineering experiences traumatized and in shock. Trust, goodwill, commitment and company loyalty lay shattered. The capacity to innovate and create wealth was often damaged, in some cases permanently.

## New Business Design

In their obsession with reducing costs, many reengineers failed to see that *declining value* was the real source of their cost problem. If you look closely you'll see that the prime candidates for reengineering in the early 1990s invariably suffered from value erosion. Reducing costs provided temporary relief but it only masked the true problem.

Worse still, focusing on cost reductions in place of adding value produced an "inside out" view of the business. As a result, Business Process Reengineering projects typically missed opportunities to move beyond process redesign and shift their focus toward business transformation. The first generation of "reengineers" did not seem to understand that a new economy demanded fundamentally new business designs and the application of new methodologies and technologies. Weighed down by their focus on costs, the reengineers of the early 1990s missed this point.

In addition, the focus on top down, "leg breaking" leadership was clearly inconsistent with the need to develop fast, flat, learning organizations. The reengineers seemed not to recognize that flexible, intelligent organizations are founded on trust, teamwork and shared commitment. You cannot force people to learn or be innovative.

## Reengineering With New Technology

Although reengineering assumes the large-scale application of new technology, particularly information systems, to redesign work processes, early advocates of the methodology were usually unsuccessful in reconciling old technology with new organizational designs. In truth, it is nearly impossible to reengineer work processes using old information technology. The old model of computing information using host-based, proprietary and often centralized information platforms was incompatible with new organizational models.

Reengineering theories also failed to seize the broader implications of large-scale business transformation. No one seemed willing to admit you cannot change the nature of work without changing the world which surrounds it. Remember, in today's world, everything effects everything else. Consequently, reengineering cannot be conducted in isolation. Retraining those whose skills are rendered obsolete by process redesign, supporting those whose roles are changing, grappling with a widening divergence of income between information haves and have nots, all this and more must be faced if reengineering is to achieve its true potential.

## Feeling Out of Control

Not surprisingly, employees buffeted and bruised by these changes feel bitter and helpless. As one Xerox employee put it, "Five years ago, I felt pretty close to comfortable, but now I feel that I'm part of a big wheel that just keeps rolling. Whatever the wheel wants to do, it's going to do." This feeling of helplessness raises anxiety, stress and disorientation. Those who find themselves unemployed, even temporarily, suffer a blow to their confidence and self-esteem. The unemployed worker loses daily association with fellow workers and is cut off not only from a source of income but also from the social system that surrounds work. The whole process is traumatic.

To make matters worse, many organizations have cut costs and laid off employees without redesigning work processes. They call it "reengineering," but the only thing they have reengineered is their budget. One organization we know responded to recessionary margin pressure with a spasm of cost-cutting initiatives. It all made sense on paper, but service levels quickly declined and customer satisfaction plummeted. As a result, when the market came back following the recovery, the firm began to lose share.

Another firm, Northern Telecom, dramatically cut its service and support functions during the early '90s. Then, when it began to experience glitches during the introduction of new products, it did not have the capacity to handle them. The company experienced record losses before restoring its former service and support levels.

Increasingly, questions are being asked about how effective restructuring and reengineering have been. In too many cases, the answers are mixed, profits do not improve, productivity remains low, and shareholder value does not increase. It is now becoming clear that many of the reengineering efforts of the early 1990s were mismanaged. Lacking any clear link to corporate strategy (sometimes reengineering *was* the strategy), these efforts became little more than brutal exercises in reducing costs.

A study by the Wyatt Company of 531 company downsizings found that few of them have produced long-term benefits. Only 46% increased earnings, 34% increased productivity, and just a third improved customer service. Another study was even more damning. University of Wisconsin researcher Kenneth De Meuse followed companies for five years, including two years before downsizing and two years after it was completed. Over the five years, the downsized companies showed profit margins of 6%, 6%, 4%, 2% and 0%. Companies which did not downsize showed margins of 6%, 6%, 7%, 6% and 5%. Recent studies have yielded similar results.

Urged on by the reengineers, the downsizing that occurred in the first half of the decade had a herd-like quality about it, with many organizations taking an ax to their own wealth creation machinery. H.J. Heinz, for example, began a cost-cutting initiative in the early 1990s which included a significant reduction in the workforce. However, quality began to decline as overworked Starkist employees began to leave tons of meat on the fish bones. Ultimately, the firm reached for a quality solution which turned conventional cost-cutting theory on its ear: quality could be improved and money made by actually *adding* employees.

At many other firms where restructuring did work and profits improved, employees found they were still subject to layoffs. If hard work and high profits can't protect your job, what *can*? Nor does it help when major corporations cut workers' salaries while making record profits and awarding executives multi-million-dollar bonuses. Feeling betrayed and burned out, many employees are withdrawing all emotional commitment from their work. Every morning they get up and just go through the motions. That is hardly a recipe for productivity or quality.

As firms renew their value propositions and jettison underperforming assets and obsolete structures, they are engaging in massive economic renewal. Unfortunately, renewal is often accompanied by layoffs and dislocation. People are inevitably caught in the middle and hurt. Ultimately, most of them take their talents to other sectors of the economy that are growing and in need of their skills. However, the transition is always painful and bloody.

## An Inevitable Reaction

We are not arguing against downsizing, which is inevitable as we transition from one economic era to another. However, we do need to keep in mind that downsizing takes place in a societal setting. It occurs because society "allows" it to happen. Such forbearance is based on the implicit assumption that downsizing will improve performance. If that turns out not to be the case, a social reaction of some sort is inevitable.

Luckily, America has a higher tolerance for this sort of disorder than other societies. It was, after all, a nation founded on revolution. But we would be foolish to assume this tolerance is infinite. If the business community pursues cost reductions or reengineering goals to the utter disregard of society as a whole, or if it makes a mess of these efforts and produces few results, a reaction of some sort is inevitable. If we are not careful, we could undermine the very trust and confidence which holds the American economic system together.

If you think that preposterous, remember what happened in the 1930s. The Depression was perceived by many as a failure of the business community. Scapegoating the private sector, citizens turned to government for solutions, and we have been living with the problems of big government ever since.

Could it happen again? Yes, but what form this reaction would take is uncertain. Today, government itself is held in such disrepute that people are unlikely to turn to the public sector for a solution, except as a last resort. But as Isaac Newton reminds us, "For every action, there is an equal and opposite reaction."

So, how would this reaction manifest itself? One indicator may be the increasing reluctance of top university graduates to work for large corporations. Generation "X" does not trust big government, but neither does it trust big business. A deadlier sign of discontent is the rise of extremist, anti-immigrant, anti-trade, and anti-big business political constituencies. To the right of this movement are even more dangerous elements—radical, nihilist groups who are against all forms of social order or governance. Like the anarchists of the 19th century, they are *against* everything and *for* nothing. With bombings, shootings and violence their trademark, this far right fringe has become an ever greater threat to American society.

## Challenge and Response

In summarizing their lifetime study of history, Will and Ariel Durant found that challenge is the chief source of renewal. A challenge successfully met propels society forward. The greater the challenge, the greater the potential "renewal."

When asked what determines if a challenge will be met, they answered: "It depends upon the presence or absence of initiative and of creative individuals with clarity of mind and energy of will. . . . "

To these two criteria, we venture to add a third: the *moral conviction* to do what is right. Arguably, we have more need of strong moral leadership today than ever before.

As we pass from one economic era to another, our society is being challenged to redefine itself. In such a period of flux, nothing is guaranteed—not even the free market system. The case for democracy and capitalism must continually be made in the form of actions, not just good intentions.

As citizens and leaders, we must go to great lengths to explain to employees and communities why today's painful changes are necessary and what the ultimate benefits will be. We must take time to explain the big picture to our employees, suppliers and the community. We should not take for granted that everyone understands the forces driving these changes; in fact, most people *do not*. They are too busy reacting to these forces to give much thought to their origins.

## Redefining Leadership

Explaining *why* will not, by itself, be enough. Business leaders must also act responsibly in undertaking large-scale restructuring and change, and they must offer leadership suitable for these unsettled times. It may be necessary to redefine the very dimensions of modern leadership. This redefinition is likely to take us back to such basics as courage, honor, fortitude, and most importantly, leading by example. Leaders involved in large-scale change must share not only information, but also hardships and risks with those they lead.

If this sounds a little old-fashioned and idealistic, *so be it*. It works. Nineteen- and twenty-year-old corporals understand implicitly they cannot lead people who do not trust or respect them. Why is this truth so hard to understand for a 50-year-old executive with above-average intelligence, a couple of degrees, and years of experience?

## The Core of Commerce

Subject to the torque and stress of change, organizations and institutions must hold together or risk being torn apart. Like the wing of an aircraft in turbulence, they must flex without breaking. Webster's dictionary defines cohesion as "the act or state of uniting or sticking together, the property of unity." The military has done extensive studies on why some units come apart under pressure, while others grow closer and stronger. The one most important factor which emerges from these studies is *trust*. The larger and stronger the radius of trust, the greater the cohesion.

When you think about it, trust has been at the core of commerce and business since the very first exchange of goods. Without trust, there can be no commerce. When you strike a bargain, you trust it will be honored. When you pay the agreed amount, you "trust" that you will receive the contracted goods or services. The person selling you the product trusts you to pay the agreed amount and trusts that the currency is genuine.

At another level, the seller is trusting that the central bank which issued the currency will redeem it at face value and/or protect its underlying value. If chaos, dishonesty or incompetence undermines this base level of trust, the whole system quickly unravels, as we saw happen in Germany in the 1920s. This explains why inflation has such a pernicious impact on the economy—it undermines "trust" in the currency, one of the pillars supporting commerce.

For a free market system to work, there must be a foundation of trust which underpins the economy. The rules must be clear, the judiciary honest, and corruption minimized. People must believe their money is safe in banks and its value will not depreciate without warning. They must trust the bulk of their suppliers, customers, and employees, since no one could possibly hire enough guards and spies to oversee them all. Without trust, the whole wealth-creation process disintegrates.

## A Major Competitive Advantage

What is true of the economy in general turns out to be true, too, within organizations. A recent study by a major consumer products firm sought to discover the most important cause of "regretted turnover"—people leaving whom the company had wished to retain. The number one factor was a low trust relationship with their boss. In another study involving many firms, employees were asked what qualities they most valued in leaders, and the most frequent response was "credibility." In a third study, researchers concluded that corporate culture can have a significant impact on a company's bottom line and that a key aspect of performance-enhancing cultures is their trustworthiness. These are just three of many directional signs pointing toward trust as a critical factor in organizational success or failure.

When value is pouring into an industry, it is possible to be profitable in almost any corporate culture. Thus, bad habits frequently become embedded in the culture. When value begins to shift, trust becomes imperative, and most employees today don't think their workplace manifests trust. *Industry Week* in a survey a few years ago showed that 87% of the workers polled believe it is "very important" that management be "honest, upright and ethical," but only 39% believed that described their leaders.

Trust, says management author and speaker Gordon Shea, is the "miracle ingredient in organizational life—a lubricant that reduces friction, a bonding agent that glues together disparate parts, a catalyst that facilitates action." Conversely, low trust begets poor results, and poor results can't be tolerated, especially when an organization is chasing value.

Over the long haul, then, trust is a major competitive advantage. To survive and prosper in today's and tomorrow's global economy will be difficult, if not impossible, for organizations in which people do not trust one another.

Organizations desperately need ideas, innovation, risk taking, open communication, and collaborative problem solving. Employees, for their part, want to feel cared about and to feel worthwhile because they are making a significant contribution.

Low trust inhibits both sets of goals. Risk taking, innovation and collaboration suffer while suspicion and defensiveness increase and worker energy is diverted into non-productive political behavior. Thus, creativity and resourcefulness are squandered.

## What Can Leaders Do?

Lack of trust is ultimately lethal. An organization lacking trust will eventually be found dead in the water. The good news is that lack of trust can be cured. Trust can be built by an organization by scrupulously underscoring trustworthy policies: telling the truth all the time, keeping agreements, and making sure everyone stays well informed. Individuals also have a large role to play in trust building.

Too many managers, even top managers, when discussing trust in their organization, speak in the language and hopeless tone of victims. They seem to be saying they are powerless to change it. That mindset becomes a self-fulfilling prophecy.

Since the level of trust fluctuates over the history of an organization, *something* causes it. External buffeting has an effect, of course. It is clear that the sum of individual human decisions and action can push trust in either direction. Far from being helpless victims, we can help create our own future.

The basic unit of trust in a relationship is between two individuals. The prevailing organizational culture bears upon each such pair. Yet, the reverse is also true: each high trust relationship models the possibility of trust and sends that message back to the culture. If enough individuals set about building a high trust relationship, the culture cannot remain unaffected. Over time, it will absorb the trust and enshrine the behavior which produced it.

Our model of trust is a temple with four pillars: Openness, Honesty, Credibility and Respect, undergirded by the need for Consistency.

*Openness* means sharing one's thoughts and feelings and being receptive to the same in others. It's self-disclosure as opposed to guardedness. As that openness is reciprocated, the trust level in the relationship is nudged higher.

*Honesty,* as used here, means giving truthful, complete feedback to others, for better or worse. "Feedback," says Ken Blanchard, co-author of *The One-Minute Manager* and other motivational books, "is the breakfast of champions." People want and need to know how they are doing. Employees will trust those who consistently talk to them straight.

*Credibility* means making and keeping agreements. You do so by (1) making only those agreements you intend to keep, (2) avoid making, or accepting, unclear or fuzzy agreements, (3) give early notice if an agreement must be broken, and (4) if you *must* break an agreement, make sure you initiate the renegotiation and try to mend your chipped credibility.

*Respect* means honoring five unspoken requests that people make of each other in any relationship. They are:

1. Listen non-judgmentally.
2. Acknowledge differences without assigning blame.
3. Give credit to others for their unique and special qualities.
4. Look for positive intentions.
5. Tell others the truth compassionately.

If you honor all five unspoken requests, the other person will consistently feel respected, even cared about. When you are able to employ all four pillars—openness, honesty, credibility, and respect—your relationships will tend to be high-trust ones.

When all the employees of an organization follow suit—with sponsorship and role models offered by management—the corporate culture gains the critical competitive advantage of everyone working together to create a successful enterprise. This is a powerful medicine for any organization.

## Dialogue Across the Centuries

Executives today must walk a thin moral line when undertaking needed restructuring. They must redesign their business to meet the customer's perception of value. They must also be fair to those hard-working employees affected by these changes. Most executives do not set out each morning to wreck people's lives, but they do have hard economic choices to make.

In making these difficult choices, they undertake a moral debate as old as mankind itself. What is the *right* thing to do? Do you wait and hope things improve on their own, or aggressively overhaul your business to better conform to shifting perceptions of value? When you act, whose interests do you protect?

It is our belief that you are on shaky moral ground if you undertake painful and disruptive restructuring or reengineering for the sole purpose of adding short-term value for shareholders. On the other hand, to make difficult changes in order to keep an organization healthy and competitive is an argument with moral weight. It is at least an argument you can take to employees and the community and expect to receive a fair hearing.

The outcome is the same either way, but the grounds for making the decision are entirely different. One caters to the needs of a single stakeholder group, while the other tries to balance the long-term interest of all parties. Knowing *why* you are undertaking major change is vitally important because it profoundly impacts the implementation. If your only goal is to enrich shareholders, you need not involve other stakeholders in the decision-making process or explain to anyone the reasons for your actions; you simply "do it to them" and hope the inevitable resistance can be overcome.

On the other hand, if you believe your decision is in the best long-term interest of the organization, you must involve all stakeholders. You must keep them informed, seek their assistance, do your utmost to support those adversely effected by the change. As the leader of such a change effort, you would have to model your behavior on that of the 19-year-old corporal we discussed earlier. You must provide physical leadership and be present with those impacted and share in their hardships and disappointments. This requires a higher order of leadership than just maneuvering a restructuring plan through the board of directors.

So it all comes down to making an informed moral decision, one you can live with as a human being and sell to all stakeholders. Such decisions are characterized by:

1. A superb communications plan. Do not skimp here.
2. Effective strategies for supporting those affected.
3. A process for involving stakeholders in developing and implementing the plan.
4. Openness and honesty. Do not be afraid to make yourself vulnerable.
5. Explaining the "why" again and again.
6. Sharing the hardship. Be physically present as often as possible.
7. Sending the right signals. Do not pay yourself wads of bonus money, for example, while others must endure pay cuts.
8. Managing the change so as to enhance, not erode, teamwork.
9. Trying to present a hopeful picture of the future.

In our focus on economic drivers, new methodologies, and state-of-the-art technology, it is easy to forget the metaphysical and spiritual side to change. In doing so, we take enormous risks. The lessons of history are clear and compelling: institutions which ignore the human and moral components of change are destined to fail.

New studies indicate that balancing the interests of stakeholders appears to pay off. James Heskett and John Kotter of Harvard University studied 32 companies over 11 years to determine the characteristics of high-performing cultures. One of their most striking conclusions was that firms which consistently produce superior business results share one fundamental characteristic: the leadership does not let the short-term interest of the shareholders override all other business considerations. Decisions in these firms are made with an eye toward long-term impact. This is not the sort of thinking that lends itself to a crowbar approach to reengineering.

And how can it be otherwise? Can any institution undertake rapid change without first being cohesive? Can we dispense with trust and teamwork in our rush to get the job done? These are simple but profound questions to which most executives would instinctively be sympathetic. But if we believe trust is important, why do we do so little to reinforce it in times of change?

Adam Smith, whom many people do not realize was first and foremost a professor of moral philosophy, built his theories on the basis of a moral community. According to Smith, while the market has a way of separating the efficient from the inefficient, it was never meant to be a substitute for moral responsibility. We would do well to reflect on the difference.

# Part IV
# Big Government's Value Crisis

# 10

# Why the Public Sector Is Hemorrhaging Value

*Great nations are never impoverished by private, though they are sometimes by public, prodigality, and misconduct.*

*—Adam Smith*

Government, not only in America but throughout the world, is in crisis. Value is bleeding out of the institution of government at an astonishing rate. Simply put, government as we know it—by not reacting quickly enough to the present value crisis—is *flirting with extinction.*

Up to now, we have discussed the movement and transformation of value primarily as economic phenomena transforming business. But it's impossible to discuss the movement of value without touching on the public sector, which is experiencing the greatest decline of all. Unlike the value problems in business, though, the crisis in government involves more than just issues of strategy and technique.

Government faces a crisis of legitimacy and relevance which is every bit as serious as the one it faces regarding its performance. Big government's problems extend beyond the erosion of value that results from not meeting customers' expectations or falling behind the information value-added curve. The truth is, big government today finds itself on the wrong side of powerful economic and historical forces. The shift in power toward a global, knowledge-driven economy and away from the old, national, analog economy is rendering government less relevant each day. This loss of relevance is at the root of today's crisis in the public sector.

As long as a product or service is relevant, value can always be added. But when something *no longer matters*, value erosion is inevitable. When declining relevance combines with high prices and poor performance, value decline is instant and massive. This is precisely the lethal combination government faces today.

While governments still have power and can perform important functions, they are clearly becoming less relevant in the eyes of many constituents. This explains why huge portions of the voting population don't bother to vote. There was a time when these non-voters were largely disenfranchised and poorly educated. Today, the profile of non-voters is changing. Increasingly, well-educated citizens are casting a vote of no-confidence by dropping out of the electoral process. This is a sure sign of declining relevance.

To understand why big government is losing relevance and hemorrhaging value, we must go back to the fundamentals of government. Remember, at the center of the nation-state's relevance are national security and control of finance and trade. Today, war is increasingly a transnational business, as the Gulf War coalition showed. And control of money is no longer a national prerogative; Alan Greenspan, chairman of the Federal Reserve, has conceded as much.

Thus, in a world riding the power curve into the global knowledge quadrant, the nation-state and its government apparatus must redefine their role and discover new sources of value and relevance. In short, government must redefine why it exists.

## Reasons for Loss of Relevance

Why is government in trouble? Some of the reasons are obvious:

1. *Obsolete systems.* The operating systems and structures of big government are rooted in another era. Its structure, based on large command-and-control bureaucracies, is archaic and incapable of quickly learning or adapting. Today's economy is infinitely more complex than in the 1930s and '40s, when the structural and philosophical foundations of big government were laid.

Back then, people thought of the economy as a great machine. Today, we know it more closely resembles a great ecosystem. Thus, an Information Age economy, like a marsh or tropical rainforest, is too complex to be designed, regulated or controlled by any bureaucracy. To live, the system must evolve spontaneously. Who planned the Amazon rainforest? For that matter, who planned the personal computer or software industries?

2. *Obsolete theories.* It is also apparent that government's basic operating theories are outdated. The idea that government can engineer a social revolution with tax and fiscal policy is based on flawed theory. It assumes laws will impact society and the economy in the ways intended by its authors. Just the opposite has often proved true.

Well-intentioned efforts to eliminate poverty and support the less privileged have produced unexpectedly perverse results. Instead of promoting economic self-sufficiency, some of our support programs encourage dependence, family breakup, and single parenthood. As a result, single parenthood has emerged as the single biggest contributor to rising poverty in America, especially among children. Similarly, efforts to redistribute wealth, provide health care, and enhance the quality of workers' lives through high payroll taxes have led to a decline in full-time employment and a rise in the number of part-time or free-lance workers who don't have health care or other benefits—again, just the opposite of what was intended.

3. *Big cost-small payoff.* We are not wiser, healthier, safer or happier as a result of 50 years of big government. Nor is society necessarily more just. However, we do pay more. In most developed economies, people now work half the year just to pay off their tax obligations. In the United States, workers' income from January through the first of June belongs to the government and that amount is growing. (If the indirect costs of government—such as tariffs and the cost of regulations—are included, the figure extends to July 1.)

Not surprisingly, according to a recent Harris poll, nearly two-thirds of Americans feel the American Dream has become harder to achieve. Why? They lay the biggest blame on government spending (73%) and high taxes (61%). This represents value erosion on a historic scale.

In jurisdiction after jurisdiction, citizens have begun to resist the state's claim on national wealth and with good reason. All indications are that big government doesn't work. In countries where the government controlled virtually all national assets, their economies have collapsed amid revolution and chaos. In democratic states, the reaction has been more muted, but the tide of resistance and resentment is rising.

4. *Coming rollback in transfer programs.* Big government still retains some relevance to those who receive money from it. Increasingly, the whole focus of government consists of transferring money from some population groups to others. That game, like a great Ponzi scheme, is about to collapse.

Why? Because this process impedes economic growth and is no longer affordable on today's scale. Governments throughout the developed world are discovering, though belatedly, that there are indeed limits on their ability to tax, borrow and spend. This realization will soon lead to a retreat of the welfare state and a rolling back of entitlement programs. In time, this retreat could become a rout as governments are forced to abandon expensive transfer payments.

As Peter Drucker points out in his book, *Post-Capitalist Society*, "In every single developed country, governments have reached the limits of their ability to tax and their ability to borrow. They have reached these limits during boom times when, according to modern economic theory, they should have built up sizable surpluses. The fiscal state has spent itself into impotence."

Government has mostly failed in its attempts to redistribute wealth. Instead, the overwhelming evidence points to productivity and economic growth as the keys to wealth redistribution. It turns out growth, not government, is the great equalizer.

5. *The dawn of the age of abundance.* Another reason government is losing relevance is that we are moving toward an Age of Abundance made possible by an explosion of knowledge. Ideas, like capital, cannot be contained within the borders of any single nation. Today, there is no such thing as national knowledge. Information and knowledge have become global assets.

Government is an institution rooted in an ethos of scarcity. Government *regulates, allocates* and *controls* on the assumption it must do so because resources are limited. But what happens when the economy shifts to an abundance cycle and resources become readily available, perhaps even unlimited? The answer . . . government loses relevance.

Winning in this Age of Abundance will require governments to think globally and focus increasingly on growth and wealth creation. Those governments and other institutions which fail to transition from managing scarcity to managing abundance will become increasingly irrelevant. They will bleed value and be pushed out of the way, something we will discuss again in Chapter 12.

## Microcosm of the Crisis

The reasons central governments were created in the first place are going away and with them, so is a portion of government's relevance. To reverse this situation, central government must redefine its role and reason for being. It must find a new source of relevance. Governments must ask, "Why do we exist?" or even "Why does society allow us to exist?"

To see a microcosm of government's crisis of relevance in a digital economy, just follow the debate in Washington on regulating the Internet. The Beltway has been hungering to get its hands on the Internet since rumors of its existence first reached Capitol Hill. Now, under the guise of protecting our children from smut, legislators propose regulating content on the Net. This, in turn, could lead to the creation of something like a Department of the Internet, staffed with high-tech bureaucrats and cybercops. The next step might be to try to tax the Internet.

But regulating the Internet will not work. The Internet is a classic by-product of the information-driven, global economy. It does not reside in any single country; it is everywhere and it is nowhere. It has no single center of gravity, no real headquarters and its output moves around the world at the speed of light. Attempts by a slow moving, industrial age institution, such as government, to capture the Internet will prove as futile as capturing quicksilver. In truth, the Internet, like capital and knowledge, has slipped the leash and gone global; and there's little that government can do about it.

A telling example of government's dilemma in trying to regulate the global economy can be found in the debate over the now infamous "Clipper Chip." The Clipper Chip is a special semiconductor designed for use in voice-encryption systems. It became a focal point in a tug-of-war between the forces of national sovereignty and global consumer sovereignty.

As more people do business over cordless phones, the need to protect privacy has become increasingly important. Thus, many companies have begun marketing voice encryption systems to ensure private conversations can't be listened to. However, these scramblers also make it more difficult for law-enforcement officials to bug the phones of suspected criminals.

So the U.S. government proposed that all voice encryption systems made in the United States be built around the Clipper Chip, which has a built-in port allowing authorities to decode the conversation. That made sense from the viewpoint of national sovereignty but from the perspective of a Third Wave global economy, it was absurd.

No one with the interest and money to buy a voice encryption system was going to buy one which was "compromised" from the beginning. If the U.S. government forced American manufacturers to use the Clipper Chip, consumers around the world would opt overwhelmingly for French or German equipment. Needless to say, the United States was in no position to force foreign manufacturers to adopt the Clipper Chip.

So the only way the Clipper Chip would work was if it were adopted as a global standard—and that was not about to happen any time soon. Meanwhile, U.S. manufacturers were outraged at the government's threat to cripple them, and the Feds, mystified by all the fuss, eventually backed off.

Skirmishes between old national sovereignty and new global consumer sovereignty will become common in the next few years. One such confrontation took place recently in Europe, where the German government raided the offices of CompuServe. The German government was concerned that 200 of the newsgroups carried by CompuServe were disseminating child pornography. CompuServe denied these charges but under pressure from the Germans, suspended these services to their German subscribers. CompuServe's remaining 3.75 million customers will go on receiving these services. What no one in the German government has yet acknowledged is that these banned services are available to German subscribers through other Internet providers operating globally or even through CompuServe in other countries.

Another example of how the rules have changed is found in the controversy on regulating derivatives, those arcane financial instruments which have the financial world in such a tizzy these days. Derivatives are sold globally, and no single nation can control them. Congress held hearings but concluded that any attempt to suppress or closely control derivatives would just force the market offshore. Thus, the problem would not go away, it would just go elsewhere.

To see yet another example of the nation-state fighting back, just look at China's attempts to control business news and the Internet. This represents a classic rearguard action by the nation-state. Desperate to limit the free flow of information, China has made it illegal to operate on the Internet except over government-controlled lines. To put the likelihood of this working in perspective, the central government has also made satellite dishes illegal but 500,000 are sold every year in China. The Internet ban is likely to be even less successful.

These are just the opening shots in what promises to be a gigantic tug of war between national sovereignty and global consumer sovereignty.

## So What *Is* the Role of Government?

Does central government have a role to play in a global, information-driven world? Yes, but it's not the role it has played for the past 300 years. If government is to stay in business, it must redefine why it exists and reengineer how it operates.

Government will not disappear overnight; history doesn't move that quickly. Defense concerns will remain important, central banks will continue to operate, and the State Department will still execute foreign policy, at least for the foreseeable future. And because the competitive free market system necessarily creates winners and losers, some government probably needs to be around to help those who are thrown out of work, injured on the job, or otherwise get caught in the gears of capitalism. In that limited sense, government may always be needed to serve as something of a support arm for the private sector. But government's role in the economy will change as it is forced to shift its focus from managing scarcity to managing growth.

However, managing growth will not be easy. To succeed, government must redefine its role and function as an institution in a most profound way. Such a metamorphosis will not come easily, especially in today's environment where, sadly, there is an inherent withering of the spirit in much of government. In the early, heady days of many agencies, an enviable idealism and an entrepreneurial fervor exist, akin to that seen in young companies. The mandate is clear and fresh. Workers are full of zeal, and enthusiasm pervades. Many of big government's finest moments have been in such settings—the early Peace Corps, NASA, Civilian Conservation Corps, and the Works Progress Administration

(WPA) where getting the job done took precedence over just getting by. Theirs was an élan, a vigor that was palpable.

Then something happens. Enthusiasm fades and the barnacles of bureaucracy grow. Without the stimulus of competition, without the lure of substantial reward, and without the sword of possible extinction hanging over the heads of all involved, the pace slows and the spirit dims. Soon, the agency loses sight of why it exists—and then it begins acting as if it exists for its own sake. We then get a by-the-numbers performance where we once may have had energized people with ideas.

Can that be changed? Our best thinkers ought to be working on that. They should look, for example, at civil service—another well-intentioned idea that has largely backfired—and how incompetent civil-service employees could be more easily fired. Or whether, under a proposal offered by Charles Peters, editor-in-chief of *The Washington Monthly*, 50% of all government workers should be political appointees. That, Peters says, would give citizens more control by allowing them to toss out the elected officials—and their bureaucrats—if levels of service were perceived as poor.

Another idea worth taking a look at is whether semi-autonomous commissions—along the lines of the recent military-base closing commissions—could help government make some of the tough decisions which pork-barrel politics now prevents. These questions are mounting and require urgent attention.

## Technology as Key Enabler of Reform

If politicians and public sector administrators can muster the courage to redefine the role of government and the public sector, then information technology can assist mightily in this transformation. Note the order here: first the role and function of government must be redefined, then information technology can become a key enabler of change. The order is important because it would be futile to use information technology to buttress the old order. We would only be throwing good money after bad.

However, once the "revolution of the mind" had occurred and government opened itself to new thinking, then exciting new possibilities would immediately become evident. For example, government could take advantage of digital disintermediation to eliminate layer after layer of unnecessary middlemen. Departments could be merged and functions concentrated in centers of excellence. This is precisely the kind of successful reengineering which new technology made possible in the private sector. Using digital technology, government services (many of which are information intensive) could be delivered electronically at a local level, close to the customer.

Proper use of information technology would enable governments to move away from multi-level bureaucracies which operate in "silos" and move toward distributed team structures linked by reengineered, horizontal work processes. A new *infostructure* would constitute the skeleton of a new, reinvented government with dramatically lower costs and improved levels of service.

Consider for example what might be done with entitlement programs. Although a rollback in entitlements is inevitable, these programs will not go away entirely. Social Security and Medicare alone distribute more than $400 billion a year to nearly 40 million citizens. Even if these programs were frozen today (an idea we hardly endorse), the distribution of benefits would remain a monumental task.

Today, these transfers are largely paper driven; the whole process resembles a 19th century paper and rule factory, with about the same economies of scale. The potential to revolutionize these programs by digitizing the transfer, tracking and reporting mechanism, is enormous. The same goes for food stamps, veterans' benefits and virtually all entitlement programs.

Properly employed, information technology would enable governments to centralize programs involving the distribution of all entitlement benefits. Then, using distributed systems, these services could be downloaded to local agencies . . . but why stop there? Why not download to local banks, churches, grocery stores or any institution which is close to the customer and relevant to the community? If American Express can consolidate its worldwide finance function, reducing its centers from 30 to 3 (in Phoenix, New Delhi and Brighton) and still service local agencies in Cairo, Kuala Lumpur and Mexico City, why can't government do something similar? The potential savings and service improvements from such a restructuring would be staggering. Digital transfer, coupled with smart cards and electronic audits, would also greatly reduce the potential for fraud.

In short, government should take advantage of disintermediation and transmigration rather than fighting these trends. Using information technology, governments could redefine their service offerings and revolutionize their delivery. Rather than resisting privatization, (which is, after all, just a form of disintermediation), governments should make it work for them by integrating new players into the total delivery process using state-of-the-art information systems.

Think about it! If a person can buy a $25,000 car using Circuit City's CarMax on-line service without ever leaving home, why should he or she have to take a day off from work and wait in line just to get a $25 driver's license? It makes no sense.

But be warned, none of these improvements is possible in the context of today's archaic political and governmental apparatus. A system in entropy cannot be saved simply by applying new whiz-bang technology to solve old problems. At best, this would result in marginal improvements to a dying order. New technology will only perform well in the context of new thinking, new structures and new strategies.

## Less Than Competent

Unfortunately, even as government contemplates renewal, it stands condemned by its own performance record. The sad fact is government has proved less than competent at most of the things it does beyond its core regulatory, law enforcement, and defense functions. Think about it: from the post office, through Medicare, Medicaid, Social Security, food stamps, education and on and on, government has turned into a second-rate supplier of goods and services. That's not our verdict but the verdict rendered by most of its customers today. Even in its regulatory function, it is often an obstacle to wealth creation rather than a help.

For example, virtually anyone starting a business in the United States must get licenses and permits from a plethora of agencies. A manager of even a small chemical company is required to have a business license, a permit for hazardous material storage, a permit for an air pressure tank, a permit from the Occupational Safety and Health Administration for a liquefied petroleum gas tank, a compressed gas permit, a hazardous waste permit from the Environmental Protection Agency, and a resale number.

Moreover, the trend points alarmingly toward more rather than fewer regulations. In *Reinventing Government*, Al Gore notes that forest rangers in the 1960s could carry the list of rules in their shirt pockets. Now they must consult several volumes of fine print.

Similarly, while OSHA has compiled more than 4,000 detailed regulations, safety in the American workplace is about the same as it was 25 years ago when the agency was created. (About 50% of all OSHA violations are for not keeping the forms correctly.)

The Interstate Highway System, the largest U.S. public works program since World War II, was authorized by a 1956 statute that ran 28 pages. By contrast, a transportation act passed by Congress in 1991 was 10 times longer.

One Congressional witness estimated that contractors routinely bid government work 10–30% higher than similar work in the private sector because there is at least eight times more paperwork. In fact, the federal government itself has estimated that 289 million hours are spent each year complying with its procurement procedures.

Government's slowness in the area of information value-added also impedes the economy. Take for example, the new air traffic control system which the Federal Aviation Administration is supposed to install across the country. This $17-billion project is already years behind schedule. Meanwhile, the old system, based on 1960s technology, is falling apart under the strain of burgeoning air traffic.

Short of a catastrophe, which becomes more likely every day, no one seems to know how to speed up the process of installing the new system. At this rate, by the time the new technology is in place, billions over budget and years behind schedule, it will already be outdated.

## The Value Equation

The value equation (Value = Quality/Price) applies to government just like any other institution. Most citizens today would be inclined to say that relative to the enormous investments and public money being committed to government, customer expectations have generally not been met. Thus, value is in decline. An inability to meet the customer's quality and price expectations *always* results in a decline in value. Unless this decline is checked or reversed by improved quality or lower prices, large-scale value loss is inevitable.

Dissatisfaction with government has been underscored by improvements in the private sector. To survive, America's private sector has had to smarten up in recent years. Costs have come down and quality has gone up, but not so with government. Unfortunately, government agencies are at a natural disadvantage when performing any commercial or service-delivery function. Lacking a true price

mechanism, public institutions are slow to perceive shifts in customer requirements. Public institutions cannot count on margin erosion, lost market share, or declining stock values to issue wake-up
calls. Few public enterprises have any long-range customer satisfaction and/or value sensors in place. As a result, by the time a value
problem is finally recognized, a full-blown crisis is usually at hand.
This is where many government agencies find themselves today.

## A System in Entropy

Citizens are unhappy with big government because their experience
with it tells them it works less well every day. It consumes more and
more and produces less and less value. From an historical perspective, big government today looks suspiciously like a system in
entropy, winding down.

Systems experiencing entropy are slowly dying. To stave off the
inevitable, they consume more and more resources, but all this does
is slow the process of decline. Often, these dying systems behave
dysfunctionally as the end nears. As an old saying has it, "Those
whom the Gods would destroy, they first make mad."

The average American knows some madness is afoot when total
spending on welfare at the federal, state and local levels averages
over $35,000 per recipient per year—and the problems of poverty
and dependency only worsen. Where does the money go? Who
*knows* for sure? But it clearly does not appear to be going to poor
people.

Meanwhile, the American people look on in bewilderment as
the deficit gets worse, even as taxes go up. In 1963, 3% of Americans
were in the 28%-or-greater tax bracket; today it is 36% and climbing.
Our 17,000-page tax code is so complex, it costs American business
and households between $180 billion and $200 billion a year just to
comply with the paperwork. In fact, it is so complex even the IRS
does not know how to interpret every aspect of it.

Meanwhile, Congress has only completed one budget on time
since 1974. Deadlines are regularly missed and spending-ceilings
routinely are ruptured. There really are no rules in federal budget-
ing, just exceptions; they have become the rule. No wonder people
are losing confidence.

Old spending programs never die; they just grow—even when
the reason for their being has long since passed. So we continue to

subsidize wool production for uniforms even though wool is no longer used to make them. Medicaid began life in 1967 at a budget of $1.2 billion; today, it is nearly a $100-billion program. Medicare, begun as a $2.7-billion effort, is on its way to $200 billion. Social Security was introduced in the 1930s to supplement the income of poor retirees. In 1965, its total budget was $17 billion; today, the average retiree has an income higher than the rest of the population, and the Social Security budget is approaching $250 billion.

At its worst, this sort of entropy moves beyond dysfunction and becomes pathological. Rather than moving toward reform and revitalization, the system behaves in ways which hasten its demise. Consider Congress' inexorable drive to raise taxes, spend more and borrow against the future through the deficit. Almost every sensible economist in the country knows this to be a terminal game, which sooner or later has to end. Yet, Congress cannot seem to stop itself.

Meanwhile, the American people looked on in astonishment as the House of Representatives proved incapable of managing its own small bank or post office. When the House books were finally audited, the audit firm could not even render an assessment because the accounts were in such disarray. It was, according to one member of the audit team, "The worst mess I've seen in my whole career." Only an institution blinded by arrogance or harboring a death wish would behave in a manner so designed to affront the sensibilities of the American voting public.

# Doing Some Things Right

Like all value shifts, today's shift in perceived value away from government is complex and multi-dimensional. For example, it would be a mistake to characterize all value shifts in government as moving against the institution. It is "big government" which is in trouble more than "all government." For example, value within the public sector is moving toward local government and locally controlled services. Some parts of government and the parapublic sector are even experiencing a surge in value. This is certainly true of law enforcement, medical services provided outside the normal hospital setting, and education. Need and relevance is strong in these areas, although in many cases, local governments are at a loss as to how to capture this new value. Those doing the best job of it are experimenting with privatization, competition and deregulation, and these experiments are mostly taking place at the local and state levels.

It is largely at the state and local levels that authorities are finding new ways to provide services which drive up quality and push down cost. Sometimes, though, it takes a crisis as a catalyst. For example, after the 1994 earthquake toppled Los Angeles freeways, California suspended its thick book of procedural guidelines and, using federal aid, authorized financial incentives for speedy work. Instead of a four-year trudge through the government maze, private contractors were able to re-build the Santa Monica Freeway in just 66 days—and to a higher standard than the old one.

Across the country, local authorities are experimenting with privatized road services, garbage collection, fire departments, transportation services, prisons and a host of other services once provided exclusively by public sector employees. In theory, state and local governments are well positioned to benefit from the present value crisis, if they can get their act together.

## Education: The Epicenter of Crisis

In fact, one area where local government definitely should seize the initiative is public education, which is clearly experiencing value erosion at a time when public concern for education is at an all-time high. Why are people concerned? Because education is vital to success in a knowledge-intensive economy. A worker equipped with a first-class education and appropriate job training has a significant competitive advantage over someone who is illiterate or untrained. All things being equal, better-educated, more highly skilled employees are more productive and consequently earn more. Unfortunately, public education, the institution we most rely on for this purpose, is facing a crisis of legitimacy. A recent poll of school superintendents showed 68% believed schools were doing a good job of preparing students for the workplace, but only 4% of business executives agreed.

## Shoring Up Monopolistic Prerogatives

Admittedly, broad generalizations regarding the state of public education are unfair to those pockets of excellence which do exist within the system. But having some schools which work doesn't change the fact that the bulk of the system is perceived as a failure by its customers, the parents and citizens whose taxes pay the bills. These consumers, not surprisingly, have already rendered a verdict on the public system, and it's not a vote of confidence.

Parents are fleeing the "free" public education system on an unprecedented scale. Many are putting their children in parochial schools or private schools at enormous personal expense, or even educating them at home. Proposals for vouchers and other privatization schemes abound. If a private company experienced this level of share loss, the management team and board of directors would be beside themselves with panic. Educators seem not to be. On the contrary, most of the intellectual energy within the system seems to be devoted to shoring up its monopolistic prerogatives. Whether accurately or not, the public perceives the teacher unions as more interested in fighting vouchers than improving the system.

It's only a matter of time before citizens start to balk at paying for a system they are not using and which produces such consistently poor results. Meanwhile, public education and its associated bureaucracy go blithely along, as if nothing were wrong. At best, they are prepared to entertain improvements at the margin of the system.

Teachers, administrators and unions are kidding themselves if they believe the status quo is sustainable. There is simply too much at stake, when it comes to education. Like it or not, public education will be pushed, pulled or dragged into a period of radical reform within a few years. Why? Because we cannot fix the U.S. economy without fixing U.S. education.

To see how closely these are tied together, just reflect on these facts from the National Alliance of Business report on marketplace trends:

- In the 1980s, 20–40% of those displaced from jobs were functionally illiterate.
- Over one-fifth of all dislocated workers lack a high school education.
- By decade's end, 5–15 million manufacturing jobs will require different skills from today's, while an equal number of service jobs will be obsolete.

Unless public education is improved, our society will continue to split into two worlds. One will be well educated, computer literate and well paid . . . the other will be poorly educated, computer illiterate and poorly compensated. Those who cannot hold jobs will become dependent on government assistance or resort to crime. Over time, those who work and pay the bills will grow increasingly resentful of those who do not work. In such a scenario, conflict is inevitable.

The ancient Greeks had a saying, "What is necessary is possible," and so it is today with public education. With the right incentives and willingness to experiment, U.S. public education can be put back on a sound footing. Tinkering with the system will not be enough. What's required is wholesale reform and this cannot happen until incentives are altered. A voucher system may not be a panacea, but it's not a bad place to begin.

## Redefinition, Not Reform

There is considerable talk these days about reforming or reinventing government. These debates will become louder and more shrill as government drifts toward ever greater irrelevance. But reforming government does not mean fixing or improving the existing outdated apparatus. Something larger is required. Government must redefine its reason for being and rediscover new sources of relevance.

It has been suggested that information technology can be used as a means of reforming government. Such suggestions completely miss the point. Information technology alone cannot reform an obsolete system. High-tech interventions can no more reverse value decline in government than the Gutenberg press could have been used to save the Holy Roman Empire. What's required is a revolution of the mind, as government redefines itself in the context of growth and abundance. Once the rethinking of government's role has been achieved, then information technology can become a key enabler of reform and revitalization. But this role as a catalyst for change can only work once new fundamentals are in place.

Even with an ecosystem-like economy, there is a role for government. But it lies less in "doing" things for people than it does in generating the conditions for wealth creation. This, very often, means less government, not more. Government's primary role has changed from one of social engineering in an age of scarcity to creating the conditions for wealth in an age of abundance. Until government recognizes the dramatic nature of this shift in roles, it will continue to hemorrhage value.

The public sector must overhaul itself as dramatically as the private sector did over the past decade, perhaps even more so. It must endure its own storm of creative destruction. In preparing itself for the coming changes, the public sector would be well advised to learn from the private sector's renewal experience and begin where it did, in a search for value. The private sector recovery of the 1980s was rooted in a value revolution activated by dramatic changes in customer requirements . . . and this "new" value was derived from knowledge and information. This would be a good starting place for governments interested in undertaking a process of renewal.

# 11

# In Search of a New Value Formula for Government

*A little rebellion now and then is a good thing.*
—*Thomas Jefferson*

Perhaps the most dramatic reflection of the value crisis in government is seen in how people think. Not so very long ago, in the 1960s and early '70s, most of us *really believed* government could solve the complex problems faced by modern society. In those days, we thought government could positively impact poverty, education or income inequality.

Today, as a result of bitter experience, fewer and fewer see government as a source of solutions to complex social problems. Many people, in fact, are coming to view government as a source of problems rather than solutions. There is rising doubt about government's capacity to add value for society. If government is to stay in business, it must begin today to change people's minds by changing its performance.

Time is running out. Whatever the present level of cynicism regarding government, it will only increase in the coming years as governments throughout the Western world are forced to abandon insolvent entitlement programs.

In North America, this default on a 50-year-old promise will have the same shattering effect on confidence as a major national or corporate default. A whole generation of citizens raised on the promise of government's capacity and willingness to provide for them are in for a shock. When the reality of this default sinks in, it will explode what's left of government's institutional credibility. The value hemorrhage which government institutions are already experiencing will be dramatically accelerated by the coming failure of middle-class welfare programs, such as Medicare and Social Security. It will shatter confidence for a generation. In our lifetime, people are not likely to ever again trust government with critical social and economic mandates. The blank check will be withdrawn and legal constraints put on government's propensity to pledge tomorrow's revenue against today's political imperatives. The proposed balanced-budget amendment is only the first and most spectacular of what will be a series of attempts to constrain government's spending capacity. These constraints are already being put into place in a number of U.S. states and Canadian provinces.

The present efforts to balance the U.S. budget over seven years are a step in the right direction. Unfortunately, we have let the problem of the deficit drift for so long, some pain is now inevitable, as we work our way out of the problem. Fortunately, it should not be unbearable. Mexico, under Carlos Salinas, or the United Kingdom, under Margaret Thatcher, did not implode with agony when they balanced their budgets. Nations with balanced budgets are not shabby, unhappy places. To the contrary, the opposite is usually true; those whose finances are out of control usually suffer the most. In any case, we can not put the problem off any longer. We need more jobs, more business opportunities, and a rising standard of living—and all of this presupposes we can get our fiscal house in order.

## Objectives on the Road to Restoring Value

Government, if it wishes to stay in business, must actively seek out a new value-added formula to promote long-term growth. Like any institution in trouble, it must rethink its existing strategies and be prepared to experiment with new alternatives. By way of advice, government should keep in mind the following objectives as it seeks to reverse the loss of value:

1. *Retrench.* Like any organization which has overreached itself, government should pull back to is core competencies. It must get out of activities for which it has little competence, and it should stop reinforcing failure by pursuing initiatives which are clearly not working. As it assesses which businesses it should be in, government should strive to "contract out" as many services as possible to the private sector. Why? Because history shows that government has a better chance of proving itself competent as a regulator and developer of policy than as an implementer.

2. *Nurture growth.* Government should stop using economic policy as a tool for social engineering. The aim of economic policy should be to nurture long-term growth. That, in turn, will generate wealth, a portion of which can be taxed and allocated to social programs. Wealth must first be created before it can be redistributed. When governments forget this sequence and mix the two, they inevitably distort the economy and slow the wealth-creation process.

On the monetary side, the central bank should focus primarily on protecting the integrity and purchasing power of the currency. The implications of living by these two principles are profound because these will not allow politicians to subordinate economic imperatives to social and political ones. Adhering to these policies creates a whole new game.

3. *Focus on the truly needy.* Government's social agenda should focus primarily on those who need help—the poor, particularly children in poverty. And those programs should foster independence, not dependency. Entitlement programs for the middle class and wealthy, such as Medicare and Social Security, must be scaled back and means-tested. We cannot go on spending 10 times as much public money on old people as we do on children. No society with such skewed priorities can produce a healthy economy and/or long-term stability. Pulling off this policy shift will necessitate an honest and extended dialogue with the American people.

4. *Get closer to the customers.* Government services should be provided as close as possible to the constituents who use them. It's no accident the level of dissatisfaction with government increases in direct proportion to the distance from its customers. Nor is it surprising that cities and counties have generally been the most innovative in exploring new methods and alternatives for delivering services. Most of the successful examples of "contracting out" and "self-help" programs have been carried out at this level of government.

5. *Find new models.* We must seek out new models and have the courage to experiment with new approaches. In addition, we must be prepared to confront powerful constituencies who will oppose any reform that limits their ability to obtain transfer money, no matter how beneficial for the nation or the economy.

## Adopting Growth-Oriented Policies

In the new millennium, government is going to have to compete for capital in a global marketplace, just like corporations do. No longer will government bonds with low interest rates be gobbled up by capital markets in search of security. Investors learned the hard way in the early 1980s that governments can and do default on debts.

Meanwhile, today's global marketplace provides an array of investment alternatives. Investors are *consumers*, too—they are buying something, whether it's growth, security, dividends, or tax advantages. And like all consumers, they have more options today.

If today's investor wants to buy government securities, he or she can shop around the world for the right product. Treasury bills are no longer the only game in town. This means that nations or states which create unpleasant or unwelcome environments for capital will find it increasingly hard to attract money.

Creating an environment which welcomes capital and encourages capital formation applies to states and provinces as well as to nations. There was a time when states, provinces, or cities could exploit their power of place to soak the local tax base. Today, such policies are self-defeating. You no longer need to be located in California's Silicon Valley or outside of Boston to launch a high-tech company. You no longer need to have your headquarters in New York to be taken seriously in advertising or financial services.

That's why states such as California, New York, and Massachusetts continued to lose jobs and investment even during the last recovery. It's no accident these are the highest-taxed states in the union. Governments everywhere are going to have to learn to help, not hinder, capital formation and the creation of wealth—or, they are going to get less of it.

The World Economic Forum, a respected Swiss research institute which holds an exclusive annual meeting in Davos, Switzerland, each year to assess global competitiveness, recently ranked government policies and their impact on competitive out-

comes. It determined, for example, that the ten countries whose policies were most conducive to competitiveness in order of ranking
were: Singapore, Hong Kong, New Zealand, Malaysia, Switzerland,
the United States, Chile, Thailand, Australia and Mexico. Those at
the bottom of the list, such as Spain, Turkey, Belgium, Greece and
Italy are, not surprisingly, experiencing relatively high unemployment and low levels of growth.

This ranking should be alarming to industrialized countries. Of
the top ten countries compared on this basis, only five are in the
OECD and none are members of the European Union. On the other
hand, four of the bottom ten are members of both the European
Union and the OECD.

## Turning Away the Transfer Seekers

What is the antidote to the outflow of value from governments?
Principally, it is to cure government of its endless quest for growth
and wean ourselves from the need for more and more government.
If government's imperative to grow is part of the problem, then the
other side of the coin is the desire of large segments of the public to
feed at the public trough.

Decades ago, German psychologist and libertarian, Frans Oppenheimer, discovered that there were only two ways of gaining wealth;
the first is production, the other is plunder. As he put it, "By one's own
labor or by capturing the labor of others." According to Oppenheimer,
one is an economic process, the other a political process. It can be
added that one is a productive activity, the other a redistributive activity. The producer gives to society, the transfer seeker takes. The latter
is accomplished either by theft or by manipulating government regulations or laws. Transfer seekers have made a conscious decision to
enhance their living standard at the expense of others.

There was a time when manipulating government for one's
own benefit was a game for the wealthy and well-connected. Today,
almost everyone is becoming expert at this game—it has become the
pastime of thousands of special interest groups across our country.
Businesses seek tariffs against competition, and unions seek minimum wage laws and laws against hiring permanent replacements
for strikers. Farmers seek subsidies. Environmentalists seek regulations on industry. Plaintiffs seek damages. Postal workers seek bans
on competition. Lobby groups like the AARP (American Association

of Retired Persons) fight to enhance Social Security funding regardless of the long-term consequences to the economy. Trial lawyers lobby to stop tort reform which would limit their ability to prey on corporate America with class action lawsuits. Farmers argue against welfare reform because it might impinge on food stamps.

Mancur Olson in his 1989 book, *The Rise and Decline of Nations*, said a society goes into decline when special interest groups so paralyze the political and social apparatus that it is unable to adapt to new circumstances. In other words, a society attacked by transfer seekers can become so debilitated that it's incapable of responding to new challenges and begins to die.

Only when transfer seekers, the carriers of what author Jonathan Rauch has called *demosclerosis*, are rooted out of the body politic, can the society regain its health. Making this same point, Olson wrote, "It follows that countries whose redistributional coalitions have been emasculated or abolished by totalitarian government or foreign occupations should grow relatively quickly after a free and stable legal order is established."

This would explain, for instance, why societies which have had their political structure destroyed, such as Germany and Japan after the Second World War, tended to grow quickly once order was restored. In such devastated societies, special interest groups which would otherwise slow the process of adaptation are temporarily stunned or eliminated, thus allowing the society to move forward.

Special interest groups have certainly not been eliminated or even temporarily stunned in the United States. They are multiplying like rabbits . . . or, more precisely, like cancer cells. Over the last several decades, there has been an enormous increase in the number of special interest groups and political action committees (PACs) within the United States.

## The Redistributive Game

In *Demosclerosis*, Jonathan Rauch refers to the development of PACs and special interest groups as the evolution of a parasitic class within society. As Rauch points out, "In the economy, as in nature, the parasite is set apart from a mere freeloader by its ability to force its target to fend it off. You may walk away from a freeloader, but you must stop and fight a parasite."

A common characteristic of these transfer-seeking groups is a disregard for the future of the country. They want the financial needs of their special interests met regardless of the long run implications for the economy. Despite the pious rhetoric surrounding their pleas, these groups don't give a hoot about justice, fairness, the economy, the country, or our children's future. They only want to go on collecting money. And make no mistake, all this redistributive game playing costs money. More importantly, this money produces no value-added for society.

Politicians have learned to play this redistributive game extremely well. They understand that simply by introducing legislation which affects an industry ("shaking the trees") they can produce a flood of interest and money from various PACs, either in favor of or opposed to the legislation.

America is not alone in playing this redistributive game. Brussels, home of the European Parliament, has 11,000 registered lobbyists and the number is growing weekly.

## Distorting the Economy

Health care offers an example of how transfer seeking distorts the economy. Health care represents 14% of GNP and is the single largest sector of the economy. Consuming almost a trillion dollars a year, U.S. health care has more economic clout than most countries. (Only Japan, Germany, and the United States have GNPs greater than a trillion dollars.)

Like the public and quasi-public sector overall, health care is experiencing a value crisis. Having been allowed to eat up one additional point of GNP every six or seven years for several decades, health care threatens to gobble up most of the economy some time in the next century. To make matters worse, much of this increase in GNP has been achieved by price increases, rather than by overall enhancements in value. Health care's share of GNP has doubled in the last 30 years, but we're not twice as healthy as we were in 1965.

In fact, as prices go up, satisfaction with the system tends to go down. By the late '80s, almost every major constituency was unhappy with the status quo. Industry complained health care costs were undermining competitiveness. Workers were afraid to leave their jobs for fear of losing health care benefits (which hindered America's otherwise efficient labor markets). As for patients, statistics indicate that individuals paid almost as much out-of-pocket money for non-conventional medical treatments, as they did for traditional health-care expenses. This shift in spending is a classic sign of value moving out.

Meanwhile, a significant sector of the U.S. population, including millions of children, remained underinsured or not insured at all. Such a situation could not go on for long in a democratic society. There was bound to be a reaction and it came in the early 1990s. The revolt manifested itself in the election of a government committed to health care reform. Beginning somewhat earlier, large corporations made it clear they were no longer willing to fund the old health care/insurance indemnity system. This opened the way for the introduction of integrated health care and capitated payments.

This revolution is only in its infancy, but is already showing signs of considerable promise. Private health care costs have been dropping for several years now and the momentum of reform is increasing. Unlike government and education, which are still largely in denial, health care is moving to reverse value declines. In fact, there is considerable reason for optimism regarding U.S. health care's capacity to reform itself. Not only are costs likely to fall, but there is a very good chance the United States—not Canada, Europe, or Japan—will emerge as the model for health care reform in the 21st century. (For a more detailed discussion of this issue, see *Don't Blink or You'll Miss It: The Reformation of U.S. Health Care Is Underway*, The Atlanta Consulting Group, 1995).

One reason American health care costs have soared out of control in recent years, is that health care benefits have been exempt from income tax. This amounts to a huge subsidy for health care consumption. Consider this: If your company were to give you an extra thousand dollars as a cash bonus, you would have to give a large chunk of it to Uncle Sam in taxes. If the firm gave you the same amount in added health care benefits, you would pay no additional tax. Such a policy encourages people to take compensation in the form of health care benefits instead of salary. Not surprisingly, this is precisely what's happening—as wage increases have slowed, the cost of providing health care benefits has soared. This subsidy artificially diverts resources into health care and away from other sectors of the economy, thus feeding health care inflation.

When an important service such as health care is subsidized in this way, it creates a "bellows effect," which fans raging demand. This economic distortion might be worth tolerating in such cases as health care, if it resulted in better health care for society; but it does not.

The added money flowing into the industry does not necessarily improve or expand the level of service. For example, the additional funds pouring into Medicare in recent years have not necessarily helped older people. When more money is pumped into a system which has no incentives to limit consumption or improve performance, it flows through to the industry like a windfall inheritance. It enables practitioners and hospitals to raise prices, provide unnecessary services and invest in buildings and equipment they do not need. In this way, unreformed programs like Medicare mutate and drift away from their original purpose of helping the elderly. They instead become a subsidy for the industry. Attempts to alter this subsidy bring on a chorus of appeals for "fairness, compassion and protecting the public interest." Such self-serving reactions are not new. Adam Smith commented in the 18th century that merchants who claim that subsidies and tariffs are a patriotic duty "were by no means such fools as those who believed them."

Remember, you always get less of what you tax and more of what you subsidize. So if you subsidize health care consumption or mortgage debt, you are going to get a lot more of both.

## Hard to Get Rid Of

Once in place, special transfers like subsidies or tariffs are almost impossible to remove. The honey subsidy introduced a half century ago, for heaven knows why, proves the point. No less than three presidents have tried to remove this silly subsidy, with no success. Finally in the early 1990s, it was struck from the books after an incredible battle in Congress. But lobbies never sleep. By the time the honey subsidy was killed, the lobbyists were already back at work seeking import restrictions on low-cost honey from Asia.

In Washington, almost no subsidy or tariff is ever eliminated. Once in place, it stays there forever. Each program instantly gives birth to an organized special-interest group whose members benefit and who will do everything in its power to keep the wealth transfer mechanism in place. That's why subsidies such as those for honey, wool, and angora have remained in place for decades, even though there's no rational reason to continue them. In fact, there probably was not a very good reason for starting them in the first place.

The *demosclerosis* phenomenon warns us that the threat to our democracy comes not from without, but from within.

# Public Ready

As usual, the people are ahead of the politicians. The country is more ready to face up to the needed reform than their leaders are to confront them with it. For example, a recent poll showed that when asked whether they would like a tax cut or a lower deficit, most people put aside self-interest and chose a lower deficit. Even retirees, by far the largest recipients of transfer payments, stated a readiness to sacrifice some of these payments for the good of the country.

What can we learn from this? It is important not to confuse interest groups with the public interest, or the AARP with retired people, or the Veterans of Foreign Wars with veterans, or the teachers union with teachers. In the end, *they are all citizens.* We must push aside special interest groups and open up a mature dialogue directly with the citizens of the country. A great democracy, when given the right information, will usually make the right decision.

# Available Antibiotics

Interestingly, one of the most powerful medicines for battling transfer seekers is *trade.* When a country expands trade, it automatically weakens interest groups that can thrive only within sealed borders. Winning anti-competitive favors on a world wide scale is almost impossible, at least for the present.

The best single parasite antidote in the world is the General Agreement on Tariffs and Trade (GATT), and the new World Trade Organization. By weakening lobbies, trade can help invigorate democratic government, not just in the United States, but all over the world. Under GATT, dozens of countries join in weakening each others' vested interests.

Other likely medicines are an *overhaul of our tax system,* a *balanced budget amendment,* and *radical reform of campaign financing.* We need to revamp our tax system to better support and sustain long-term growth. The U.S. tax code now subsidizes consumption and debt, while taxing savings and investment. This impedes economic growth because fast-growing economies need more savings and investment, not less. Always remember, you get more of what you subsidize and less of what you tax. So, if you tax savings and investment, you'll get less of it.

The tax system subsidizes debt and consumption in a host of ways, such as deductibility for mortgage interest and health care premiums. At the same time, it punishes savings, investments, and earnings through double taxation of dividends and taxing capital gains. The income tax itself impedes growth because it discourages citizens from earning income or taking compensation in the form of income.

The balanced budget amendment would reduce the size of the pie which parasitic transfer seekers can attack. It would also put the future off limits by preventing transfer seekers from running up debts for our children to pay.

In the end, the democratic process may solve the problem by simply shrinking the amount of resources available to government. As value moves away from government and government services, people will be less and less inclined to hand over nearly half the total wealth of the nation to this badly mismanaged sector of the economy. It is a safe bet that government, at least at the federal level, will shrink in the years ahead. This may make transfer seeking less lucrative.

As for campaign reform, the democratic process will continue to be viewed with skepticism so long as people believe elections can be bought. Congress has taken a stab at introducing election campaign reform, but only half-heartedly. The present system is so lucrative, no one on the inside really wants to upset the apple cart or should we say, the gravy train. If we are to get comprehensive campaign reform, the American people are going to have to get hopping mad and insist on it.

## Finding Models That Work

Benchmarking is a Total Quality Management tool which allows organizations to compare their processes and performance with the "best-in-class." By learning who does what best, we can adopt their methods and achieve similar or better results. This tool played an important role in America's quality and competitive recovery in the 1980s.

In national economic terms, this means finding and comparing ourselves to economies that are improving productivity, creating jobs, reducing income inequality, raising living standards and expanding economic growth. Once found, our task is to identify the underlying principles behind their success and then adopt or adapt them to our own situation. Inversely, if we find examples of economic failure, we should avoid mimicking them. Benchmarking may sound simple and obvious, but do not be deceived; the technique is extremely powerful.

There are plenty of people out there doing things right. The question is: are we willing to learn? We know from experience that benchmarking only works when the investigating organization is willing to *act* on what is learned from the benchmarking analysis. Up to now, it has not been national benchmarking models we lack, but the will and courage to implement the findings.

If we look at successful models of economic growth—countries which have sustained growth rates above 6%—we find they have a number of things in common. For one, they tend to have a smaller share of GNP controlled by the public sector. Secondly, in these fast-growing economies, public investments are concentrated in high-leverage areas like education, basic health care, and infrastructure. Thirdly, marginal income tax rates also tend to be lower than in slow-growth economies. Capital gains, if taxed at all, are taxed at low rates while the rate of savings tends to be high.

Would our economy grow faster if we adopted such a model? Yes. Then why haven't we done so? Because it will require significant and painful adjustments in our tax and fiscal policy and in how we think about the economy. As long as we view tax policy as a redistributive tool instead of one to promote growth, as long as we see a cut in the capital gains tax as a giveaway to the rich instead of a strategy for wealth creation, then a high-growth economic model will never be adopted.

Our reluctance to change our wrongheaded thinking and take appropriate action ought to be a source of shame as we look around the world at the sacrifices people in Eastern Europe, the Pacific Rim, or Central and South America are prepared to make in order to establish and secure their economies. Take for example, Mexico, which has balanced its budget and reduced its public debt as a percentage of GNP to 23%, compared to 50% in the United States and over 90% in Canada. To achieve this financial discipline, Mexico endured the equivalent of *five fully-implemented Gramm/Rudman budget-balancing bills*. Chile balanced its budget years ago, and Singapore constantly runs a balanced budget. Meanwhile, our government leaders seem unable to accomplish the same feat here. In short, Chile, Mexico and Singapore can do it, but the United States and Canada *cannot*! Does this sound reasonable to you?

Our resources in North America are so much greater and the sacrifices required of us are proportionally so much smaller, there is no excuse for not acting. The reason we have not acted up to now is because we have been able to sidestep the problem by borrowing against our children's future with ever-increasing deficits. Global bond markets will soon close off that avenue of escape for spend-thrift governments.

As the global economy shifts into an abundance cycle, government's primary role will be to change from redistributing wealth to creating the conditions for wealth creation. Only by doing so can government regain some measure of relevance and reverse the deterioration of value. Luckily, there are models out there of governments which are doing this successfully, but few are found within the clubby environment of the OECD (Organization for Economic Cooperation and Development) where the most developed countries in the world reside. As usual, tomorrow's models are emerging on the periphery, far from the traditional centers of power.

If central government's role changes, so must its basic design. To perform different functions, it must take on different forms and adopt different philosophies. These forms and philosophies are already taking shape in a handful of countries around the world.

## New Zealand: Best-in-Class Candidate

Typical business benchmarking categories are inventory management, customer service, logistics, operations and costs. For governments, the categories might include levels of growth, income inequality, pension plans, taxation levels, quality of education and fiscal reform.

The most comprehensive models of government fiscal reform have come not out of Europe or North America, but from the Pacific Rim. For example, New Zealand is emerging as a model for how a developed economy can restore fiscal discipline. Having basically gone broke in the early '80s because of irresponsible government spending, New Zealand turned over a new leaf and is now a model of fiscal discipline.

Its Fiscal Responsibility Act seeks to encourage its politicians to pursue policies in the country's long-term economic interest, rather than short-term political ones. It requires the government to maintain financial accounts similar to the private sector. These capital and operating accounts allow citizens to see how much is being spent on long-term infrastructure investments—such as roads, airports, schools, hospitals, and water-treatment plants—and how much is being spent on pork-barrel and transfer payments, which provide little long-term payback. Separating the capital and operating accounts makes it more difficult for politicians to buy votes with transfer payments because the process is more visible and accountable. To prevent politicians from, say, disguising pork barrel programs as capital expenditures, the government's books are audited yearly by an independent agency which publishes its findings.

Thus, these accounts have two benefits: they lessen the likelihood of fiscal trickery and they encourage governments to focus on the longer-term consequences of their policies. In addition, the act states that government must run a surplus until debt is reduced to prudent levels, and then the budget must stay in rough balance over the economic cycle. The New Zealanders defined "prudent" levels as a ratio of net debt to GNP below 30% in the short term and 20% in the long term. The act requires full disclosure of information to allow for closer scrutiny of budget policy by Parliament, the press, and the public. For example, the government must publish a fully audited assessment of its finances just before an election to reduce the risk of a pre-election spending binge.

When coupled with New Zealand's Reserve Bank Act, a model of central bank independence which has greatly enhanced the credibility of the country's monetary policy, New Zealand now probably has the best framework for monetary and fiscal policy anywhere in the world. This all came about when the citizens put the tax-and-spend government apparatus under trusteeship. They then put legal constraints on government's capacity to ever again break loose and plunge the country into financial chaos. It is a harbinger of things to come.

## East Asian Miracles

Other powerful and contemporary models are also found on the Pacific Rim. A recent World Bank study entitled *The East Asian Miracles* analyzed the factors contributing to the phenomenal growth of Taiwan, Korea, Hong Kong and Singapore. Interestingly, the report's conclusions dispute conventional wisdom that industrial policy and government direction of the economy were central to the success of these states.

On the contrary, it would appear that government direction, industrial policies and public subsidies played secondary roles to what the report's authors call "economic fundamentals." High savings rates, high investment rates, low taxes, fiscal discipline, convertible currencies, access to capital markets, and secure property rights are all included under this heading and were viewed as being much more important to the success of these economies than government industrial policies.

These governments also helped their economies grow by investing in sectors and activities which provided high economic leverage, such as education, health care, and infrastructure (such as roads, utilities, airports, sewage systems, and telecommunications.) It is these fundamentals, coupled with access to rich markets such as the United States, which propelled these small Asian nations from underdeveloped to developed status in one generation. The World Bank study gives considerable credit to the United States for providing these developing economies with access to markets at a critical time in their development.

Singapore, one of those East Asian "miracles," has turned itself into an "intelligent island." Investing heavily in education, it has wired the whole city-state for high-tech communications. In fact, it is the only state in the world which is 100% wired for ISDN (Integrated Systems Digital Network) protocols, which allow simultaneous voice and data transmissions. Singapore also has invested heavily in digital-systems infrastructure such as its "Portnet," which has helped make it the most efficient container port in the world. It has set up similar systems for financial services.

## Doing Things Right

Chile, as much a part of the Pacific Rim as of Latin America, has propelled itself toward developed status with astonishing speed and confidence. Inflation is now in the single digits and falling. Foreign exchange reserves are high and growing. The government consistently runs a healthy budget surplus.

By the mid-1990s, exports were growing at 25% a year, foreign investment accounted for almost 10% of gross domestic product, and unemployment was less than 6%. The population living below the poverty line had declined from more than 40% to less than 28% and continues to drop.

Meanwhile, Chile's privatized national pension plan is considered by many to be the best in the world. It has raised the national savings rate and created a badly needed pool of domestic capital for investment. On every count, Chile's pension plan is a model that North America's unfunded and underfunded public pension plans would do well to emulate.

How was all this accomplished? By doing things right. For starters, taxes were lowered, the percentage of GNP controlled by the state was rolled back from 33 to 23%, and state industries were privatized. At the same time, the economy was largely de-regulated, tariffs lowered, and foreign investment welcomed.

Chile's road to prosperity has not been without bumps. In the 1980s, it experienced a run on its currency similar to what Mexico endured in 1995. But from that experience, Chilean authorities concluded they needed policies to encourage domestic savings, discourage short-term capital coming in and out of the economy, and make long-term investment welcome.

## Morality and Balance

To the economic principles evident in these foreign success stories, we must add a moral one: successful economies seem to be rooted in a value system which places a premium on future prosperity. Decisions regarding present consumption are always weighed against future economic health. Applied to America, this means we have a responsibility to leave behind to our children an economy and a world at least as viable as the one we received from our parents. It is immoral to pass on inter-generational debt, environmental degradation or an education system which will not adequately prepare them for the 21st century. They will have enough to contend with in the future without being burdened with problems we refused to face in our lifetime. To do justice to our children, we must bring the federal budget into balance and keep it there for some time, as we grow our way out of our fiscal bind.

Balancing the budget should not and need not be done on the backs of the poor. It's important that we maintain a sense of balance and fairness. History teaches that, if left unaltered and untended, the gap between rich and poor will widen indefinitely. This, in turn, leads to social disorder. One of the great lessons which historians Will and Ariel Durant drew from their monumental lifetime study of civilization is that societies which allow the gap between rich and poor to grow indefinitely face the prospect of social disintegration. Thus, it's essential that we focus attention on raising productivity and maintaining redistributive programs aimed at the truly needy.

Here is our quandary. Without some concerted effort to reduce the gap between rich and poor, it will grow indefinitely, to the point where social disorder and even collapse are likely. If taxes are raised too high or public consumption grows too quickly, it slows growth and makes social inequality even worse. Remember, the gap between rich and poor is widest in economies with slow growth and declining productivity.

Our problem, then, is one of balance. In our desire to do good things for people, we forgot that the list of good things to do is limitless, while the resources of society are not. In our desire to say "yes" to everyone and every need, we mustn't unwittingly say "no" to future prosperity by undermining society's capacity to create the very wealth needed to meet those needs.

We must strive to restore balance. While not eliminating all redistributive programs, we must roll back many of them, especially those not aimed exclusively at helping the poor. The bulk of government redistributive programs today direct money not to the poor, but to the middle class and even the wealthy. To sustain our middle class welfare system, we are overtaxing the productive sectors of our economy to the point of diminishing returns, and piling up debt for our children and grandchildren to pay. Meanwhile, it can be persuasively argued, the United States does not do enough to help its poor children. As we said, a society which spends 10 times as much on old people (who vote) as it does on children (who do not) is headed for trouble. This clearly represents an unsustainable situation, but luckily, it is fixable, if we have the courage to step up to the challenge now.

The key is to acknowledge that what we're doing at present is no longer working. The vast majority of the public already knows that truth. It is just a question of Washington, or Ottawa, or Paris admitting what everyone already knows—and then having the courage to do something about it. Until they do, political partisanship will inhibit our ability to form a consensus for action.

The moment a politician of conscience, on either side, steps up to the problem of entitlements, the other side sees it as an opportunity for demagoguery. This may be good politics, but it's bad nation-building, and it's going to catch up with us sooner or later. It is this amoral, politics-as-usual behavior which has led to increased cynicism and loss of confidence in government. That erosion of respect only worsens today's value crisis in Washington.

However, this is not unique to our era. In the 4th century B.C., the Athenian philosopher Sophocles wrote *Antigone*, a tragedy about a ruler who, with the best of intentions, makes an unwise decision and is doomed ever after to choose between two equally evil alternatives. The only way out of this dilemma is to admit the initial mistake, but the doomed leader cannot bring himself to do so. *Antigone* is an old story which tells a timeless truth. Sadly, the tragedy of *Antigone* is being played out today in capitals throughout the western world.

# Part V
## Transitioning to Tomorrow

# 12

# Coming to Grips With the Age of Abundance

*This time, like all times, is a very good one, if we but know what to do with it.*

*—Ralph Waldo Emerson*

Huge consumer superstores spring up in every town . . . and the Berlin Wall comes down. NAFTA passes . . . and the Internet mushrooms. The Mexican peso collapses . . . and the software industry explodes.

At first glance, such events may seem random and unrelated; however, they are not. Like billiard balls scattering in all directions and ricocheting noisily off one another, these seemingly purposeless happenings all have been set in motion by strong, definable forces. But in the billiards game we call the world economy, there are no pauses to chalk up the cues or study the table. And there is no point in waiting for the balls to slow down so we can reflect and learn. They *will not*.

In this global game, we must learn on the go. The challenge for us, as players and observers, is to find the patterns which link these events and provide some measure of coherence. A new world order really is taking shape right before our eyes. Power is shifting from place to people, from the nation-state to the global market, and *especially* from producers to consumers. These changes are overpowering institutions, protocols, procedures, and assumptions rooted in an earlier, slower-moving era.

Today's economy is as different from that which President Kennedy inherited as the Age of Napoleon was from that of Charlemagne. The most important factor in this change is *knowledge*. At one time, knowledge doubled every thousand years. Then in the 19th century, the span shrank to every 100 years. Now it's said to double every year—and the interval narrows with each passing day.

Causes and effects in the global economy are not going to slow down because knowledge isn't slowing down. In fact, one reason knowledge is growing so quickly is because it's *moving* so quickly. The minute someone introduces an important idea anywhere, it is almost instantaneously communicated around the world.

Givenchy can come up with a fashion design in Paris in the morning, and by mid-afternoon, it's being talked about in New York. And within a week, someone in China will be knocking out cheap imitations for sale to mass merchandisers. Today's ideas move quickly and can be replicated easily if the right technology is available—and if it is not, it soon will be.

## Speed and Availability

An economy driven by information is characterized by two things—*speed* and *availability*. Speed is something we now take for granted. We expect packages delivered overnight, photos developed in an hour, and financial transactions performed in nanoseconds. Availability, on the other hand, is a relatively new phenomenon.

Our mindset is still shaped by an Industrial Age paradigm of scarcity, and our way of working is largely a by-product of this thinking. We focus energy on *managing resources, allocating materials, extracting efficiencies,* and *managing risk*. All of these are scarcity-related terms and reflect scarcity-related thinking.

These terms and this way of thinking are not about to disappear overnight, but they will lose some of their potency in the years ahead. Tomorrow's focus will shift increasingly toward abundance-related terms and concepts like *growth, adding value, creating wealth,* and *exceeding customer expectations*. In large measure, we are leaving behind the scarcity of the Industrial Age and embracing the abundance of the Knowledge Age. In fact, that transition is already under way.

# Knowledge vs. Abundance

There is a direct relationship between knowledge and abundance. An economy based on exploitation of resources must, of necessity, be focused on managing scarcity. After all, raw materials aren't inexhaustible.

For example, there is a lot of oil in the world. In fact, there is far more than the average person realizes. However, the supply is finite, and that fact has provided the backdrop for economic and political planning in the Industrial Age. The fortunes of countries, the design of products, the aims of diplomacy, and even the willingness to wage war have ebbed and flowed according to perceptions about the supply of oil.

Corporate policy, in general, has centered on improving the efficiency with which raw materials and other resources could be exploited. Successful economies, such as those in North America, Japan and Europe, were able to extract ever-increasing efficiency and value from these resources, thus driving up living standards.

How did they do that? By applying more and more knowledge to the exploitation process. Smart economies produced more GNP with fewer raw materials. That was the key to creating wealth in the Industrial Age.

But what happens when knowledge is no longer a means to an end but becomes an end in itself. When knowledge replaces raw materials as both the *source* and *object* of production, the economy has changed forever. That's where we are today.

We are no longer just applying knowledge to resources to create efficient output. Instead, we are applying knowledge to knowledge to create yet more knowledge. Knowledge has become both the critical input and output of the economy. Making knowledge productive has become an economic imperative for both business and government.

In a knowledge-driven economy, technology is the most tangible manifestation of knowledge; it is knowledge in physical form. With knowledge as the key source of value, technology can dramatically raise returns on investment and living standards. That's why developed economies in the West have sustained robust growth, sidestepping the law of diminishing returns decreed by traditional economic theory. By applying even more knowledge to the wealth-creation process, mature economies can continue to expand—*if* they encourage high rates of investment.

# The Abundance Cycle

Investments in knowledge and people make technology more valuable. By training people and better preparing them to use new technology, the speed of adaptation is greatly enhanced. Paul Romer and other growth theory economists have shown that the application of technology tends to increase the return on investment. Thus, in a classic virtuous cycle, knowledge and technology raise the return on investment—and investment spurs more knowledge and technology. The result: abundance.

In the Industrial Age, this process of leveraging knowledge to create wealth showed us how to exploit resources more efficiently. This old cycle is still running its course., even as it's overtaken by new cycles of abundance. The final contribution of the old industrial cycle may be to enable us to produce energy from almost nothing—which is precisely what cold fusion will do. In fact, it is not the laws of physics but the application of sufficient knowledge that now stands between us and cold fusion. We are only one idea away from an economy in which energy will be practically free.

Meanwhile, in the Information Age economy of abundance, the power of computers and software is increasing while the cost of computing time drops. By the year 2000, computer time will be as inexpensive as using the phone today. At that rate, by the early 21st century, it will be practically free. Think of what limitless energy, combined with limitless, expanding and inexpensive knowledge will do to the economy! The combined effect will act like an afterburner propelling the economy forward with tremendous force and speed.

Economist Paul Romer has explained how, at its core, this abundance cycle allows for a ratcheting down of the basic cost per input of production. Objects in the old industrial and agricultural economy had a near-constant price per unit. Take oranges as an example. The direct cost of producing the first 1,000 oranges is a proportion of the whole. The 999th costs about the same as the 1000th orange because each additional orange requires nearly the same amount of land, fertilizer and water as the first.

Producing ideas, on the other hand, entails a different formula. Ideas may, and often do, require a lot of investment up front. Developing software, for example, is not cheap, but once it's developed, it can be replicated quickly and often cheaply. The same applies to new production methodologies, brand concepts, or fashion ideas. This means the cost of producing future knowledge-driven wealth will decline. So, as knowledge becomes both the critical input and output of the economy, we will get richer, faster.

The cost of producing tomorrow's wealth is going to drop dramatically, even as the speed of production increases. This will bring on an Age of Abundance, at least for those who trade in ideas and their by-product, technology. However, managing in an Age of Abundance will require entirely new institutional arrangements, pricing, and distribution systems. Society will also have to adjust by creating environments which actively encourage the development of knowledge and technology.

The key to business success in an Age of Abundance will be coming to grips with the two-edged sword of availability. There will be more *customers*, more *purchasing power*, more *options*, and more *opportunities*—but also more *competition*. The only way out of this conundrum will be to add more *value*.

An Age of Abundance might sound far-fetched. But already there are signs of the coming abundance if you look for them. Even in these early manifestations, there are hints of what will separate winners from losers in the new economy.

## Imperatives in an Age of Abundance

*1. Invest in learning.* The primary means of adding value in the new economy will be information and knowledge, and the primary output will be yet more information. Just as Industrial Age organizations invested heavily to improve productivity and reliability, we now must invest in the capacity to learn. This will require a shift in thinking.

It is not hard to get an executive to buy a new machine to drive down costs. But investment in knowledge is still viewed as unorthodox. Existing accounting practices only encourage this bias. For example, investments in equipment can be capitalized and written off over a number of years, but not so investments in knowledge. Most of these are treated as an expense which adds no residual value. As a result, new software purchases are usually treated as having no more residual value than pencils or paper. Investments in education and training are viewed by steely-eyed comptrollers as expenses to be minimized.

This blind spot regarding the value of information manifests itself in perverse ways. For instance, companies which spend millions on new products and services often lack reliable information on the customers they hope will buy these products. Yet, in the corporate boardroom, eyes glaze over at the mere mention of customer profiles and customer perception of value. In fact, most organizations know surprisingly little about the 20% of customers who provide 80% of their profits.

One is reminded of the early days of the quality movement when executives would look you in the eye and say, with a straight face, "We can't afford quality right now. It would cost too much." In short, they didn't *get* it. Today, that has all changed. Most Fortune 500 executives can explain why and how quality saves money, so as a result, quality is no longer a tough sell in the boardroom. Ultimately, the same will be true about investments in learning and market information.

This breakthrough in thinking will result in new strategies to operate in knowledge-intensive environments. That, in turn, will lead to the development of sophisticated listening systems to measure customer loyalty, customer perception of value, competitive cost performance, comparative process performance, and if relevant, brand equity. To know where value is going, industry must know where the customer's marginal dollar is going and why.

In an Age of Abundance, the race for success will be run on a dual track, embracing both the present and the future. Companies will need to find ways to add more value to existing customer relationships, while investing in tools to track value and identify where tomorrow's customers are heading. Playing this dual-track game will be very knowledge-intensive. Slow learners or those convinced they already know the answers will not be able to keep up.

Getting this information will be vital to business success. In short, businesses will learn fast and keep on learning. Or they just won't survive.

2. *Think global; think information.* Organizations which resist or get stuck in the old national, analog economy will be at risk. They will see margins evaporate, profits erode and growth possibilities disappear. In fact, any institution—commercial, political or non-profit—which stakes its future on the old analog, nation-based economy is taking a big chance.

In an Age of Abundance, institutions built to manage in an environment of scarcity will inevitably come unglued. Government, the ultimate scarcity manager—and just as often, scarcity creator— will likely find itself under particular pressure.

Scarcity, you might say, is built into the DNA code of government. Thus, it has a special knack for creating it, often with the very best of intentions. Government's capacity to create shortage—for example, through price controls, tariffs and taxation— easily rivals Mother Nature at her worst. If you want to see something become scarce, just place it under the control of a government marketing board which limits production or fixes prices below market value. If that doesn't work, try taxing it at confiscatory levels and see what happens? It will disappear. From the famines in Africa to the long gas lines in the United States during the so-called energy crisis, government—not nature—has been the prime source of scarcity.

This explains why government is having such a difficult time adjusting to the new Age of Abundance. Neither its thinking nor its tools are designed for such an environment. This, in part, explains why traditional economic tools appear inept and ineffective in a global economy based on abundance. Both the old tools and the system for using them are beginning to wind down.

For example, efforts by government to solve unemployment with more spending—a classic Keynesian response—often backfires today because it raises the deficit and pushes up interest rates, which further slows the economy. Seeing politicians struggling with the challenges of the nascent Age of Abundance brings to mind Herbert Hoover's famous quote when asked, during the depth of the Depression, what Lincoln would have done. Hoover replied angrily, "If Lincoln were in my shoes, he would be just as perplexed as I am."

One cannot help but feel some measure of pity for national politicians and central bankers who know things are slipping out of control, but who are at a loss as to what to do about it. In desperation, they keep applying the old tools, only to find they no longer work and very often make things worse.

*3. Use new measures of success.* Another herald of the new era is the breakdown of traditional measurements. Nowhere is this more evident than in the yardsticks of national wealth such as GNP, trade statistics, and productivity. In a global economy where multinational companies move ideas, designs, and products around the world with incredible ease and speed, national accounts—GNP, GDP, trade balances, and productivity—are getting harder and harder to measure.

Within free trade areas, which are essentially single economic units, does it really matter what the balance of trade is? Within NAFTA, for example, does it matter how much Ontario exports or imports from New York any more than it matters how much New York exports or imports from Vermont? Not long ago, the answer would have been unequivocally, "Yes, it matters a lot." Today, the issue is far less clear.

That's true of productivity measures, too. Today's methods for tracking productivity are relics of the Industrial Age when things were easier to count. At best, our present productivity measures accurately reflect only what's going on in the manufacturing and agricultural sectors. But those sectors now account for less than one-third of the economy.

We are still in search of a new algorithm which reflects the true value of knowledge and technology. Part of the problem is we have no way of gauging increased quality, convenience, or safety. For instance, copiers, computers, and semiconductors have all been declining in price over the past decade, even as their power, efficiency and reliability have increased exponentially. Traditional productivity figures cannot capture this tremendous increase in value. The real breakthroughs have come in performance and reliability which are difficult to measure.

The problem gets even more difficult when it comes to idea-driven products, such as software. How do you measure the increased productivity or value of a new generation of software? Economists may not know, but the stock market does. This may explain why successful software companies enjoy such high market valuations.

Clearly, we will need new tools for measuring economic activity in a knowledge-driven economy. Precisely because these tools are so badly needed, we will almost certainly get them. One by one, you will see these new tools come on line over the next decade.

4. *Expect more competition.* A knowledge-driven economy uses fewer and fewer resources to produce more and more output. This greater availability of supply will manifest itself in more competition. As retailers or car dealers, for example, are forced to lower prices and abandon suggested retail prices, they will likely point to "intense global competition" as the cause; few will have the pre-

science to view the phenomenon as stemming from greater availability of output (i.e., abundance).

During these early stages of an abundance cycle, much of the economy will remain focused on managing scarcity, even as the trends point in the opposite direction. There will be some confusion and lack of certainty as the economy lurches in one direction today, then reverses itself tomorrow.

5. *Anticipate consumer power.* Even more than we have already seen, consumers will be in the driver's seat in the Age of Abundance. Armed with vast amounts of information on more readily available products and services, consumers will drive quality up and prices down.

They will insist on more and more for less and less. They will wrest power from both corporations and the nation-state.

6. *Emphasize growth.* A rising number of new corporations, new patents, new copyrights, and a plethora of new products and services will also accompany the coming increase in supply. Suddenly "growing" your way to success will become more important than "cutting" your way there. In such an environment, governments and corporations will be increasingly obsessed with promoting innovation, creative thinking and growth.

Just as importantly, such an environment will transform the very nature of economic value. Even more than we have already seen, value will move in new directions and take on new forms. Value-added will increasingly mean information added, and knowledge will begin to displace capital, labor, and raw materials as the key to wealth creation.

7. *Make way for more democracy.* The arrival of an Age of Abundance will coincide with the ascendancy of democracy on a global scale. Democracy now is on the march in Latin America, in Eastern Europe and much of Asia.

This trend represents a triumph of the individual over the state and signals a growing recognition that liberty, open markets, and the rule of law are inextricably linked to growth and prosperity. Popularly elected governments, bound by laws, subject to the oversight of the electorate, the press, and the international community are more likely to create the conditions necessary for wealth creation than are despotic or totalitarian regimes.

All other things being equal, history shows that open, democratic societies can take in and synthesize more information more quickly than closed societies. They learn faster. Thus, they create wealth more quickly. This conclusion is supported by recent studies prepared by the Institute for International Economics and by World Bank economist Surjit Bhalla. In studying 90 countries from 1973 to the early 1990s, Bhalla concluded that for all its faults, democracy seems to provide the surest foundation for prosperity and growth. This was not an ideological conclusion, but a statistical one.

Lee Kuan Yew, Singapore's leader for many years and one of the world's most successful policy makers, once said that for a country to develop, it needs discipline more than democracy. While this may be true for developing economies, once a country achieves developed status, the case for democracy becomes more and more compelling. In fact, the historical evidence suggests the best possible combination for growth is democracy *with* discipline.

*8. Create new national and global agendas.* The need to create learning societies capable of thriving in an Age of Abundance will dramatically alter corporate, national and international agendas. As firms seek to stay ahead of shifting value and become learning organizations, society will be forced to pay more attention to the ingredients needed for wealth creation. Governments will focus less energy on using outdated Keynesian formulas for managing business cycles and focus more on managing long-term growth. This means issues like education, infrastructure, and investment will take precedent over efforts to redistribute wealth or spend our way out of each cyclical slump.

Internationally, we will begin to set a new global agenda and develop institutions capable of implementing it. Our biggest issues— international finance and banking, pollution, terrorism, nuclear proliferation, AIDS, population control, war and peace—are all global in nature. No single nation-state can manage these problems alone and no existing international institutions appear up to the task. The International Monetary Fund, World Bank, OECD and even the United Nations are ill-equipped for the job ahead. These institutions are magnificent relics of the post-war Pax Americana. For all the good service they've provided, they are old, out of date, and hopelessly underpowered when compared to the global challenges of the 21st century. The U.N. is a prime example. Despite the good it does, the U.N. is slow, hierarchical, and too-often corrupt. It mirrors the 20th century nation-states which gave it birth 50 years ago.

However, the importance of having common rules and standards in areas such as global trade and commerce, is becoming clearer each day. The rules, regulations and protocols being hammered out for regional free trade areas are the beginnings of this global process. Simultaneously, we are seeing individual groups and businesses, tired of waiting for national and international institutions to get their act together, acting for themselves to set tomorrow's rules. For instance, multinational businesses have come together to set a code of conduct to deal with child labor, pollution and community responsibility. On a global scale, we now have protocols in transportation and postal services, air transportation and air safety, and telecommunications. The Law of the Sea sets standards of behavior for shipping lines. The list grows every year.

This is just the beginning. Under the auspices of a reformed and renewed United Nations, or some other agency with an appropriate mandate, the rules governing tomorrow's global economy will take shape over the next decade. There is a catch-22, though, to the global growth game. *Order is required for growth—and growth is a prerequisite for order.* We must have both. It's not sufficient to set international environmental rules, for example, if the world is too poor to care. As Gandhi pointed out, an empty stomach is a poor foundation on which to build democracy.

That point was driven home in a study by two Princeton University economists on the environmental impact of NAFTA. Correlating the levels of two major pollutants with per capita income, they found that the level of pollution rises until income reaches $5,000 per head (in 1985 dollars adjusted for purchasing-power parity), and then starts to fall. The same pattern holds true for population growth—family size increases until income reaches about $5,000 per head, then falls. What this tells us is that as countries get richer, they can better afford to reduce pollution and people are less likely to have large families.

The challenge, then, for leaders in the Age of Abundance will be to slowly harmonize international standards to the highest common denominator. The worst possible outcome would be a process which forces standards downward, thus forcing the United States to lower living standards and increase pollution to compete with developing countries. Such an outcome would be unsustainable environmentally and unacceptable politically, if for no other reason than it would lead to rampant isolationism and protectionism in the developed world.

The best outcome would be to steadily raise living standards and environmental protection in developing countries. And studies convincingly show that this can only be achieved *through growth.*

9. *Foster innovation and trust.* Innovation must be nurtured as the ultimate font of new wealth. That will be the ultimate competence that businesses—and society—will need in order to grow. Rules to protect patents, copyright and brands will be a prerequisite to global growth. Countries or regions which fail to protect the ideas of inventors, be it their own or their trading partners, will impede global growth and undermine their own wealth-creation capacity.

On another level, trust becomes the adhesive of growth because ideas cannot be created in a vacuum. There must be collaboration, sharing, and learning to produce ideas, and none of this can be accomplished in a world without trust.

10. *Reduce the power of governments.* Government can only retain relevance in the new economy by giving up some of its power. To come out of this a winner, government must yield some of the functions and prerogatives it has spent a half-century garnering for itself. To succeed, national governments must retrench and retreat toward those basic defense, law enforcement, and regulatory functions first envisioned in America by Jefferson, Madison and John Adams. Where services are needed, government must learn to buy them from the private sector rather than to provide them itself.

Government must develop a core competency for contracting-out functions. It lacks this competency today. For example, the cost of doing business with the government is very high because the contracting process is so painfully long and expensive. Ironically, this tortuous contracting process does not seem to improve performance. Certainly, it does not appear to have helped defense or health care suppliers. Think about it: what other customer but the government has to employ thousands of auditors and FBI investigators to police, fine, and occasionally imprison its suppliers of vital services?

Government must rethink the way it does business and have the wisdom to give power away in order to get it back. The operative word here is *give.* If power must be wrenched from government by an angry electorate, it is unlikely to be given back any time soon.

In addition, governments everywhere must also begin paying much more attention to issues of growth. None can afford to take wealth or wealth-creation for granted any longer. In an Age of Abundance, the electorate will very quickly grow impatient with governments which do not deliver prosperity. As a wave of prosperity and growth makes itself felt in region after region around the world, the electorate in slow-growing economies will soon begin asking, "Why not us?" Politicians unable to provide a reasonable answer to this question will find themselves headed for early retirement.

## Not Nirvana

It is important, though, to be clear about this: the coming abundance will not be uniformly distributed. While the world generally will get richer and living standards will improve, some regions, some workers and some businesses will suffer a lot in the immediate future. The rising tide will lift most boats but some will rise a lot faster and higher than others—and *some* will not rise at all, until their education catches up.

Availability, the hallmark of abundance, should not be confused with absolute accessibility. For instance, the availability of high-quality jobs will not guarantee universality of high-quality employment. Those workers lacking the necessary skills may see their earnings under pressure, and many may be unable to find employment above the minimum wage level.

Nor will business emerge unscathed. Abundance, as we mentioned, will take the form of much more opportunity, but also will bring much more competition. As more and more companies enter the market, margins will come under relentless pressure. The only way to stay ahead of margin erosion will be to innovate and find ways to add value.

Thus, businesses will need to spend every hour of every day in search of ways to drive down costs, drive up quality, and increase overall value. Those not quick enough will be eliminated.

Such pressure will not only affect large, global competitors but, increasingly, local firms, too. Globalization will up the ante. Even small, local companies will find themselves forced to meet quality, cost, and service standards dictated by the world's best companies. Those unable to compete will be bought, merged, or forced to close their doors.

Thus, abundance means *more*—but it doesn't mean *more of the same*. It's a safe bet that the sales volumes of some old-line firms will decline, along with margins, as buyers switch to new types of products. For example, the sales of automobiles may decline while demand for electronics, home computers, and software increases.

Governments, especially central governments, will find the Age of Abundance uncomfortable. They will be under increasing pressure to keep up with fast-moving private-sector standards. In a world suspicious of slow-moving bureaucracies, government will be challenged on every front to justify its activities. This will dramatically impact public policy as government is forced to abandon or contract-out more of its functions.

On a macro-economic level, governments which adopt *anti-growth* policies will find **they work**. Growth will shudder to a halt. As growth slows, local constituents will become cranky and demanding. Global financial markets will be even harder to appease. Money will be increasingly indifferent to national borders. Finance ministers accustomed to finding ready buyers for their bonds may be shocked one day to find they can no longer sell them, even to their own citizens, who are busy investing in other markets.

## Why Incomes Are Diverging

Perhaps the biggest challenge democratic government faces in coping with this new age of abundance is the potentially unequal distribution of income flowing from a world of information haves and have nots. We must also determine what constitutes sustainable growth. The first problem, unequal income distribution, is already making itself felt politically in much of the developed world. People without access to technology, adequate education, or those dependent on government transfers or protection, as well as those tied to dying sectors of the old economy, are all experiencing considerable downward pressure on their incomes.

The press tends to view this divergence of income as historically unique, but it is not. Such splits in income have occurred before during periods of transition between epochs. When an old order goes into decline, those whose incomes are tied to it inevitably come under pressure. Today's shifts in income distribution largely reflect the economy's transition to a higher plane of knowledge intensity. This shift is driving up the demand for high knowledge labor and lowering the value of low knowledge labor, and this is happening on a global scale.

Some view this as a problem resulting from trade and the global economy. But this is a serious misreading of the facts. The problem of divergent income is endemic to the workings of any modern, high knowledge economy which does not have a correspondingly high knowledge workforce. Any high knowledge economy which harbors a remnant of low knowledge labor is going to see incomes diverge. Unless society can miraculously transform that component of its workforce which is low knowledge to high knowledge overnight, divergence of income distribution is inevitable. Government can ameliorate the problem by redistributing incomes through tax policies. But such remedies treat only the symptom, not the cause. The true source of the problem is to be found in the workforce itself, where some workers lack the skills or knowledge to transition from the old economy to the new. But make no mistake, this problem *can be fixed*, but it can't be fixed overnight. It will require significant investments in education and an end to our present ethos of entitlement. The one thing which won't work is a trade war.

Not surprisingly, those who feel themselves at risk are anxious about the future. They easily fall prey to unscrupulous politicians who seek to blame someone for the situation. In the mid 1990s, we have seen a return to the anti-trade, anti-immigrant rhetoric of the late 1920s and early '30s. This sort of scapegoating may make good politics, but can easily lead to disaster if rhetoric becomes policy. It was precisely this sort of wrong-headed thinking which plunged us into the Great Depression of the 1930s. Trade wars kill jobs, they don't protect them.

We are facing a classic battle between those who benefit from yesterday's status quo and those who will benefit from tomorrow's. What we are witnessing is not just a divergence of income, but a divergence of interests. If not managed, this divergence could easily take on the trappings of an economic civil war.

Short of stopping the future from arriving, the only reasonable answer lies in managing this historic transition by supporting those most at risk. And yes, *this would almost certainly involve a role for government*, as well as business and the community. Financial, education and moral support for those affected will be required. If we just abandon those left behind by the new economy, they will become saboteurs, doing their best to slow this important economic transition at every turn. The accompanying tension between those striving for the future and those clinging to the past will put tremendous pressure on our democratic institutions in the years ahead.

On the issue of sustainable growth, we will need new measures of economic success. The original concept of national accounts is more than half a century old. Simon Kuznets, the man who first developed this concept, pointed out in the 1930s that "the welfare of the nation can scarcely be inferred from a measurement of gross national product alone." Clearly, Kuznets was right. More things contribute to national well-being than simply raw economic growth, as important as it may be. Pollution, crime, family stability, community cohesion are all important factors in determining well-being. Clearly, we need new measures and metrics for determining our success as a society. These metrics must take account of growth, but they must also measure other things important to society. Determining this new scale of measures will be important as we head into the 21st century.

## Turning Economics on Its Ear

Although the world has already begun to shift to an abundance cycle, economic theory has yet to catch up. Traditional economic theory has it that the economy's output is a function of capital and labor. Of course, we know from recent, real life experience this is mostly nonsense.

Studies now show that *knowledge* and its surrogate, *technology*, are the real catalysts for growth. Properly applied, knowledge acts as a multiplier which significantly increases the payoff from investment and raises the productivity of labor.

Knowledge and technology must be acquired in much the same way other factors of production are obtained. They must be paid for by deferring current consumption. In short, societies must actively *invest* in knowledge and technology.

Luckily, knowledge and technology are brought on by the same factors which stimulate investment—open markets, competition, and the rule of law. This means societies which limit competition or mute markets with protection, or in some way discourage profits through taxation or legislation will be in trouble. Conversely, efforts to free up and enlarge markets, enhance competition and create profit-making opportunities will spur growth faster than under traditional economic theory.

## The Coming Hysteria

As we approach the end of the decade, we are closing out a century as well as a millennium. Further, we're bringing to a close an historic epoch: the post-war era of Soviet-American competition and the struggle between democracy and communism. Even now, the Cold War is hard to explain to our children, only a few years after it ended. To them, NATO is as distant a reality as the League of Nations.

With so much coming to an end at once, we can expect the lunatic fringe and even a few mainstream commentators to begin scaring the wits out of everyone with talk of a great reckoning, with dire prognostications about the end of economic life as we know it. Such shrill voices have always been with us. With the passing of the millennium, we should brace for an above-average dose of hysteria.

This generation of pessimists will use the same old Luddite themes but wrapped in new rhetoric. Expect to hear somber messages about the end of the middle class, irreversible wage disparities, mass unemployment and the rise of high-tech oligopolies. Movies like *The Net* and a host of copycat productions will bring us to the edge of our seats as we contemplate the dangers of a digital world.

However, anyone with a knowledge of economic history knows that wage fluctuations and sectoral dislocation are by-products of economic transition. We've seen it all before and we will likely see it all again. Even the temporary concentration of economic power in the hands of powerful corporations is a pattern repeated again and again in history. The so-called robber barons who controlled the railways, shipping lines and banks before the turn of the century were as powerful an oligopoly as the world has ever seen. Off the coast of Georgia, at Jekyll Island, you can see where they wintered together in luxury, year after year. But for all their power, where are they today? Do the Cranes, DuPonts, Vanderbilts, or Mellons control today's economy? Not by a long shot. Their influence is negligible and has been receding for more than three quarters of a century.

In the early 1960s, economist John Kenneth Galbraith and others were predicting the world's wealth would soon be concentrated in the hands of a small number of giant, multinational corporations. At the time, they had in mind paragons of corporate success like Sears, General Motors and IBM. Well, just the opposite happened. Economic power fractured globally, splintering in a thousand different directions.

Remember, all of this is just a rehash of *How to Survive the Coming Bad Years, Closing Circle,* and *Zero-Sum Society,* stuff heard at the end of the 1970s. Then, we were going to run out of oil, minerals, farmland, food, and even air to breathe. OPEC was going to own the whole world and the West was doomed to slow, inexorable decline. Well, guess what? It didn't happen. (Naysaying seems to be a growth industry in every era. In 1963, a professor told Congress that America was becoming satiated with consumer goods like refrigerators and televisions. He predicted that as demand declined, automation would eliminate 40,000 jobs a year—and that at that rate, *every job in America would be eliminated by 1999!*)

Don't believe the new Cassandras. There will be lots of jobs and opportunities in tomorrow's economy for those with the right skills. Sure there will also be lots of problems and challenges, but don't confuse dislocation with decay. As we leave one economic era and enter another, some disruption is inevitable, even desirable. It has occurred in every major economic transition in history. Why should things be different this time around?

Thanks to the changes we are seeing today, the world is positioning itself to better manage these issues. Think about it! How could we expect to attack international pollution or nuclear proliferation when we were locked into a deadly cold war? Our biggest concern was not attacking pollution but *being attacked* by the Soviet Union. In those days, everything took a back seat to this deadly competition. Now that threat has passed.

## Positive Harbinger

Increasing trade is one of the world's more positive harbingers of future growth. We are only now returning to the level of trade as a percentage of global output that characterized the belle époque, that era of rapidly expanding prosperity and global market integration in the late 19th and early 20th centuries. That process of growth was derailed by a series of cataclysms—including two world wars and the Great Depression. The present trend toward rising living standards and globalization appears to be a continuation of what was interrupted three-quarters of a century ago.

Today, free of the Cold War, the world is positioning itself to deal with a new generation of problems. Those problems are "better" than the ones they are replacing. Instead of focusing on the Cold

War, we can concern ourselves with pollution, nuclear proliferation, and global financial stability. We are surrounded by opportunities. The world, in its own jerky fashion, is moving toward, not away from, solutions to its problems.

What we are witnessing today is not an end, as so many are likely to predict in the next few years, but a *beginning*. The present turmoil signals the dawn of a new century, a new millennium, and a new economy. These developments are, for the most part, overwhelmingly positive. In an Age of Abundance, anything is possible. So we should stop wringing our hands about the future and get on with shaping it.

## "Tomorrow Country"

The great message which emerges from a study of today's transformation of value and the emergence of a new economic order is that America has an unprecedented capacity to adapt and change. This should not surprise anyone, America has always been about change.

Ours is a nation of vast diversity, a cauldron of hopes, dreams and entrepreneurial energy that remakes itself every generation by taking in new people and new ideas. America is not just a country of immigrants, it is also a country of optimists— "tomorrow country," Walt Whitman called it. This bent for optimism remains as true today as when he wrote about it a century ago. So long as America maintains its optimism and sense of purpose, it can cope with almost any set of challenges.

In 1980, we faced a host of problems including the Cold War (which was heating up with the Soviet invasion of Afghanistan), the energy crisis, the Iran hostage crisis, a sick dollar, runaway inflation, astronomical interest rates, stagflation (high inflation combined with high unemployment), declining competitiveness, poor-quality products, and low morale in the military and the country. On the whole, it was a pretty scary time.

In his first presidential inaugural address, Ronald Reagan said, "Our problems will not go away overnight, but they will go away." And although it was not a clean sweep, the problems which most vexed Americans in those dark days have, indeed, gone away. True, we now have a new set of problems and challenges to face. But it is also true that over the past decade, the United States successfully dealt with every one of the issues which were at the top of the national agenda in 1980. All in all, it was an impressive performance. And it was not a victory attributable to any political party or any one leader, it was a victory attributable to the American people and the amazingly flexible American economy.

America in the 1980s successfully transitioned from an analog-, industrial- and service-based economy to one driven by information and knowledge. As value shifted and transformed itself, so did American business. The '80s turned out to be a period of "re-industrialization" for the United States rather than deindustrialization, as so many gloomsters predicted. We made this transition faster and more comprehensively than any region on earth. This does not guarantee *anything* in the future, yet it remains an impressive accomplishment for a country that was supposedly down for the count.

Tomorrow's problems are no more formidable—and probably less so—than the ones we have overcome in the last 15 years. And they pale in comparison to the challenges of the past 50 years, which included winning the Second World War, rebuilding Europe and Japan, protecting democracy, surviving the Cold War, and liberalizing world trade. America has a great track record of coming through in a crunch. In fact, the more impossible the task, the better we respond. When John Kennedy said we would go to the moon and back in the decade of the '60s, the operative technology did not exist. The plan was perceived as just another one of those crazy American dreams. But in 1969, we made the dream come true.

As we look toward the next millennium, we can confidently say the global economy is in better shape than at any time this century. Inflation is low in most of the world. Capital remains both available and affordable. We have not banished the business cycle, but we have muted it.

Asia and Latin America are booming, North America is growing briskly, and Europe and Japan are emerging from recession. Eastern Europe is getting its act together and will soon be riding a powerful growth curve. Despite a spate of ethnic conflicts in Eastern Europe, peace is trying to break out around the world—everywhere from South Africa and the Middle East to Northern Ireland. More importantly, the Cold War has ended, thereby freeing up precious resources for more productive pursuits.

There has been a dramatic expansion of regional free-trade areas in North America, South America, and Europe, as well as a strengthening of world trade through GATT and the World Trade Organization. Asia and the Middle East are beginning to set up regional free-trade areas. In fact, all around the world, free markets are in ascendance. Trade will boom in the years ahead if we can keep from stumbling into a trade war.

Politically, too, the results have turned out almost exactly as George Kennan, George Marshall, Harry Truman and the other architects of America's post-war strategy had hoped. It just took longer than they expected. Everything does.

Today, Europe and Japan are wealthy and free. The people of Eastern Europe and the former Soviet Union are able to shape their own future. Outside of Cuba, an unelected government cannot be found anywhere in the Western Hemisphere. Democracy, freedom, and market economies are on the rise everywhere.

Looking ahead, we see every reason for optimism. Yes, a lot could still go wrong, but we are inclined to believe more will go right. Certainly, few generations have been afforded a scenario so rich with opportunity. Chances are, in the next century, we will see a stronger, not a weaker U.S. economy. Jobs will increase and so will productivity. National sovereignty will erode, but global consumer sovereignty will fill the void.

Something will be lost, but a lot more will be gained. Instead of being overwhelmed by the challenges of a new global agenda, we may find facing up to them a source of energy.

Those billiard balls are not bouncing around the table helter-skelter. There are forces driving them, and if we set our minds to it, we can harness those forces. We should be confident and aggressive about the future, not gloomy and pessimistic. We are on the edge of a new era of abundance, rich in opportunity. The responsibility of seizing these opportunities rests with every individual, institution or corporation. Not all will have the wisdom to do so. But there will be far more winners than losers when the smoke clears. In any case, as Shakespeare would have it, "Our fate is in our own hands."

# Sources:
# Notes &
# Bibliography

# Notes

## Chapter 1: Through the Looking Glass

For a discussion of American competitiveness, two useful sources are: The World Economic Forum, IMED Institute, Davos, Switzerland, *Report on Global Competitiveness*, December, 1994; and *Made in America*, M. Dertouzous, R.K. Lester, R.M. Solow, MIT Press, Cambridge, Mass, 1989.

For insights into the Japanese economy, those sources which are particularly useful are: *More Like Us*, James Fallows, Houghton-Mifflin, Boston, 1989; *The Bubble Economy*, Christopher Wood, Atlantic Monthly Press, New York, 1992; *The Enigma of Japanese Power*, Karel Van Wolferen, Alfred Knopf, New York, 1989; and *The Sun Also Sets*, Bill Emmott, Times Books–Random House, New York, 1989.

For contrasting views of the post-Cold War world, we refer the reader to: *Out of Control*, Zbigniew Brzezinski, Robert Stewart Books, New York, 1993; and *Perestroika*, Mikhail Gorbachev, Harper & Row, New York, 1987.

Other sources were: *The Third Century*, Joel Kotkin and Yoriko Kishimoto, Crown, New York, 1988; *An Illustrated Guide to the American Economy*, Herbert Stein and Murray Foss, American Enterprise Institute, Washington, 1992; and *Leadership and the New Science*, Margaret J. Wheatley, Barret and Koehler, San Francisco, 1994.

## Chapter 2: The New Economy: A Value-Driven Kaleidoscope

We are indebted to Canadian economist Nuala Beck, whose brilliant analysis of the new economy, *Shifting Gears*, HarperCollins, Toronto, 1993, was immensely useful in the preparation of this book. For an outstanding discussion of globalization, we refer the reader to: *The Borderless World*, Kenichi Ohmae, HarperBusiness, New York, 1990; and *A Matter of Survival*, Diane Francis, Key Porter Books, Toronto, 1993.

For a discussion of how global currency and financial markets are eroding national sovereignty, we refer the reader to: *The Vandal's Crown, How Currency Traders Overthrew the World Central Bankers*, Gregory Millman, The Free Press, New York, 1995; and Richard O'Brien's insightful work, *The End of Geography: Global Financial Integration*, The Royal Institute of International Affairs, Pinter Publishers, London, 1992.

We are indebted to Don Tapscott's, *Digital Economy*, McGraw-Hill, Toronto, 1995, for his insightful and readable analysis of new trends including disintermediation, integration, prosumption and integration.

For a thorough analysis of East Asian economic power, refer to James Fallows' new book, *Looking at the Sun: The Rise of the New East Asian Economic and Political System*, Pantheon Books, New York, 1994.

For those interested in the process by which the American military reformed itself in the 1980s, we refer the reader to Al Santoli's very readable *Leading the Way*, Random House, New York, 1993.

For a discussion of the dramatic decline in the real cost of natural resources, see Stephen Moore, as quoted in *Market Liberalism: A Paradigm for the 21st Century*, edited by David Boaz and Edward H. Crane, The Cato Institute, Washington, D.C., 1993. Charles Handy's *Age of Paradox*, Harvard Business School Press, Boston, 1994, also provides useful insights into the rise of the contingent workforce and the changing shape of the modern workplace. Other sources used were:

- Price Pritchett, *The Employee Handbook of New Work Habits for a Radically Changing World*, Pritchett & Associates, Inc., Dallas, Tex., 1994
- *An Illustrated Guide to the American Economy*, Herbert Stein and Murray Foss, American Enterprise Institute, Washington, 1992
- NBC special documentary, "If Japan Can . . . Why Can't We?" 1980. This documentary is viewed as a watershed in the U.S. quality movement. Many view it as the emotional detonator that set off the U.S. quality recovery
- Congressional Committee presentation by Abraham Katz, director of the Council for International Business, October 15, 1994, as reported on C-SPAN

- "Global Trade Expands," *European Financial Times*, June 7, 1994
- "What Computers Are For," *The Economist*, January 22, 1994
- A. Tonelson, "Beating Back Predatory Trade," *Foreign Affairs*, July-August 1994
- "The Motown Summit," *McLean's* magazine, March 28, 1994
- "Auto Plants Hiring Higher Skills," *The Wall Street Journal*, March 11, 1994
- "1994 Inc. 500 List," 13th annual ranking of the fastest growing companies, *Inc.* magazine
- "Global Economy in Change," *Financial Post*, May 1995, Financial Post 500 Special Edition
- Mercosur Free Trade Area (Argentina, Brazil, Paraguay, Uruguay and soon, Chile and Bolivia) encompasses 200 million people with a combined GNP of nearly 800 billion dollars, AP, August 5, 1994, 18:30 EDT VO 398
- "Secret Apple Cyberdog," *USA Today*, October 24, 1994.
- "Callback Services Cut Telephone Bills to Users Abroad," *The Wall Street Journal*, June 21, 1994
- "Japan is Dialing 1-800-Buy America," *BusinessWeek*, June 12, 1995
- Dave Winter, "Bill's Bet the Company Strategy," *Wired*, June 1995
- CNW Market Research, as quoted in *The Wall Street Journal*, May 3, 1995
- "Austrians Look to Drive a Bargain Across the Border," *European Financial Times*, August 23, 1995
- The Gorman and Huey quotes are from *Fortune*, "Waking Up to the New Economy," June 27, 1994

## Chapter 3: What Causes Value to Shift?

To better understand the Xerox story, we refer the reader to *Prophets in the Dark*, David Kearns and David Nadler, Harper Business, New York, 1992. For those interested in Harley Davidson, Peter C. Reid's very readable book, *Well Made in America*, McGraw-Hill, New York, 1990, provides an excellent source.

For insights into the impact of information on the banking industry, read "Why Banks Keep Bulking Up," *BusinessWeek*, July 31, 1995. For a discussion of shifting buying patterns for automobiles, see "Six Reasons People Are Buying Fewer Cars," *The Wall Street*

*Journal*, Wednesday, May 3, 1995, and "Detroit Is Retooling Its Economic Models," *The Wall Street Journal*, August 7, 1995.

For a fascinating and insightful discussion of the interaction of technologies and ideas, read James Burke's *Connections*, Little, Brown & Co., Toronto, 1978.

For those interested in the impact of new materials on value, read Thomas Forester's *The Materials Revolution*, MIT Press, Boston, 1988. Other sources were:

- Gerhard D. Mensch, "Stalemate in Technology: Innovations Overcome the Depression," Ballinger, Cambridge, Mass., 1979
- CNW Market Research, as quoted in *The Wall Street Journal*, May 3, 1995
- "GM Takes Steps to Overhaul Dealership System," *The Wall Street Journal*, June 26, 1995

## Chapter 4: What's So Different About Today's Value Shifts?

For an outstanding discussion of the interaction between quality, brand power, market share and ROI, read *Managing Customer Value*, Bradley T. Gale, The Free Press, New York, 1994.

For a discussion on the birth of the cruise industry, John Maxtone-Graham's *Liners to the Sun*, Macmillan, New York, 1985; and *Crossing and Cruising*, Scribner, New York, 1992, are excellent sources.

For details on the new technology "house calls," see "Business Bulletin: PC House Calls Catch on With Electronics Retailers," *The Wall Street Journal*, November 9, 1995, p. 1.

For definitive discussion of the role of industry-wide chains of value in creating competitive advantage, read *The Competitive Advantage of Nations*, Michael Porter, The Free Press, New York, 1990. Other useful sources were:

- "McKesson Systems, New Division of PCS Health Systems," *Business Week*, February 23, 1994
- "The Information Wars," *Fortune*, July 12, 1995
- "Laboratory in Your Lounge," *The Economist*, May 6, 1995

# Chapter 5: Why Even Smart Companies Sometimes Act Dumb

For a more thorough analysis of the Encyclopedia Brittanica story, see Gary Samuel's article, "CD-Rom's First Big Victim: Encyclopedia Brittanica, Inc.," *Forbes* magazine, February 28, 1994, p. 42.

We found Barbara Tuchman's *The March of Folly*, Cardinal Books, New York, 1990, both useful and inspirational in the preparation of this chapter. *Discontinuous Change*, by David Nadler and Robert B. Shaw, Jossey-Bass, San Francisco, 1995, was also helpful.

The Primal Change Model was the by-product of the Atlanta Consulting Group/CPC Study, Implementation/Change Benchmarking Study conducted with IDS and American Express in November 1993. (This study pointed to *need* as being the overwhelming driver of successful change.)

Tolstoy's description of General Kutuzov's decision to originally defend and then abandon Moscow, contained in his classic work, *War and Peace*, Leo Tolstoy, The Modern Library, Random House, New York, 1994, remains, in our view, the quintessential description of what real time executive decision making looks like. As Tolstoy shows, the process is often surrounded by chaos, pressure and inadequate information.

Margaret Wheatley's wonderful book, *Leadership and the New Science*, Barret and Koehler, San Francisco, 1994, provides outstanding insights into why organizations resist learning and are so slow to change, even in the face of overwhelming need.

Lawrence Miller's book, *Barbarians to Bureaucrats*, Clarkson & Potter Publishers, New York, 1989, was immensely useful in analyzing the causes of organizational decay.

Those interested in the American Express story may wish to read *The Credit Card Catastrophe, The 20th Century Phenomenon That Changed the World*, Marty Simmons, Barricade Books, New York,1995; *A Piece of the Action: How the American Middle Class Joined the Money Class*, Joseph Nocera, Simon & Schuster, New York, 1994; *American Express: The Unofficial History*, Peter Z. Grossman, Crown, New York, 1987; and "American Express Applies for a New Line of Credit," Stephen D. Solomon, *The New York Times Magazine*, July 30, 1995.

To give context concerning the chronology of acquisitions and mergers at American Express: Between 1981 and 1987, American Express purchased a number of financial institutions which added to or expanded the company's reach into retail brokerage, investment banking, portfolio management and life insurance. American Express bought Shearson Loeb Rhodes, the fourth-largest brokerage firm in the country in 1981; IDS Financial Services in 1983; Lehman Brothers in 1984 and E.F. Hutton in 1988. Shearson, Lehman and Hutton became known as Shearson Lehman Brothers. In 1987, before the acquisition of Hutton, American Express sold off 46% of Shearson Lehman Brothers. It repurchased all of the outstanding shares of Shearson Lehman in 1990 to protect the viability of the firm, its clients and its assets.

The purchase of E.F. Hutton in 1988 was the major cause of Shearson's downturn. Shearson's tangible net worth was seriously diminished by Hutton's extensive liabilities. This exacerbated the effects of the recession that cut across the securities industry, and placed an even heavier financial responsibility on American Express as Shearson's parent company.

For a discussion of the doom cycle, see *Discontinuous Change*, Nadler and Shaw (cited earlier). For insights into the Kodak/George Fisher story, see "New Chief, George Fisher, Pushes Kodak Into Digital Era," *The Wall Street Journal*, June 9, 1995, pp. B1–4.

A useful source for change management is Peter F. Drucker's "The Five Deadly Business Sins," *The Wall Street Journal*, October 21, 1993, editorial page. For a thoughtful discussion of the impact of disruptive technologies on change, see "Disruptive Technologies: Catching the Wave," Joseph L. Bower and Clayton M. Cristensen, *Harvard Business Review*, January-February, 1995.

# Chapter 6: Recognizing and Tracking the Movement of Value in Your Industry

Economic Value Added™ (EVA), as discussed in this chapter, is a proprietary product trademarked to Sterns, Stewart and Company, New York.

The work of Corporate Decision, Inc. (CDI) was very helpful in those sections of the chapter dealing with value inflow and outflow, as well as value migration. The latter term, value migration, is trademarked to CDI.

Discussions of the enigma code can be found in *The Enigma War*, Joseph Garlinksi, Schribner, New York, 1979; *The Eagle Against the Sun*, Ronald H. Spector, The Free Press, New York, 1985; and *A Man Called Intrepid*, William Stevenson, Harcourt, Brace, Jovanovich, 1976.

The use of the Primal Change Model in this chapter is the result of findings from an Atlanta Consulting Group/CPC Study, Implementation/Change Benchmarking Study conducted with IDS and American Express in November 1993.

For a discussion of GE's forcing mechanisms, see *Control Your Destiny or Someone Else Will*, Noel Tichy and Stratford Sherman, Doubleday, New York, 1993.

For an understanding of the importance of demanding customers, read *The Competitive Advantage of Nations*, Porter (cited earlier). According to Porter, one of the most important factors in developing a world-class industry is to have demanding, world-class customers.

The four ring model used in this chapter was derived from *Firing on All Cylinders*, Jim Clemmer with Barry Sheehy and Associates, Business-One Irwin, New York, 1992.

The diagram, "The Payoff From Keeping Customers," was reprinted with permission from *Fortune* magazine, special issue, Autumn/Winter, 1993, p. 57.

Joel Rosenfeld and the Strategic Planning Institute's Profit Impact Market Strategy (PIMS) database was immensely helpful in the course of this work. The PIMS database is the largest and oldest of its kind and provides an outstanding platform for measuring the interaction between quality, ROI and market share.

For the specifics of how Whirlpool misjudged European consumers see "Whirlpool's Bloody Nose," *Forbes*, Marcia Berss, March 11, 1996, pp. 90–92.

The Value Landscaping™ tool developed by the Atlanta Consulting Group is based upon established Jungian psychological theory, which confirms that each customer has a set of psychological tendencies that determine his or her behavior in the marketplace. A psychological questionnaire is used to provide fresh insights into customers through personification. This moves customers beyond familiar, dictated perceptions of value—like generally used product attributes and benefits—into the realm of what customers believe and feel. In a study conducted by the Advertising Research Foundation, the theroretical framework upon which the Value Landscaping methodology is based was proven to be the best indicator of actual, real-market sales and customer loyalty.

For further discussion of the need to move beyond traditional customer research techniques, see Rosabeth Moss Kanter's book, *Fad Surfing in the Boardroom*, particularly the chapter entitled "The (Inharmonious) Voice of the Customer."

# Chapter 7: Using Old Tools to Get a Handle on New Value

Useful sources in preparing this chapter were *Firing on All Cylinders*, Jim Clemmer with Barry Sheehy and Associates, Business-One Irwin, New York, 1992; *The Search for Quality, An Anthology of Works*, Executive Excellence Publishing, Provo, Utah, 1995; and *The Competitive Advantage of Nations*, Michael Porter, The Free Press, New York, 1990.

The cellular industry discovered that its best customer segments were ten times more profitable than its worst segments. Moreover, 20% of customers accounted for 60 to 80 percent of revenue in the industry. (Duncan McDougall, "Know Thy Customer," *The Wall Street Journal*, August 7, 1995.) Other useful sources were:

- "Term Info Letter," *USA Today*, March 29, 1995
- "Quality, the Only Source of Sustainable Competitive Advantage," Quality Progress, June 1993
- B. Ray Helton, "The Baldie Play," Quality Progress, February 1995
- Barry Sheehy and James D. Robinson III, "Staying the Course," published in Executive Excellence, The Atlanta Consulting Group, 1995
- *Economic Value Added*, a registered trademark of Stern, Stewart & Co., New York
- "The Real Key to Creating Wealth," *Fortune*, September 20, 1993
- NBC special documentary, "If Japan Can . . . Why Can't We?" 1980
- Frederick F. Reichheld and W. Earl Sasser Jr., "Zero Defects," *Harvard Business Review*, September-October 1990

- Heskett, Jones, Loveman, Sasser & Schlesinger, "Putting the Service Profit Chain to Work," *Harvard Business Review*, March-April 1994
- Bradley T. Gale, "Quality Comes First When Hatching Power Brands," *Planning Review*, July-August 1992
- Aldo Papone, "Brand Value vs. Commodity Appeal," speech presented to the 34th IAA World Advertising Congress, Cancun, Mexico, May 17, 1994
- Michael Beer, Russell Eisenstat and Bert Spector, "Why Change Programs Don't Produce Change," *Harvard Business Review*, November-December, 1990
- Regis McKenna, "Real-Time Marketing," *Harvard Business Review*, July-August, 1995

# Chapter 8: Learning Drives the Quest for Value

For the general characteristics of the learning organization, the best sources remain Peter Senge's *The Fifth Discipline*, Doubleday Books, New York, 1992, and Margaret Wheatley's, *Leadership and the New Science*, cited earlier.

For insights into the difference between a "knowing" and "learning" organization, we refer the reader to *The Smarter Organization*, Michael E. McGill and John W. Slocum, John Wiley & Sons, New York, 1995.

For an understanding of Mikhail Gorbachev's learning dilemma, read *Perestroika*, Harper & Row, New York, 1987, and Gale Sheehy's, *The Man Who Changed the World*, HarperCollins, New York, 1990; and *At the Highest Levels: The Inside Story of the End of the Cold War*, Michael R. Beschloss and Strobe Talbott, Little, Brown & Co., Toronto, 1993.

For a discussion on the impact of competition on innovation, a useful source was *Hot Rivalry Drives Good Practices*, Canadian Conference Board Report as cited in *Toronto's Globe and Mail*, November 16, 1993, B-26.

For a detailed discussion of the NUMMI experience, as well as insights into the recovery of the American automobile industry, see *The Reckoning*, David Halberstam, William Morrow & Co., New York, 1986, and *Rude Awakening*, MaryAnn Keller, William Morrow & Co., New York, 1989.

# Chapter 9: Something Gained . . . Something Lost

For invaluable insight into the changing nature of American working demographics, see *The New American Workplace*, Eileen Appelbaum and Rosemary Batt, The ILR Press, Ithaca, New York, 1994, and *G Forces, Reinventing the World*, Frank Feather, Summerhill Press, Toronto, 1989 (also provides information regarding the changing nature of work).

For reengineering, the most popular primer remains *Reengineering the Corporation*, Michael Hammer and James Champy, Harper-Business, New York, 1993.

Further evidence indicating reengineering efforts have not been very successful can be found in the work of Steven Pressman, published in *Challenge, The Magazine of Economic Affairs*, November/December 1994. Pressman concludes that 3 out of 4 of the success stories cited in *Reengineering the Corporation*, actually do worse than their industry average. In contrast, the October 18, 1993, *BusinessWeek* story, "Betting to Win on the Baldie Winners," showed that an investment in the stocks of Baldrige-winning firms on the day each won the award turned in an 89.2% total gain compared with a 33.1% figure for the S&P 500 stock index.

Francis Fukuyama's new book, *Trust, The Social Virtues and the Creation of Prosperity*, The Free Press, New York, 1995, was particularly useful in its discussion of social cohesion and its impact on capitalism.

Works we found particularly helpful with regard to the moral dilemmas which business leaders in a capitalist society must face are *The Executive's Compass*, James O'Toole, Oxford University Press, New York, 1993; *The Lessons of History*, Will and Ariel Durant, Simon & Schuster, New York, 1968; *A Study of History*, Arnold Toynbee, Dell Publishing Company, New York, 1946; and Hyler Bracey's book, *Managing From the Heart*, provided useful background for discussion of the goal of leaders in a modern economy.

For those interested in understanding the impact of the Great Depression on public policy, we recommend *The Age of Uncertainty*, John Kenneth Galbraith, Houghton-Mifflin, Boston, 1977; *The Great Crash*, John Kenneth Galbraith, Quantum Books, New York, 1979; and *The Day the Market Crashed*, Donald Rogers, Arlington House, New York, 1971.

We are indebted to Don Tapscott's, *Digital Economy*, McGraw-Hill, Toronto, 1995, for his moving description of the dark side of reengineering.

For the power of integrity as a business strategy, we refer the reader to "The Caring Company," *The Economist*, June 6, 1992. Other sources were:

- "Corporate Downsizing Amid Record Profits," *The Wall Street Journal*, May 4, 1995
- Barry Sheehy, "Cutting Costs Without Cutting Your Throat," *White Paper*, The Atlanta Consulting Group, 1995
- "IBM Slashes Secretaries Salaries," *The Wall Street Journal*, May 19, 1995
- "Making Change Stick," *Fortune*, April 17, 1995
- "Today's Layoffs," *The New York Times*, June 25, 1995
- "Scheme to Reengineer American Business Goes Off Track," *Chicago Tribune*, as quoted in the *Savannah News Press*, April 23, 1995

## Chapter 10: Why the Public Sector Is Hemorrhaging Value

Statistics on disenchantment of government came from Harris Poll, as reported in "Term," *The Wall Street Journal*, February 21, 1995, volume 4, number 2, page 4. Good discussions on the fundamental problems faced by government on the cusp of the 21st century can be found in *Post-Capitalist Society*, Peter Drucker, HarperBusiness, New York, 1993, and Charles Handy, *Age of Paradox* (cited earlier).

For a profound discussion of why government's actions so often produce perverse results, read *The Death of Common Sense: How Law Is Suffocating America*, Philip K. Howard, Random House, New York, 1994.

For an excellent discussion of the challenges facing American education, read *Educating America*, James Bowsher, John Wiley & Sons, New York, 1989.

Two sources on health care reform which we found particularly useful were: *Restructuring Health Care*, David Phillip Lathrop, Jossey-

Bass, San Francisco, 1993 and *Revolution: The Healthcare System Takes Shape,* Russell C. Coile, Whittle Direct Books, San Francisco, 1993. We also refer the reader to The Atlanta Consulting Group's white papers, *Don't Blink or You'll Miss It: The Reformation of U.S. Health Care Is Underway; Managing the Cost Imperative in Health Care;* and *U.S. Health Care: The Big Squeeze.*

## Chapter 11: In Search of a New Value Formula for Government

For an outstanding discussion of the challenges and failings of modern liberal democracy, we found *Democracy Against Itself,* Jean-Francois Revel, Macmillan, New York, 1993, most useful.

*The Rise and Decline of Nations,* Mancur Olson, Yale University Press, New Haven, 1989, and *Demosclerosis: The Silent Killer of Government,* Jonathan Rauch, Random House, New York, 1994, provided valuable insights into the pernicious impact of vested interests on the democratic process.

The World Bank Policy Research Group report, *The East Asian Miracles,* Oxford University Press, New York, 1994, provided valuable insights into the Asian tiger's sources of success as did The World Economic Forum, IMED Institute, Davos, Switzerland, *Report on Global Competitiveness,* (cited earlier). Other useful sources were:

- "The Great Escape," *The Economist,* April 1, 1995
- "Economic Miracle or Myth," *The Economist,* October 22, 1993

## Chapter 12: Coming to Grips With the Age of Abundance

In understanding the importance of democracy and the rule of law in building prosperity, sources that were particularly valuable were *Trust: The Social Virtues and the Creation of Prosperity,* Francis Fukuyama (cited earlier), and *Why Voting Is Good for You* ("Economic Development and Democracy," in *The Economist,* August 27, 1994).

To contrast the ideas associated with scarcity versus abundance, we refer the reader to *The Wheels of Commerce, Civilization and Capitalism, 15th to 18th Century,* Fernand Braudel, Harper & Row,

New York, 1979; George Gilder's extraordinary work, *Wealth and Poverty*, Basic Books, New York, 1981. The relationship between economic growth and environental protection is discussed in *Fortune*, "Growth Helps the Environment," March 23, 1992.

The work of economist Paul Romer was indispensable to the development of this chapter. For those interested in reading more about new growth theory, we refer them to: *Forbes* ASAP, quarterly report, "A Tax Companies Might Like," *Forbes*, November 1, 1993, as well as "Unraveling the Mystery of Growth," *The Economist*, January 4, 1992.

Other articles by Romer which we found useful were "New Goods, Old Theory, and the Welfare Costs of Trade Restrictions," *Journal of Development Economics* 43, 1993; "The Origins of Endogenous Growth," *Journal of Economic Perspectives* 8, Winter 1994; "Economic Growth," *The Fortune Encyclopedia of Economics*, David R. Henderson (ed.), Time Warner Books, New York, 1993; "Ideas and Things," *The Economist*, September 11, 1993; "Beyond Classical and Keynesian Macroeconomic Policy," *Policy Options*, July-August 1994; and "Economic Growth and Investment in Children," *Daedalus* 123, Fall 1994.

Other useful sources were: *The Coming Global Boom*, Charles Morris, Bantam Books, New York, 1990; *G Forces, Reinventing the World*, Frank Feather, (cited earlier); and *Powershift*, Alvin Toffler, Bantam Books, New York, 1990.

# Bibliography

## A

*The Age of Diminished Expectations*, U.S. Economic Policy in the 1990s,
  Paul Krugman, MIT Press, Cambridge, Mass., 1991.
*The Age of Paradox*, Charles Handy, Harvard Business School Press,
  Boston, 1994.
*The Age of Uncertainty*, John Kenneth Galbraith, Houghton-Mifflin,
  Boston, 1977.
*American Express: The Unofficial History*, Peter Z. Grossman, Crown
  Publishers, New York, 1987.
*At Dawn We Slept*, Gordon W. Prange, McGraw-Hill, Toronto, 1981.

## B

*Bankruptcy 1995: The Coming Collapse*, Harry E. Figgie, Little, Brown
  & Co., New York, 1993.
*Barbarians to Bureaucrats*, Lawrence Miller, Clarkson and Potter
  Publishers, New York, 1989.
*Beyond the Hype*, Robert G. Eccles and Nitin Nohria, Harvard
  Business School Press, Boston, 1992.
*The Borderless World*, Kenichi Ohmae, HarperBusiness, New York, 1990.
*The Breakthrough Strategy*, Robert Schaffer, HarperBusiness, New
  York, 1988.
*The Bubble Economy*, Christopher Wood, Atlantic Monthly Press,
  New York, 1992.

## C

*The Change Agent's Handbook*, David Hutton, ASQC Quality Press,
  Milwaukee, 1994.

*The Coming Boom,* Herman Kahn, Simon & Schuster, New York, 1982.
*The Coming Global Boom,* Charles Morris, Bantam Books, New York, 1990.
*Competing for the Future,* Gary Hamel and C.K. Prahalad, Harvard Business School Press, Boston, 1994.
*The Competitive Advantage of Nations,* Michael Porter, The Free Press, New York, 1990.
*Connections,* James Burke, Little, Brown & Co., Toronto, 1978.
*The Credit Card Catastrophe, The 20th Century Phenomenon That Changed the World,* Marty Simmons, Barricade Books, New York, 1995.
*Crossing and Cruising,* John Maxtone-Graham, Scribner, New York, 1992.

# D

*The Day the Market Crashed,* Donald Rogers, Arlington House, New York, 1971.
*The Death of Common Sense: How Law Is Suffocating America,* Philip K. Howard, Random House, New York, 1994.
*The Debt and the Deficit,* Robert Heilbroner and Peter Bernstein, W.W. Norton, New York, 1989.
*The Decline of Capitalism,* Arthur Jones, Thomas Crowell, New York, 1976.
*Deming Management at Work,* Mary Walton, Putnum & Sons, New York, 1990.
*The Deming Management Method,* Mary Walton, Pedigree Books, New York, 1986.
*Democracy Against Itself,* Jean-Francois Revel, Macmillan, New York, 1993.
*Demosclerosis: The Silent Killer of Government,* Jonathan Rauch, Random House, New York, 1994.
*Digital Economy,* Don Tapscott, McGraw-Hill, Toronto, 1995.
*Discontinuous Change,* David Nadler and Robert B. Shaw, Jossey-Bass, San Francisco, 1995.

# E

*The Eagle Against the Sun,* Ronald H. Spector, The Free Press, New York, 1985.

*Economics,* E.K. Hunt and Howard J. Sherman, Harper & Row, New York, 1978.

*Educating America,* James Bowsher, John Wiley & Sons, New York, 1989.

*The End of Geography: Global Financial Integration,* Richard O'Brien, The Royal Institute of International Affairs, Pinter Publishers, London, 1992.

*The End of Order,* Charles L. Mee, E.P. Dutton, New York, 1980.

*The Enigma of Japanese Power,* Karel Van Wolferen, Alfred Knopf, New York, 1989.

*Economics on Trial,* Mark Skousan, Business-One Irwin, Chicago, 1991.

*The Executive's Compass,* James O'Toole, Oxford University Press, New York, 1993.


# F


*The Fifth Discipline,* Peter Senge, Doubleday Books, New York, 1992.

*Firing on All Cylinders,* Jim Clemmer with Barry Sheehy and Associates, Business-One Irwin, New York, 1992.

*Five Economic Challenges,* Robert Heilbroner and Lester Thurow, Prentice-Hall, Englewood Cliffs, N.J., 1981.

*For Good and Evil, The Impact of Taxes on the Course of Civilization,* Charles Adams, Madison Books, New York, 1993.

*Free to Choose,* Milton and Rose Friedman, Harcourt Brace Jovanovich, New York, 1980.

*Future Perfect,* Stanley M. Davis, Addison-Wesley, New York, 1987.


# G


*G Forces, Reinventing the World,* Frank Feather, Summerhill Press, Toronto, 1989.

*The Great Crash,* John Kenneth Galbraith, Quantum Books, New York, 1979.

*The Great Depression of 1990,* Ravi Batra, Simon & Schuster, 1987.


# H


"Hot Rivalry Drives Good Practices," *Toronto's Globe and Mail,* November 16, 1993, B-26.

# I

*The "I" of the Hurricane: Creating Corporate Energy*, Art McNeil, Stoddart, Toronto, 1988.

*An Illustrated Guide to the American Economy*, Herbert Stein and Murray Foss, American Enterprise Institute, Washington, D.C., 1992.

*Innovation and Entrepreneurship*, Peter Drucker, Harper & Row, New York, 1985.

# J

*Japan: The Coming Collapse*, Bryan Reading, Weidenfeld & Nicholson, London, 1992.

*Job Creation in America*, David Birch, The Free Press, New York, 1987.

# L

*Leadership and the New Science*, Margaret J. Wheatley, Barret and Koehler, San Francisco, 1994.

*Leading the Way*, Al Santoli, Random House, New York, 1993.

*Le Défi américain*, Jean Jacques Servan-Schreiber, Editions Denofi, Paris, 1967, Hamish Hamilton, London, 1968.

*The Lessons of History*, Will and Ariel Durant, Simon & Schuster, New York, 1968.

*A Life in Our Times*, John Kenneth Galbraith, Houghton Mifflin, Boston, 1981.

*Liners to the Sun*, John Maxtone-Graham, Macmillan, New York, 1985.

*Looking at the Sun, The Rise of the New East Asian Economic and Political System*, James Fallows, Pantheon Books, New York, 1994.

# M

*Made in America*, M. Dertouzous, R.K. Lester and R.M. Solow, MIT Press, Cambridge, Mass., 1989.

*Made in Japan*, Akio Morita, E.P. Dutton, New York, 1986.

*Making It in America*, Jerry Jasinowski and Robert Hamrin, Simon & Schuster, New York, 1995.

*Managing Customer Value*, Bradley T. Gale, The Free Press, New York, 1994.

*The March of Folly*, Barbara Tuchman, Cardinal Books, New York, 1990.

*Market Liberalism: A Paradigm for the 21st Century*, edited by David Boaz and Edward H. Crane, The Cato Institute, Washington, D.C., 1993.

*The Materials Revolution*, Thomas Forester, MIT Press, Boston, 1988.

*A Matter of Survival*, Diane Francis, Key Porter Books, Toronto, 1993.

*Megatrends 2000*, John Naisbitt and Patricia Aburdene, William Morrow & Co., New York 1990.

*The Misunderstood Economy*, Robert Eisner, Harvard Business School Press, Boston, 1994.

*The Money Lenders, Bankers and the World in Turmoil*, Anthony Sampson, The Free Press, New York, 1991.

*More Like Us*, James Fallows, Houghton-Mifflin, Boston 1989.


# N


*The New American Workplace*, Eileen Appelbaum and Rosemary Batt, The ILR Press, Ithaca, New York, 1994.

*The Next Canadian Economy*, Dian Cohen and Kristin Shannon, Eden Press, Montreal, 1984.

*The Next Century*, David Halberstam, William Morrow & Co., New York, 1991.

*The Next 200 Years*, Herman Kahn, William Morrow & Co., New York, 1976.


# O


*Out of Control*, Zbigniew Brzezinski, Robert Stewart Books, New York, 1993.

*Out of the Crisis*, W. Edwards Deming, MIT Press, Cambridge, Mass., 1986.


# P


*Paper Money*, Adam Smith, Summit Books, New York, 1981.

*Pathways to Performance*, Jim Clemmer, Prima Publishing, Toronto, 1995.
*Peddling Prosperity*, Paul Krugman, W.W. Norton, New York, 1994.
*Perestroika*, Mikhail Gorbachev, Harper & Row, New York, 1987.
*A Piece of the Action: How the American Middle Class Joined the Money Class*, Joseph Nocera, Simon & Schuster, New York, 1994.
*Post-Capitalist Society*, Peter Drucker, HarperBusiness, New York, 1993.
*Powershift*, Alvin Toffler, Bantam Books, New York, 1990.
*Prophets in the Dark*, David Kearns and David Nadler, Harper-Business, New York, 1992.

# Q

*Quality Is Free*, Philip Crosby, New American Library, New York, 1979.
*Quality or Else*, Lloyd Dobyns and Claire Crawford-Mason, Houghton-Mifflin, Boston, 1991.

# R

*Reagonomics: Supply-Side in Action*, Bruce Bartlett, Arlington House, Westport, Conn., 1981.
*The Reckoning*, David Halberstam, William Morrow & Co., New York, 1986.
*Reengineering the Corporation*, Michael Hammer and James Champy, HarperBusiness, New York, 1993.
*Reinventing the Corporation*, John Naisbitt, Patricia Aburdene, Warner Books, 1985.
*Report on Global Competitiveness*, World Economic Forum, IMED Institute, Davos, Switzerland, December 1994.
*Restructuring Health Care*, David Phillip Lathrop, Jossey-Bass, San Francisco, 1993.
*Revolution: The Healthcare System Takes Shape*, Russell C. Coile, Whittle Direct Books, San Francisco, 1993.
*The Rise and Decline of Nations*, Mancur Olson, Yale University Press, New Haven, Conn., 1989.
*The Rise and Fall of Great Powers*, Paul Kennedy and Unwin Hyman, Random House, New York, 1988.

*The Rising Sun*, John Toland, Random House, New York, 1970.
*Rude Awakening*, Mary Ann Keller, William Morrow & Co., New York, 1989.

## S

*The Search for Quality: An Anthology of Works*, Executive Excellence Publishing, Provo, Utah, 1995.
*The Service Edge*, Ron Zemke, New American Library, New York, 1989.
*Shifting Gears*, Nuala Beck, HarperCollins, Toronto, 1993.
*A Short History of Financial Euphoria*, John Kenneth Galbraith, Whittle Books, New York, 1990.
*The Silent War*, Ira Magaziner and Mark Patinkin, Randon House, New York, 1989.
*The Smarter Organization*, Michael E. McGill and John W. Slocum, John Wiley & Sons, New York, 1995.
*The Sorcerer's Apprentices*, Peter Foster, Collins, Toronto, 1982.
*The Spirit of Enterprises*, George Gilder, Simon & Schuster, New York, 1984.
*A Study of History*, Arnold Toynbee, Dell Publishing Company, New York, 1946.
*The Sun Also Sets*, Bill Emmott, Times Books–Random House, New York, 1989.

## T

*Taurus, the Car That Saved Ford*, Aeric Taub, Dutton Books, New York, 1991.
*The Third Century*, Joel Kotkin and Yoriko Kishimoto, Crown, New York, 1988.
*The Third Wave*, Alvin Toffler, Bantam Books, New York, 1981.
*Total Customer Service*, W.H. Davidow and Bro Uttal, Harper & Row, New York, 1989.
*Trust, the Social Virtues and the Creation of Prosperity*, Francis Fukuyama, The Free Press, New York, 1995.
*Tyranny of the Status Quo*, Milton and Rose Friedman, Harcourt, Brace, Jovanovich, New York, 1984.

# V

*The Vandal's Crown: How Currency Traders Overthrew the World Central Bankers*, Gregory Millman, The Free Press, New York, 1995.
*The VIP Strategy*, Art McNeil and Jim Clemmer, Key Porter Books, Toronto, 1988.

# W

*War and Peace*, Leo Tolstoy, The Modern Library, Random House, New York, 1994.
*Wealth and Poverty*, George Gilder, Basic Books, New York, 1981.
*Well Made in America*, Peter C. Reid, McGraw-Hill, New York, 1990.
*What Went Right in the 1980s*, Richard B. McKenzie, Pacific Research Institute for Public Policy, San Francisco, 1994.
*The Wheels of Commerce, Civilization and Capitalism, 15th to 18th Century*, Fernand Braudel, Harper & Row, New York, 1979.
*The World After Oil*, Bruce Nussbaum, Simon & Schuster, New York, 1983.
*The World Challenge*, Jean-Jacques Servan-Schreiber, Simon & Schuster, New York, 1980.
*The Worldly Philosophers*, Robert L. Heilbroner, Simon & Schuster, New York, 1972.

# Y

*Yen! Japan's New Financial Empire*, Daniel Burstein, Simon & Schuster, New York, 1988.

# Z

*Zero Sum Society*, Lester Thurow, Basil Books, New York, 1980.

# Index

# About the Authors

**Barry Sheehy**, a principal of The Atlanta Consulting Group, has a unique ability to predict major economic trends and their effects on a variety of industries and countries. He is a highly sought-after speaker and an accomplished author.

His experience in quality and reengineering implementation comes from firsthand involvement in award-winning initiatives in both the public and private sectors. As a Canadian living in the United States, he has a special perspective on the similarities and differences of what businesses are facing on both sides of the border. He most recently advised American Express on the global implementation of American Express Quality Leadership. Other clients include multinational corporations from Europe, Japan, North America, the Middle East, and the Pacific Rim.

Mr. Sheehy is co-author of *Firing On All Cylinders*, and a contributing author to *The Search for Quality* and *Game Plans for Success*. He is also frequently featured in the media and has written articles for numerous newspapers and magazines, including *The National Productivity Review*, *Asian Productivity Digest*, *the Singapore Times*, and *Executive Excellence*.

Mr. Sheehy lives in Savannah, Georgia.

As president of The Atlanta Consulting Group, **Hyler Bracey** works with organizations to create large-scale business transformation. He guides executive teams to help them focus on and gather the strategic intelligence necessary for moving their business forward.

Dr. Bracey's colorful background includes working on a tugboat, owning and managing an agribusiness firm, racing stock cars, and more recently becoming a nationally acclaimed consultant and public speaker. He has a unique talent for communicating the power of integration—the human issues merged with measurable results. He is the co-author of the internationally published best-seller *Managing From the Heart.*

For more than twenty years, he has been an expert in the field of transformation, and has been quoted and published widely in such periodicals as *Nation's Business, Executive Excellence, Entrepreneur, American Banker,* and *Hospital Progress.* He has also been featured on national television, including the CBS Evening News *Eye on America* series.

Dr. Bracey lives in Atlanta, Georgia.

As a vice president of the Atlanta Consulting Group, **Rick Frazier** specializes in business intelligence and strategic planning. His previous consulting experience includes total quality management and organizational development.

Mr. Frazier's career began in the high-tech industry where he worked for one of the first companies to manufacture word-processing equipment and one of the largest UNIX database software companies. He also co-founded an on-line information services firm where he served as CEO for five years. The story of this unique start-up company and its subsequent acquisition by a Fortune 200 firm was described in national media including *USA Today* and *Business Week.*

Mr. Frazier lives in Old Lyme, Connecticut.